THE HALBERT CENTRE FOR CANADIAN STUDIES
THE HEBREW UNIVERSITY OF JERUSALEM

THE HALBERT EXCHANGE PROGRAM
THE UNIVERSITY OF TORONTO

THE ISRAEL ASSOCIATION FOR CANADIAN STUDIES

CHANGE AND IMPACT
Essays in Canadian Social Sciences

Edited by

Sally F. Zerker

THE MAGNES PRESS, THE HEBREW UNIVERSITY, JERUSALEM

This book is published under the auspices of the Halbert Centre for Canadian Studies of the Hebrew University of Jerusalem, the Halbert Exchange Program of the University of Toronto and the Israel Association for Canadian Studies.

Distributed by
The Magnes Press
P.O. Box 7695
Jerusalem 91076
Israel

Managing Editor: Ruth Chernia, Toronto
Maps: Tamar Soffer, Jerusalem

ISBN   965-223-883-X

Printed in Jerusalem, Israel, 1994

Contents

Contributors

SALLY F. ZERKER is a Professor in the Departments of Social Science and Economics at York University, Toronto, Ontario.

KEN ATKINSON is with the School of Geography, University of Leeds, UK.

SIMON M. BERKOWICZ is with the Institute of Earth Sciences, The Hebrew University of Jerusalem.

BARRY R. CHISWICK is with the Department of Economics, University of Illinois at Chicago.

PETER CLANCY is Associate Professor in the Department of Political Science, St. Francis Xavier University, Antigonish, Nova Scotia.

JOHN C. COURTNEY is with the Department of Political Studies, University of Saskatchewan, Saskatoon, Saskatchewan.

CHRISTOPHER DUNN is in the Department of Political Science, Memorial University of Newfoundland, St. Johns, Newfoundland.

J. STEFAN DUPRÉ is Professor in the Department of Political Science at the University of Toronto.

ZACHARIAH KAY is a researcher and writer on Canada–Israel relations.

R.G. LAWFORD is Chief, Hydrometeorological Processes Division, Canadian Climate Centre, National Hydrology Research Centre, Saskatoon, Saskatchewan.

CYRIL LEVITT is in the Department of Sociology, McMaster University, Hamilton, Ontario.

PAUL W. MILLER is with the Department of Economics, University of Western Australia.

PIERRE MOHNEN is in the Département des sciences économique at the Université de Québec à Montréal.

DAVID MORLEY is Professor in Environmental Studies at York University, Toronto, Ontario.

SHEILA M. NEYSMITH is with the Faculty of Social Work, University of Toronto.

H. PETER OBERLANDER is Professor of Political Science, Simon Fraser University, Burnaby, British Columbia. He served as federal deputy Minister of Urban Affairs, 1970–73, and is currently a partner with Downs/Archambault, Architects and Planners.

BEN SCHLESINGER is Professor in the Faculty of Social Work, University of Toronto.

MILDRED A. SCHWARTZ is in the Department of Sociology, University of Illinois at Chicago, Illinois.

ROBERT SCHWARTZWALD is in the Department of French and Italian at the University of Massachusetts at Amherst.

THIJS TEN RAA is at Tilburg University, the Netherlands.

ALLAN A. WARRACK is Professor in the Faculty of Business, University of Alberta, Edmonton, Alberta.

Preface

At first sight, Canada and Israel seem to have very little in common. Where Canadian boundaries encompass the second largest national territorial mass in the world, the whole of Israel is but a small sliver of land, about the length of Nova Scotia sans Cape Breton, and approximately the width of Prince Edward Island's narrow side. Canada essentially has only one national neighbour, and a peaceful one at that. Who hasn't heard the cliché about the longest undefended border in the world between Canada and the United States? That border is also commercially increasingly less restricted and more open since the Free Trade Agreement of 1989. By contrast, Israel is in close proximity to numerous neighbouring nations—from Israel's southernmost point, four of those neighbouring countries are close to convergence at the port of Eilat—but to this day Israel's neighbours (with the exception of Egypt) are still officially at war with it. Moreover, these countries not only do not trade with Israel, they are actively engaged in an economic boycott of that nation. Where Canada is endowed with a richness in natural resources that is almost unparalleled, Israel must import many of the primary products that are essential for an industrialized society. Israel has an ancient origin, Canada a modern beginning.

This list of contrasts is by no means complete; one can easily think of other distinctions between these two very different countries. Nevertheless, at the Hebrew University of Jerusalem an institution exists and indeed flourishes that takes as its premise that each country has much to learn from the other. That institution is the Israel Association for Canadian Studies. The study of Canada by Israeli scholars recognizes those obvious differences between Israel and Canada, but takes account of important similarities as well. For example, both countries have grown out of immigrant populations, and both therefore have experienced and continue to experience problems of integration. In both Canada and Israel, the ideological influence of socialism is felt, either directly through the election to power of socialist parties, or indirectly through the concept of the role of the state in social welfare. The colonial influence of the British empire, though resisted and transformed, has left its mark in both their respective political and legal systems.

From 17 to 21 May 1992, the Israel Association for Canadian Studies in conjunction with the Halbert Centre for Canadian Studies sponsored an International Canadian Studies Conference, held at the Hebrew University in Jerusalem. The theme of the conference was "The Economy, Society and Culture of Canada." In addition to the general conference, a symposium was held on the subject of Public Services under Declining Resources and Changing Ideologies. The present volume of essays is composed of scholarly papers from various social science disciplines delivered at that conference. Those with humanities content have been published in a separate volume entitled *At the Edge*. Canadian scholars were heavily represented among the participants to this conference, but there were also contributors from Israel, India, the Netherlands, the United States and other nations, many of whom are specialists in the field of Canadian Studies in their own countries.

This collection of essays is divided according to disciplinary interest, and each section is launched by a short introductory essay. The book opens with a segment that deals with Canadian politics and public policy and it includes six essays. Professor John C. Courtney of the University of Saskatchewan has written a penetrating introduction to the first four essays all of which, in one way or another, address the subject of constitutional reform in Canada. Professor Sally Zerker of York University has added a few paragraphs of introduction to two essays that are relevant to the subject of public policy, although removed from constitutional issues. The first of these two considers cultural development policy in Québec, and the second one examines the record of Canadian policy vis-à-vis Israel.

Section two has four essays. This section is composed of three papers that are interdisciplinary in nature—in the area of political economy—while the fourth essay is strictly unidisciplinary, a work in the field of economics. Sally Zerker has written the introduction to this second section in this collection of essays.

Professor David Morley of York University introduces the third section entitled "Essays in Canadian Environment." Morley's piece is a contribution on its own, a short essay in which he investigates the state of environmental science within Canadian studies broadly speaking. The three contributing essays that Morley reviews here are seen as "hint[ing] at a major future extension of the area studies genre into the critical environment issues facing mankind." This section therefore merits special attention for Canadian scholars who are newly discovering the potential for the study of environment within the context of Canadian social sciences.

The final section deals with important Canadian social issues, such as immigrant income and language adjustments, support for aging women, the condition of one–parent families among Jewish Canadians and the question of racism in Canada. Professor Cyril Levitt of McMaster University wrote the introduction for this section. He has rightly pointed out that, while these essays do not cover all aspects of Canadian social problems, they do portray a concern with some of the most significant issues in Canadian life at the present time.

This book has been made possible, first and foremost, by 17 outstanding works of scholarship. It was evident during the International Conference in Jerusalem that such accomplishments merited a wider dissemination than that limited to the participants at the conference. This book grew out of that conviction. Secondly, the efforts by Professors Courtney, Morley and Levitt, whose expertise in their respective fields was so generously extended through their introductory essays, has helped enormously in structuring the book for accessability and clarity. In addition, Professor Arie Shachar of the Hebrew University, who originally conceived the need for this volume, has assisted the production of this book through his unceasing interest, countless discussions, advice, helpful contacts when needed and thoughtful encouragement to this editor. Daphna Oren of the Institute of Urban Studies, Hebrew University, has assisted masterfully throughout, and Ruth Chernia's editing work has added the necessary and much appreciated final polish to this combined project.

Sally F. Zerker

PART I
ESSAYS IN CANADIAN POLITICS AND PUBLIC POLICIES

JOHN C. COURTNEY

Introduction

Presented in the post–Meech Lake and pre–Charlottetown era of Canada's constitutional debate, the first four papers making up this section of the book offer several original and thoughtful insights into Canadian politics and public policy formation. They draw on the long history of federal–provincial relations, and, in so doing, they inform us about many of the issues and arguments relating to Canada's constitution that are likely to surface in the years ahead. Need it be said that nothing is certain in politics, least of all on the constitutional front? But it would be out of character for Canadian political élites to turn their backs on questions that remain unresolved at the end of the Mulroney era. Three that come to mind are the future of Québec, the demand for an elected Senate and the probability and desirability of aboriginal self-government.

The theme central to Stefan Dupré's essay warrants careful attention. In their more that 125-year history, Canadians have made remarkable achievements in the design and delivery of social, educational and health services, with scarcely any need for formal amendments to their constitution. In a paper that pays, in Professor Dupré's words, "particular attention to the historical roots of Canadian diversity," the remarkably adaptive capacity of Canada's constitution is forcefully illustrated. Examples of the constitutional adaptability that has characterized Canadian federalism range from cooperative federal–provincial programs in such areas as immigration, job training and hospital and medical care, to Québec's ability and obvious willingness to employ single-handedly and "with a vengeance" the power of the state to legislate a French-only commercial advertising policy. Two of Professor Dupré's observations on the theme of his paper are worth repeating: there is a "striking irrelevance of constitutional change to the delivery of [social, educational and health] services in Canada," and nothing of any significance with respect to the delivery of services "would have changed had Meech Lake succeeded."

To Stefan Dupré the root of the constitutional discontent and quarrelling that has marked so much of Canada's recent history lies not in the inadequacies and rigidity of an archaic document and an inappropriate division of powers. Rather it derives from the symbolic divisions of contemporary Canadian society and the attraction to the Québécois of the Myths of Imposition and Rejection following the adoption of the constitutional package in 1982 and the failure of the Meech Lake accord in 1990. The linguistic, cultural and ethnic divisions within Canadian society will be the real testing ground for the future of the country. In Professor Dupré's words, if Canada "does tear itself apart, it will not be because federalism has served it badly but because inflated symbols may be blinding Canadians to the virtues of what they have achieved without formal constitutional change." This serves as a powerful reminder of the inherent strength of the Confederation agreement and of the divisive tensions that result from perceived social differences.

In his paper, Christopher Dunn challenges the conventional wisdom that the debate over Canadian federalism should be seen largely, if not exclusively, in terms of a dichotomous choice. It is commonly asserted that the country either has strong provincial governments or a strong central one; that it is either decentralized or centralized. In his helpful review of some of the literature of the past three decades, Professor Dunn explores the variety of ways in which the constitutional reform debate has been analyzed and explained by scholars and in government publications. In his view many of the arguments in the literature tend to cancel one another out. What is needed, he claims, is a theory of Canadian federalism that draws on the principle of mutual satisfaction among intergovernmental actors.

Professor Dunn finds that a fruitful approach lies in expanding on the decade-old typology of interregional conflict as resting either on "taste" (incompatible public policy preferences) or "claim" (incompatible redistributive preferences). As national integration depends upon the successful deployment of the principle of mutual advantage and an acceptance of the need for system maintenance, he suggests that a number of "directions" could be followed in order to ensure a more stable federal system in Canada. These include constitutional minimalism, by which the author means making as few demands as possible for strict constitutional amer.dments; avoidance of changes in the division of powers; and acceptance of the desirability of asymmetrical federalism. Clearly not all of these are compatible. Nor, for that matter, are all likely to be universally acceptable. Opponents of federal asymmetry find solace in the recently popular notion of equality of the provinces, just as those who favour a substantial reallocation of jurisdictional powers often call for a major re-working of the Constitution. Nonetheless, the "directions" outlined by Professor Dunn will help to inform future discussion over constitutional reform in Canada.

For Mildred Schwartz the recent attention paid to regionalism as a component of Canada's evolving constitutional arrangement stands in stark contrast to the long-standing focus of Canadian politics on French-English and Québec–rest-of-Canada relations. In the wake of the failure of the Meech Lake accord in 1990, reports issued both by the federal government and by a special parliamentary committee on the Constitution took Canadians even further along the road to regionalism than had earlier efforts of the Mulroney era. Professor Schwartz finds that the distinction between federalism and regionalism rests on the difference between constitutional allocation of powers and resources between two governments and organizational location on an autonomy-dependency axis. In the author's words "federalism determines the form by which a country is governed; regionalism determines how its interests are divided."

Recognizing as well that regions are also systems of power, Professor Schwartz properly notes that politics is inherent in regionalism. By definition, competing political interests affect "the recruitment of elites, the mobilization of citizens and the political alignments" in the several regions. In reviewing proposals from Meech Lake to the early 1990s with respect to Senate reform and the nomination and appointment of judges to the Supreme Court of Canada, the paper implicitly and appropriately accepts the fact that, in order to put into effect regionally driven changes to the Constitution, the provincial and federal legislatures nonetheless remain the formal constitutional actors.

Noting that "local self-government operates at the whim of the provinces and has no constitutional anchor," Peter Oberlander claims that the challenge to Canadian federalism is nowhere more "vigorously felt" than in public policy relating to urban affairs. Urban policies in Canada have remained highly segmented and issue-oriented. To Professor Oberlander they have failed to capture the interdependence of contemporary Canadian society and the spatially specific and location-focused life of Canadians. Revisiting the Trudeau government's initiative of the 1970s in the area of urban policies (the Ministry of State for Urban Affairs), Professor Oberlander describes its demise after seven years as a failure to resolve the federal–provincial constitutional tension on municipal issues. According to the author, the Ministry "was sacrificed on the altar of federal–provincial relations." That brief and unsuccessful search for a national urban policy remains to this day a "short-lived hiccup" on the Canadian constitutional front.

The first four papers in this section address important, though different and unrelated, aspects of federal–provincial relations in Canada. The adaptability of the Canadian Constitution as a framework within which services can be delivered remains, as Professor Dupré argued, one of its telling features. The 125-year record suggests that there is no reason to believe that with the failure of both the Meech Lake and the Charlottetown accords adaptability will not continue to be a defining characteristic of Canada's Constitution. The generous interpretation on federal–provincial relations given by Stefan Dupré should be tempered by one of the points noted in Christopher Dunn's paper: federal development policies (of which the National Energy Program remains a prime example) often have the capacity to frustrate provincial policies. Nonetheless, national integration within a diverse federal system, according to Professor Dunn, is possible given a general recognition and acceptance of the principles of mutual advantage and system maintenance. But whether those principles will ever meet with widespread acceptance remains an open question, given Mildred Schwartz's analysis of the force of Canadian regionalism. This is particularly so in light of the special role assigned the provincial legislatures and the federal parliament in the constitutional amending formula adopted in 1982. The case for a renewed interest in a national urban policy, which Peter Oberlander makes based on the federal experiment of the 1970s, remains, at best, problematic. A legislative power staunchly defended by the provinces as exclusively theirs is unlikely to be assaulted by the federal government, given the scope and magnitude of problems facing Canadians in the 1990s.

Addition to Introduction

The last two papers in this section undoubtedly address issues of government policy and are therefore appropriately selected for this part of the book. However, these papers differ from the first four in their focus. Neither has anything to say about constitutional matters, although Robert Schwartzwald's title might mislead one to think otherwise. Schwartzwald's paper deals specifically with cultural policy in Québec, and Zachariah Kay examines the record of Canadian foreign policy as it applies to Israel.

Schwartzwald provides a critical analysis of the two most recent policy papers on culture and cultural development produced by two different Québec administrations. Significantly, the Québec governments that sponsored these two documents held widely diverse ideologies. The now-familiar *Livre bleu* of 1978 was the document on culture produced by and for the *séparatiste* Parti Québécois government. More than two decades later, in 1991, the provincial Liberal government headed by Robert Bourassa, responding to the failure of the Meech Lake accord, produced its report on culture and cultural development called *Une politique de la culture et des arts*, but more familiarly known as the Arpin Report. These two documents are the source material for Schwartzwald's examination of the province's position on the crucial question of culture.

Yet, despite the ideological differences of the sponsors of the documents, both share the view that "Québec must achieve exclusivity over cultural policy." However, as Schwartzwald demonstrates through comparing the papers from many perspectives, these documents illuminate many of the important issues on culture and cultural policy that are the subject of ongoing debate in Québec.

Zachariah Kay has written a résumé of Canadian government policy as it relates to the state of Israel. Since this paper is based on an article for a forthcoming *Encyclopaedia of Zionism*, it has the quality of a survey piece, but it is a useful canvass of the subject. Kay begins his survey with Mackenzie King's support of Britain's Mandate policy in Palestine, and follows the subsequent changes in Canadian policy. In this endeavour, Kay takes note of various issues and responses from the different Canadian administrations through the years, from the establishment of the state of Israel to the late 1980s. This includes Canadian links to United Nations' positions, Canadian debates about armament sales to Israel, St. Laurent's response to the Anglo-French action at the time of the Suez crisis in 1956, and the Diefenbaker positions in contrast to the record of Lester Pearson. Kay's report also touches on the Arab oil embargo and its significance to Canada, the growing Canadian interest in the Palestinian cause, and he ends with External Affairs Minister Joe Clark's evident break with Ottawa's traditional attitude toward the Arab-Israeli conflict. In addition, Kay provides a worthwhile bibliography of the subject. Hence, this paper is a valuable source of information about the matter of Canadian policy as it evolved in relation to Israel.

Sally F. Zerker

J. STEFAN DUPRÉ

Constitutional Change and the Delivery of Services in Canada: An Overview

Thirty years ago, when I was a young scholar, the task of introducing my strange country to a cosmopolitan audience could be easily accomplished. It was simply a matter of telling what Canadians call the elephant story. Children attending an international school were asked to write an essay about the elephant. The British child wrote about the elephant as a symbol of past imperial glory. The American child wrote about the elephant's power, efficacy and profitability. The bemused Canadian child wrote an essay entitled, "The Elephant: A Federal or Provincial Responsibility?"

Today, when my strange country, one of the wealthiest and most fortunate members of the family of nations, seems on the brink of tearing itself apart over issues of constitutional change, the elephant story somehow sounds quaint and dated. But it retains enormous relevance to my topic, Constitutional Change and the Delivery of Services. My Canadian child, as the story indicates, is obsessed with the role of the state. And coming from an eminently federal state, my child is driven to ask which of the two constitutionally ordained levels of government within that state should be doing what. Why is this so? My child is a product of her political culture, moulded by its evolving beliefs, attitudes and values.

Fittingly, therefore, I shall begin by examining the history of that culture in all its heterogeneity, paying particular attention to the historical roots of Canadian diversity. Observing that federalism was cut out to accommodate such diversity, I shall then examine the triumphs and tribulations of federal–provincial relations in Canada's constitutionally bifurcated state. These relations, at once transcending and reflecting Canada's territorially based political, economic and social differences, shaped the delivery of modern health, educational and social services. They did so without requiring more than a modicum of formal constitutional change. They offer a standing reminder that the Canadian division of jurisdiction, whose 125th anniversary took place in 1992, has abundantly met one of the most demanding tests of a sound constitution: it has enabled successive generations of Canadians to adapt an inherited legal text to changing levels of demand for public services. I consider this to be so true that I shall close by arguing that if my country does tear itself apart, it will not be because federalism has served it badly but because inflated symbols may be blinding Canadians to the virtues of what they have achieved without formal constitutional change.

Political Culture, Heterogeneity and the Role of the State

To stride through Canadian history using broad terms boldly is to encounter a country whose political culture is nothing if not heterogeneous. In the beginning, which coincided with the seventeenth-century arrival of the Puritans in what became the United States, New France was settled by pre-Enlightenment Catholics whose own westward movement was propelled by a mixture of economic appetite for fur-bearing animals and missionary zeal for the conversion of Aboriginal souls to Christianity. The Puritans of New England and the Catholics of New France were each what the late Louis Hartz called "fragments" of Europe—partial versions of the political culture of the continent whence they had come and from whose future development they were isolated by distance (Hartz 1964; with respect to French Canada in particular *see* Forbes 1987).

Thoroughgoing individualists whose values—a preview of what was later called whig liberalism—had brought persecution in England, the American Puritans constituted what Hartz called an escaped fragment, whose individualism constituted a clean break with the values of the feudal, hierarchical European past. Viewed in this light, the subsequent American Revolution was the natural expression of a liberal society shaking off the colonial authorities in their midst like the Tory impurities of the Imperial Government they represented.

Every history text read by generations of American schoolchildren cites a statutory enactment of this Imperial Government among the leading proximate causes of that Revolution. I refer to the Quebec Act of 1774. Having acquired New France by conquest in 1763, the British authorities had found themselves ruling a colony whose inhabitants were the descendants of an implanted fragment of seventeenth-century France. Far from having escaped, the original settlers had been induced by a French monarchy at the zenith of its powers to inhabit the shores of the St. Lawrence and had brought with them leaders and institutions whose collective, hierarchical values reflected Europe's feudal past. Deprived by the British conquest of a civil leadership whose members returned to France, the descendants of these settlers were left with their ecclesiastical leaders, whose influence brought the other-worldly dimension of collective feudal values to the fore.

How different these people were from the American colonists already chafing under British rule. How respectful, how congenial, how distinctive they were by comparison. The price to be paid by Britain for their assured support was to recognize their Church. This was the Church of Rome—not, to be sure, the imperially established Church of England—but tantalizingly similar in its ordered hierarchy and its collective willingness to submit to any accommodating civil authority. This the Quebec Act accomplished, thereby according the recognition of the Imperial Parliament to a distinct society north of the American colonies, a society seen by the latter as popish, illiberal and, yes, un-American.

No wonder the Quebec Act could be interpreted by the American colonists as a symbol of Imperial perfidy. No wonder too that it would guarantee for generations a continued British presence in North America. American emissaries in search of French Canadian support during the revolutionary war could not be understood across a language barrier that, even more than linguistic, was a barrier between a liberal vocabulary and a feudal one. Note well, in this connection, that "the state" is a term that is not to be found in the feudal vocabulary. Where this term is not understood, there will be no expectation that the state can, let alone should, play a role in the delivery of services. For about two centuries, indeed into the 1950s, educational, health and social services in Québec will be provided by religious orders and diocesan authorities.

Meanwhile, however, America's victory in the War of Independence had brought a new wave of settlers to Britain's remaining North American colony: the so-called Loyalists. These are Americans; as such they are liberal individualists, but they have been expelled from America as failed liberals. Their enduring loyalty to the Crown during the War of Independence had marked them as impure individualists, tainted by their attachment to a royal symbol of the European past. In these settlers Canada acquired what Gad Horowitz has called its tory-touched liberal fragment (Horowitz 1966). Expelled and expropriated by the Americans, these are liberals with a difference: individualists who expect that government, in the guise of the British colonial authorities, will assist them in return for the loyalty that accounts for their plight. The consequences for the future are profound. English Canada's liberal political culture, compromised by Tory values from its beginning, can never propel individualism to the status of the civic religion that will permeate nineteenth-century America. Moreover, it will be open to socialist values in the present century.

Geography enters to play its own role in support of English Canadian values that invite positive government. The American frontier is essentially a soft frontier, beckoning throughout the nineteenth century the gradual westward movement of American settlers to the squeak of their own wagon wheels. But the hard frontier of Canada's Great Shield presents a formidable barrier to the fertile lands beyond. The Canadian westward movement must therefore await the clickety-clack of train wheels on railways financed by government credit and concessions. These railways bring turn-of-the-century Europeans direct from the dockside of Canadian ports to the prairies and British Columbia. Indeed, the latter province has been characterized as a "radical" fragment, more akin to Australia than to the older parts of English Canada, its politics less dominated by the centre and more characterized by the twentieth-century ideological divide between left and right (Galbraith 1976).

And there is still more to the geographical heterogeneity of evolving Canadian political culture. As it emerges in this century, the prairie province of Saskatchewan, a major recipient of British immigrants whose political baggage includes the values of Methodism and Fabianism, exhibits a political culture permeated with what Martin Lipset has called agrarian socialism (Lipset 1968). Meantime, its immediate western neighbour, Alberta, the last Canadian province to receive settlers after the closing of the American frontier, becomes home to Canada's most individualist political culture, imported by American settlers who, upon finding the Great Plains occupied, veered northward (Wiseman 1991). In Alberta, Canada has its "Little America," complete with a historical appetite for the nostrums of the so-called monetary cranks of the inter-war period.

To round out this historical portrait of Canada's heterogeneous political culture, reference needs be made to Canada's oldest English-speaking provinces, those on the Atlantic Ocean. Here an absence of twentieth-century immigration—itself the marker of deep-seated conditions of economic stagnation—yields a political culture of dependency and cynicism seemingly frozen in the tory-touched liberal mould of the nineteenth century (Adamson and Stewart 1991). But as matters would turn out, the chronic have-not status of the three Maritime provinces, augmented by the addition of the former Dominion of Newfoundland in 1949, was not to be without its own impact on the federal–provincial dimensions of the role of the state.

Presently, however, my historical portrait of Canada's heterogeneity requires drastic updating in one respect: the truly remarkable changes in the post-war political culture of Québec. At work throughout the 1950s and visibly apparent from the 1960s, these changes transform Québec from the other-worldly, Catholic society of the past into a thoroughly secular, highly modernized statist society. In an elemental way, these changes are conveyed by a change in political vocabulary. *Les Canadiens*, as the French Canadians used to call themselves, become politically extinct. *Les Canadiens*, historically the majoritarian population within the boundaries of Québec but with a significant presence elsewhere, especially in eastern and northern Ontario and to a lesser extent in Manitoba, transform themselves within Québec into *les Québéquois*. This term, by which historically the residents of Québec City distinguished themselves from the residents of the cities of Trois-Rivières (*Trifluviens*) or Montreal (*Montréalais*) is appropriated by all who live within the jurisdictional boundaries of the Province of Québec, whose government has been transformed into the engine of their secularization and modernization.

At the level of the schoolroom, the secularization of Québec becomes apparent in the transformation of primary and secondary education along lines strikingly similar to those prevailing elsewhere in North America. At the level of the bedroom, modernization propels what by the 1980s had become the lowest fertility rate in Canada: 1.4 children per woman of child-bearing age compared to 1.8 in the rest of the country—2.1 being the number required to maintain population stability.

If anything, Québec becomes more North American than ever in its past: in its occupational structure, its economic orientation, its social deportment. Québec has discovered the role of the state with a vengeance. Transcending this aggressive public sector role in education, health and social services is one startling difference: the role of the state in language policy. A series of legislative enactments that culminate in the famous Bill 101 of 1976—the Charter of the French Language—moulds the provincial state into an affirmative action vehicle on behalf of language. Québec is to be as French as Ontario is English. Québec is to offer an exclusively French face to the world by mandating French as the language of commercial advertising; its private sector is "francisized" through legal measures stipulating that no offer of employment or promotion may be contingent on knowledge of a language other than French save by the consent of a regulatory agency, the Office de la Langue Francaise (see McRoberts 1988). The constitutional capacity of the Québec government to implement this affirmative action program is ample, as is its constitutional capacity, like that of other provinces, in the realm of educational, health and social services.

The Delivery of Services in the Canadian State

This leads me to elaborate upon my core observation: the striking irrelevance of constitutional change to the delivery of these services in Canada. The constitutional framework that has been in place since 1867 puts all the institutions involved with these services under the exclusive jurisdiction of the provinces. In the realm of government revenue, that same framework makes direct taxation, which includes all major taxes on income and consumption, a field of concurrent federal and provincial jurisdiction. Finally, it confers a virtually unrestricted spending power on the federal government. In brief, the federal government may make payments to provincial governments, to institutions and to individuals for any purposes, including those involving matters under provincial jurisdiction. The only apparent constitutional restriction is that such payments must be financed by the federal government's general revenues rather than from special funds earmarked for a purpose that might be deemed under provincial jurisdiction.

Unemployment Insurance

The simple restriction I have just outlined spawned the only constitutional changes to the division of jurisdiction that are material to the realm of services. So that unemployment insurance could be financed from a federally earmarked fund, it was added to the matters under exclusive federal jurisdiction in 1940. To permit the same mode of financing, in 1951 old age pensions and in 1964 survivors' and disability benefits were designated as matters of concurrent federal and provincial jurisdiction, with paramountcy assigned to the provinces in the sense that no federal law bearing on these matters can affect the operation of provincial laws on the subject (see Cameron and Dupré 1983).

Therefore, the entire Canadian labour force is covered by a single program of Unemployment Insurance whose premiums, eligibility rules, benefit levels and benefit duration are federally determined. Social assistance for those not covered by unemployment insurance, including individuals who remain unemployed after exhausting their insurance benefits, is determined by the provinces, which recover half their social assistance and service expenditures from the federal government in the form of a shared-cost transfer payment under the Canada Assistance Plan. In this setting, one finds that many provinces have creatively tailored their own social and employment policies with an eye to federal unemployment insurance. Especially where unemployment occurs on a seasonal basis, one can find provincial public works projects that are designed to employ unemployment insurance recipients upon the termination of their benefit eligibility for time spans that are just long enough to qualify these individuals for a further eligibility period at the expense of the federal government. Some might call what I have just described federal–provincial entanglement. Others might call it creative public sector management. I call it typically Canadian, eh?

Old Age Security

Turning to the realm of old age security, one encounters two distinct programs. The first, which is exclusively federal and was initiated in 1952, provides demogrants* to all Canadians aged 65 and over. Given subsequent improvements, a guaranteed income supplement is added for pensioners whose incomes are below a threshold level determined by the federal government. Yet further income redistribution is achieved because the same government, to use its own vocabulary, annually claws back the monthly demogrants it has paid to affluent individuals on its income tax return.

The second program provides earnings–related retirement, survivor and disability pensions paid from an earmarked fund financed by employer and employee contributions. It is at the inception of this program that we find two recurring themes in federal–provincial relations: provincial creativity and asymmetric federalism. In the first part of the 1960s, contributory public pensions rose to the top of the Canadian policy agenda. Among the various designs that emerged as serious candidates, the one advanced by Québec was deemed superior because, given the relatively young age structure of the Canadian population, it would generate a substantial surplus of pension plan revenues over pension expenditures for several decades.

---

*A payment granted solely on the basis of demographic characteristics.

The outcome, sanctioned by the 1964 constitutional change I have outlined and begun in 1966, was the Canadian Pension Plan in nine provinces and the Québec Pension Plan in the tenth. The contribution and benefit levels are identical. The asymmetry lies in the investment of the surplus funds. Canada Pension Plan funds are invested exclusively in the long-term bonds of the nine provinces in which this federally administered Plan applies, thereby giving these provinces a source of market-sheltered borrowing. (The interest they pay is the rate that prevails with respect to long-term federal borrowing, which is advantageous to the extent that this rate is below the rates at which provincial bonds, especially those of the smaller provinces, can find a market.) The Québec Pension Plan makes the surplus funds available for private- as well as public-sector borrowing. Here we find what is indeed the tangible expression of a modernized Québec eager to use the state as an engine of private-sector development.

For all that remains, nothing I am about to say has involved any constitutional change whatsoever. The tales I am telling are entirely stories of non-constitutional federal–provincial adaptation (National, Provincial and Municipal Finances).

Medical Insurance
In the realm of health, as was the case in contributory pensions, the story begins with provincial creativity. To Saskatchewan, the Canadian home of agrarian socialism, belongs the credit for initiating publicly financed hospital insurance in 1948. Newfoundland brought its own so-called "cottage hospital" system into Confederation in 1949. British Columbia copied Saskatchewan in 1950 as did Alberta in 1952 (Simeon and Robinson 1990, 149). All these programs were financed exclusively by the provinces involved. Then in 1955, after Ontario simultaneously announced the preparation of its own program and invited federal financing on a shared-cost basis, the federal government developed a shared-cost arrangement that was initiated in 1957 and involved all ten provinces by the time Québec mounted its own hospital insurance program in 1963.

Meanwhile, Saskatchewan's creativity had gone to work for a second time, as this provincial home of agrarian socialism mounted in 1962 a public medical insurance program with the help of the windfall revenue it recovered from the federal share of hospital insurance costs. Responding to a climate of public opinion that clearly endorsed public medical insurance, in 1966 the federal government announced a medical shared-cost program that by 1971 involved all ten provinces. "Medicare," as comprehensive hospital and medical insurance came to be called in popular parlance, has since emerged as something of a symbol of Canadian nationhood. Here I am anticipating the final section of this paper.

To round out this descriptive account, I shall simply observe that the federal role in financing a significant portion of medicare left each province entirely free—if that is the right word—to cope with the institutional configuration and availability of technologically driven health services and to confront, in the realm of physician compensation, the organized greed of their respective health professionals. Until 1984, federal medicare funding stipulated only that provincial medicare plans be comprehensive, universal, publicly administered, interprovincially portable and accessible. In that year, an additional condition essentially banned extra-billing by physicians by stipulating a one-to-one dollar reduction in federal transfers for every dollar allowed in such fees. Five provinces finance their share of medicare costs from their general tax revenues; British Columbia and Alberta charge compulsory premiums to employers and employees; and Manitoba, Ontario and Québec levy a payroll tax on employers.

Education Services
Federal financing of postsecondary education had as stormy a beginning as any episode that is to be found in the historical annals of federal–provincial relations. Relying on its constitutionally unlimited spending power, which includes a capacity to make payments directly to institutions, in 1951 the federal government initiated grants that it paid directly to universities. This gave rise to a peculiarly Canadian version of what Americans call the politics of interposition when the then premier of Québec, Maurice Duplessis, ordered Québec universities to refuse the grants. Interposition, the eminently American southern state practice invoked in that country against the enforcement of court decisions, was invoked in Canada against the federal spending power. The result was that what the Canadian constitution permits, the political canons of federal–provincial relations denied (Cameron and Dupré 1983).

What ensued was a genuinely asymmetric episode in federal–provincial finance with one set of arrangements in the nine English-speaking provinces and a different one in Québec. The essence of the federal–Québec arrangement, which was temporarily extended to certain health and welfare programs, is that Québec opted out of federal postsecondary education spending in exchange for tax room that the federal government vacated in Québec by reducing, in favour of provincial taxation, the income taxes it levies on Québec residents. Aspects of this asymmetric feature of federal–provincial finance, which symbolically yields to Québec a measure of special status, remain to the present day.

What is material to the immediate present are comprehensive federal–provincial arrangements that have been in place since 1977. Pursuant to these arrangements, which encompass both medicare and postsecondary education, federal funds flow to provincial governments through what are called Established Program transfers. These are block funding transfers unrelated to provincial expenditure levels. More than any other development, it is Established Program Financing that has made the elephant story with which I began this address somewhat less relevant to the federal–provincial domain than it used to be. With respect to postsecondary education in particular, the upshot in Canada amounts to ten distinct postsecondary education systems, each of them guided and nurtured entirely by the provincial government concerned.

Equalization Payments
Along with Established Program Financing, the same fiscal arrangements encompass another federal transfer whose significance for Canadian unity cannot be rated too highly. I refer to equalization payments. Entirely financed by the federal government, these are unconditional grants designed to raise the fiscal capacity of Canadian provinces to a representative national average. As fiscally affluent provinces, Alberta, British Columbia and Ontario do not qualify. Saskatchewan—on the geographical margin of the oil-and-gas lands that, when resource prices boom, make Alberta Canada's Kuwait—is the "swing" province, qualifying for equalization grants in some years but not in others. The remaining provinces are the consistent recipients, and the significance of these grants can be gauged by the fact that they annually represent about 10 percent of Québec's provincial revenues, 15 percent of Manitoba's and between 20 and 33 percent of the revenues of each of the four chronically have-not provinces of Atlantic Canada.

Equalization payments are enormously consequential. In tangible terms, they are what makes it possible to bring comparable levels of public services within reach of all Canadians, whatever their province of residence. They underpin the capacity of the recipient provinces to engage highly qualified public servants. And they testify to social, economic and moral ties that bind Canadian citizens in a sharing commun'ty.

That community expresses its concern for the economic well-being of deprived regions through yet another set of government activities: regional development programs. Over the decades, what is literally an alphabet soup of federal government agencies—ADB, ARDA, FRED, DREE, DRIE, ACOA and WED—have expended billions of dollars in efforts to reduce interregional economic disparities (*see* Savoie 1986).

These efforts, sad to say, have had little apparent success at a level that can be measured by macroeconomic indicators. But their effect is visibly apparent in the public sector infrastructure of Canada's have-not provinces. In such provinces, federal government spending and expertise have deeply penetrated areas of provincial jurisdiction. Here one will find municipal public works, roads and even schools federally planned and financed under bilateral development agreements concluded between federal negotiators and representatives of the provincial government concerned. In these instances, every elephant (admittedly some of them white elephants) is a jointly federal and provincial beast. Most notable of all, regional development programs, like equalization payments, are sustained and indeed celebrated as a badge of coast-to-coast Canadian nationhood.

And here is where constitutional change does enter the picture—not to permit or facilitate what has been accomplished—but precisely to celebrate it. Section 36 of the Constitution Act, 1982 is a non-justiciable declaration of commitment to the principle of federal equalization payments and to federal–provincial efforts to reduce regional economic disparities. It constitutes symbolic approbation for what has been achieved without—I repeat—any need for constitutional change.

Constitutional Change

This brings me to that doleful subject in its recent setting—constitutional discontent that has gnawed remorselessly at Canada's political fabric. This discontent has nothing to do with what this paper has described and is celebrated in Section 36. It is instead a discontent rooted in symbolism, that most delicate and intractable dimension of human affairs. The symbolic dimension of my story begins in Québec, the distinct society whose survival in North America is rooted in the Quebec Act of 1774. *Les Canadiens* are secure in their distinctiveness for as long as their traditional, Catholic, non-statist society makes this matter self-evident. But a modernized Québec becomes exactly like other modernized societies in socioeconomic values and outlook. Within North America, the only remaining difference is language in a setting where a recently discovered provincial state is the vigorous promoter of that language. In the symbolic realm, this invites a search for what might be available to give further expression to

Québec's dwindling difference. Could this be recognition of Québec within the Canadian constitutional framework as a distinct society or perhaps as an associate state? What about the trappings of a sovereign and independent nation-state?

The road travelled before and since the Constitution Act of 1982 leaves these questions hanging over the Canadian realm. The federal prime minister who more than anyone authored the Constitution Act was convinced that the answer to these questions should be a resounding "no." Pierre Trudeau sought instead, and succeeded, in entrenching a Charter of Rights and Freedoms to symbolize the unity of Canadians as rights-bearers. The success of the Charter in this regard awaits the verdict of history. What can be said about this thoroughly contemporary Charter is that the explicit recognition it accords to women, ethnic minorities and Aboriginal peoples is worn by the recipients, who transcend provincial boundaries, as badges of honour (see Cairns 1991). But the Constitution Act of 1982 was promulgated over the explicitly recorded opposition of the Québec legislature. The political agony that preceded its promulgation was therefore fated to be prolonged.

That promulgation began with a mostly futile round of negotiation on the constitutional status of Native peoples. This round, mandated by a commitment that had been entrenched in the Constitution Act, was boycotted by the Government of Québec, given the illegitimacy with which its legislature had branded this Act. Then, as is well known, the advent in 1984-85 of Brian Mulroney and Robert Bourassa—the former a new prime minister in Ottawa and the latter a recycled prime minister in Québec—created the circumstances that led to the so-called Meech Lake accord. All 11 of Canada's first ministers endorsed, in April and June of 1987, a document that met the five basic constitutional demands formulated by Mr. Bourassa: 1. distinct society status for Québec without any explicit additions to its jurisdiction; 2. the constitutionalization of an existing Québec-Ottawa agreement on immigration to Québec; 3. a limitation on the constitutional capacity of the federal government to initiate future shared-cost programs in areas of exclusive provincial jurisdiction; 4. explicit constitutional recognition of the long-established practice whereby three members of the Supreme Court are members of the Québec bar; 5. a Québec veto over future constitutional amendments involving federal institutions or the creation of new provinces, this veto being conferred through the simple expedient of requiring unanimous provincial consent to all such amendments.

Technically, the reason why the accord failed to pass into the realm of constitutional law is that, in a setting where its fourth and fifth components involved a unanimity requirement, two provincial legislatures, those of Manitoba and Newfoundland, did not ratify it (*see* Monahan 1991). Because I am addressing constitutional change and the delivery of services, I shall not editorialize except to observe that nothing I have outlined in the body of this chapter would have changed had Meech Lake succeeded, with a single exception. In the event that new federal–provincial shared-cost programs might be initiated in the future, the same asymmetric arrangements that have already yielded Québec a measure of special status in financial arrangements would be negotiated as a constitutional requirement rather than an ordinary political compromise.

In the end, the jurisdictional and financial status quo remained. The country itself hung in the balance. In Québec, the events that first yielded the Constitution Act of 1982 over the objection of its legislature and then denied the Meech Lake accord quickly hardened into two powerful myths. There is the Myth of Imposition, which envelops the Act of 1982, compounded by the Myth of Rejection, the denial of the accord being taken as symbolizing the rejection of Québec by the rest of Canada. These two myths received statutory formulation in the preamble of Bill 150, passed by the Québec legislature in June of 1991. This law mandated the holding of a referendum on Québec's sovereignty by October 26 of 1992 and further stipulated that an affirmative vote in this referendum would "constitute a proposal that Quebec acquire the status of a sovereign state one year to the day from the holding of the referendum" (Dupré 1991, 70).

The search for a solution to this impasse thereupon consumed Canada's politicians for more than a year on the path to another fruitless outcome on October 26, 1992. Along the way to this outcome, a concerned observer might have hoped that one lesson of the Meech Lake fiasco would have registered: elements of constitutional change that require unanimous consent should not be integrated in a single package with elements that require only the consent of the federal parliament and the legislatures of seven provinces with 50 percent of the population. Had Meech Lake not been an integrated package, its distinct society clause, its constitutionalized immigration agreements and its limitation on future applications of the federal spending power would already be part of the law of the Canadian constitution.

Instead, however, what transpired led to the negotiation of a mind-boggling collage of constitutional amendments—the so-called

Charlottetown accord of 1992. Here could be found not only a repetition of the Meech response to Quebec's five basic constitutional demands but changes affecting the status of Aboriginal peoples, the composition of the House of Commons, the division of jurisdiction and a change that, at the behest of Alberta, ever Canada's "little America," would yield a federal Senate that is not only elected but gives equal representation to each province. This sprawling package meant that ratification must once again involve unanimous consent (*see* Russell 1993, chs. 10–11).

In the event, the Charlottetown accord died before it could even reach the formal ratification arena. Its death-blow was delivered by a precedent-setting plebiscite on October 26, 1992, the very day originally mandated by Québec's Bill 150 as the ultimate deadline for a referendum on Québec sovereignty. The Québec statute mandating this referendum could be amended to substitute the Charlottetown accord for sovereignty as the subject to be addressed by the question but the already existing plebiscitary momentum was irreversible. At this juncture a federal statute passed for the purpose submitted the Charlottetown accord to a nationwide referendum. Its resounding defeat by the electorates of six provinces relegated the accord to the scrap heap of aborted constitutional changes. Mercifully, the Québec electorate was among these six, thereby precluding a Meech-like portrayal of the outcome as a rejection of that province's constitutional aspirations by the rest of the country. At the same time, recourse to the plebiscitary process set a precedent for future referenda that is unlikely to be overturned, at least where comprehensive packages of constitutional amendments are concerned.

The upshot is that further attempts at comprehensive constitutional changes are not part of the foreseeable future. The symbolic inflation fuelled by constitutional negotiation has been punctured by the democratically sanctioned fate of the Charlottetown accord, inviting a renewed exploration of what can be achieved without recourse to the constitution. This requires the country to deal not with symbolism but with the very tangible and quantifiable problems that currently beset the delivery of its public services. For reasons that I believe are embedded in Canada's heterogeneous political culture, its people and politicians have proven to be relatively immune to the ideological nostrums of Reaganism and Thatcherism. But they must cope with economic conditions that make the immediate climate one of exceptional fiscal stringency.

In practical terms, this climate has led the federal government to freeze the cash transfers of its Established Programs Financing and to place a 5 percent ceiling on the annual growth of the shared-cost transfers that its Canada Assistance Plan provides to the so-called "have" provinces that do not qualify for equalization payments. This same climate is leading all governments to contain their expenditures not by cutting service levels but instead by reducing public sector compensation. More generally, it makes creative public sector management, especially in the delivery of health, social and educational services, a Canadian imperative. Other papers in this volume explore many of these delivery issues. For my part, I am not reluctant to bet that the requisite creativity will be forthcoming and that it will be driven by the extent to which, for all its heterogeneity, Canada is indeed a sharing community.

Here I return to the relevance of Section 36 of the Constitution Act of 1982. As I have observed, what is celebrated here as badges of Canadian unity are the principles of federal equalization payments and of federal–provincial efforts to combat regional disparities. In a similar vein, the least controversial portion of the ill-fated Charlottetown accord was a nonjusticiable social charter that celebrated a Canadian commitment to preserve adequate public services, including notably its medicare system.

The creative public sector management that the sharing community commands invites further exploration of the asymmetric federal–provincial relations that developed in the 1960s. Public services such as labour market training can potentially be delivered in a manner that, through the very asymmetry that has been achieved in the past without constitutional change, bridges the heterogeneity of "have" provinces, "have-not" provinces and a Québec whose distinctiveness is accommodated through fiscal adjustments (*see* Maxwell 1993).

It remains not unlikely that the near future may yield a Québec referendum on sovereignty. But such a referendum must be won and, at least as measured by public opinion polls, the chances of a sovereigntist victory are anything but robust when poll respondents are informed that sovereignty means exclusion from Canada's sharing community (Dion 1993). In this light, I am more than willing to wager that future generations of Canadian children will be writing elephant stories whose federal–provincial content varies with each child's province of residence and that these stories, not least because of Quebec's constitutional capacity to promote French, will continue to be written in both of Canada's official languages.

References

Adamson, Agar, and Ian Stewart. 1991. Party Politics in Atlantic Canada: Still the Mysterious East. In *Party Politics in Canada*, edited by Hugh G. Thorburn. Scarborough: Prentice-Hall Canada.

Cairns, Alan C. 1991. *Disruptions: Constitutional Struggles from the Charter to Meech Lake*, edited by Douglas E. Williams. Toronto: McClelland & Stewart.

Cameron, David M., and J. Stefan Dupré. 1983. The Financial Framework of Income Distribution and Social Services. In *Canada and the New Constitution: The Unfinished Agenda*, edited by Stanley M. Beck and Ivan Bernier. Vol. I. Montreal: The Institute for Research on Public Policy.

Dion, Stéphane. 1993. La Sécession du Québec: Evaluation des probabilités. Conférence présentée lors du colloque international, Les élections au Canada 1993. Centre de recherche sur l'Amérique du Nord de l'Université Autonome du Mexique, 12 novembre.

Dupré, J. Stefan. 1991. Canada's Political and Constitutional Future: Reflections on the Bélanger-Campeau Report and Bill 150. In *"English Canada" Speaks Out*, edited by J.L. Granatstein and K.W. McNaught. Toronto: Doubleday Canada.

Forbes, H. Donald. 1987. Hartz-Horowitz at Twenty: Nationalism, Toryism and Socialism in Canada and the United States. *Canadian Journal of Political Science* 20 (June):287–316.

Galbraith, Gordon S. 1976. British Columbia. In *The Provincial Political Systems*, edited by David J. Bellamy et al. Toronto: Methuen Publications.

Hartz, Louis. 1964. *The Founding of New Societies*. New York: Harcourt, Brace and World.

Horowitz, Gad. 1966. Conservatism, Liberalism and Socialism in Canada: An Interpretation. *Canadian Journal of Economics and Political Science* 32(May):143–71.

Lipset, S.M. 1968. *Agrarian Socialism: The Co-operative Commonwealth Federation in Saskatchewan*. New York: Garden City.

Maxwell, Judith. 1993. More Carrots Please: Education, Training and Fiscal Federalism. Conference on Fiscal Federalism for the Future. Kingston: School of Policy Studies, Queen's University, November 5.

McRoberts, Kenneth. 1988. *Quebec: Social Change and Political Crises*. 3d ed. Toronto: McClelland & Stewart.

Monahan, Patrick. 1991. *Meech Lake: The Inside Story*. Toronto: University of Toronto Press.

Russell, Peter H. 1993. *Constitutional Odyssey: Can Canadians Become a Sovereign People?* 2d. ed. Toronto: University of Toronto Press.

Savoie, Donald J. 1986. *Regional Development: Canada's Search for Solutions*. Toronto: University of Toronto Press.

Simeon, Richard, and Ian Robertson. 1990. *State, Society, and the Development of Canadian Federalism*. Research Studies of the Royal Commission on the Economic Union and Development Prospects for Canada, no. 71. Toronto: University of Toronto Press.

The National Finances (annual) and *Provincial and Municipal Finances* (biennial). Much of the information in this essay draws from these two altogether indispensable publications of the Canadian Tax Foundation in Toronto.

Wiseman, Nelson. 1991. The Pattern of Prairie Politics. In *Party Politics in Canada*, edited by Hugh G. Thorburn. Scarborough: Prentice-Hall Canada.

CHRISTOPHER DUNN

Centralism, Provincialism and Constitutional Politics in Canada

One of the major themes of Canadian federalism for the past 30 years has involved provincial and, to a lesser extent, federal demands for new powers. Yet there have been few theories of federalism that suggest how to deal with such demands according to the principle of mutual satisfaction among intergovernmental actors. Demands for new provincial powers usually generate governmental and academic literature that asks readers to choose between strong provinces or a strong central government, between centralization and decentralization and between the historical records of different levels of government. The arguments in the literature, moreover, tend to cancel each other out. This paper argues that such dichotomies are unimaginative and that other approaches to Canadian federalism that escape from traditional dichotomies deserve more attention. It also argues that such reasoning is more in keeping with the public mood, as revealed by the 1990–92 consultation process in Canada.

A few caveats are appropriate at the beginning. References are made to recent history and to current controversies, but the paper does not purport to deal with them in any substantive way. It does not deal specifically with the role of Québec in Confederation, although some of its "solutions" may be applicable to the Québec question. Our major emphasis is to isolate and critique general trends in Canadian argumentation about division of powers; our major assumption is that in isolating these some perspective can be gained for use in future constitutional debates.

The agenda for Trudeau-era constitutional reform usually placed division-of-powers questions at the bottom of the list after entrenchment of rights and institutional reform. The Meech Lake accord proposal advanced the division-of-powers question more to the forefront, although in rather oblique fashion. The question of provincial power shares—in both the *de jure* and *de facto* senses—became an important item in constitutional talks once again.

The question of whether or not to increase provincial power has, of course, already been with us for some time. In the modern era it was spearheaded by the Lesage government—successfully, as it turned out, in the particular areas of pensions policy and the 1965 option-out provisions. Québec continued to push for attention to reform of the division of powers during the 1968-71 constitution conferences, challenging the federal agenda for the talks. The first ministers considered changes in the division of taxing and spending powers in 1969, as well as considering respective roles in the field of income security and social services. In June 1971, Québec made some radical proposals for reallocation of federal and provincial responsibilities for social security; the Victoria Charter of 1971 made some limited concessions to Québec in this area and others that Premier Bourassa ultimately rejected.

In the mid-to-late 1970s other provinces joined the call for provincial control of varying degrees over a sizeable list of matters: immigration, language policy, resource taxation, the declaratory power, annual first ministers' conferences, creation of new provinces, culture, communications, federal spending power, equalization, reservation and disallowance, implementation of treaties, fisheries, natural resources and appointment of judges of the provincial Supreme Courts. Consideration of *other* aspects of federal power was to follow this as well! The other provinces had joined Québec in the challenge to the federal agenda. What they did not get on this list in the 1980–82 and 1987 constitutional negotiations—and they got some items—they continued to seek on the judicial, regulatory, fiscal and policy fronts.

In the spring of 1991 the Allaire Committee of the Québec Liberal Party demanded that Québec be given exclusive control of 22 jurisdictional matters; this new emphasis on the division of powers was echoed by the Québec Legislature's Bélanger-Campeau Commission. Perhaps seeking to mollify Québec without violating the principle of provincial equality, the federal government's proposals of September 1991 suggested recognizing exclusive provincial jurisdiction over tourism, forestry, mining, recreation and municipal affairs as well as sharing authority in areas like manpower training, culture and immigration. Of course, these suggestions were counterbalanced by some centralizing provisions in the federal package. Reflecting a Trudeau-era theme, the federal proposals suggested a new head of federal power to pass laws for the efficient functioning of the economic union that would be subject to approval by a new "Council of the Federation."

This burst of activity on the division-of-powers question generated a growth of scholarly literature on the same subject. The literature, while often acknowledging that wider conceptualizations of federalism were possible, tended to drift towards discussions of the relative merits of centralization and decentralization. A review of this literature will give us an idea of the restricted nature of the debate.

Debates about Jurisdictional Power
Constitutional Directives and Constitutional Change
A common method of arguing that provinces have too much power is to concentrate on constitutional matters. One may note how provinces have blocked needed constitutional change or else have weakened constitutional arrangements that had bona fide reasons for being installed in the first place. Some opponents of the growth of provincial power argue that in a federation provisions that allocate foreign affairs to the national government and that provide for an economic common market within the union make political and economic sense. To weaken them would not. As well, constitutional change that would provide for autarkic constitutional development was resisted in the past because of provincial self-interest; there is little indication that this reflex has been abandoned and so provinces should not be accorded more of a hammerlock on future constitutional change. Of course, these arguments can be challenged.

The Internal Common Market
An argument can be made that provinces have blunted constitutional directives promoting an internal common market. Section 121 of the *Constitution Act, 1867* says that "All articles of Growth, Produce or Manufacture of any of the Provinces shall, from and after the Union, be admitted free into each of the other Provinces." However, as is well known, provinces have erected a wide variety of barriers to the free flow of interprovincial commerce, such as technical and product standards, procurement policies, and conditions set on the sale of raw natural resources. Until prevented by section 6 of the *Constitution Act, 1982*, provinces also engaged in analogous restrictions to the mobility of labour in Canada. The reason for these blockages is to promote development—an economic policy that results in the enhancement of employment and provincial per capita income, that decreases net out-migration and that expands forward, backward and final

demand linkages in the area of staple goods. Such restrictions are contrary to economic efficiency, say opponents, and they are contrary to the specific intent of the Fathers of Confederation. The clear implication is that regional development policies that feature interprovincial trade barriers should be de-emphasized at the provincial level.

The argument can be turned around, however. Federal as well as provincial policies may result in a failure of national economic integration. Centralized regional development policies may hinder rather than facilitate economic adjustment to technological change and market conditions. The industrial structure may remain inappropriate to changing patterns of comparative advantage if it is propped up by ill-advised development grants. However, Canadian nationalists tend to turn a blind eye to such facts, and concentrate instead on "provincial protectionism" (Leslie 1987, 91).

The Appropriate Division of International Responsibilities
Although the 1867 Constitution was unclear on the division of international responsibilities in Canadian federalism, there is some indication in Section 132 (Empire Treaties) that Ottawa was intended to play the major role in international treaties and undertakings. Since the 1937 *Labour Conventions Case* the responsibility effectively has been curtailed: Canada did not have the right, by concluding an international treaty, to commit a province to carrying out the matter agreed to therein if it fell within provincial jurisdiction. Left ambiguous in this 1937 Judicial Committee decision, however, were the respective rights of the federal and provincial governments to negotiate international agreements; and Québec has at times asserted its right to do so. Given the vast range of provincial "transnational activity," it is not beyond the realm of possibility that other provinces one day might claim similar privileges.

It is instructive to review the federal defence of "one voice" in international affairs during the heyday of the controversy in the late 1960s:

> Ottawa's case was that the prerogative power to enter into international arrangements and to conclude agreements binding in international law resided in the federal executive alone.... The federal authorities make much of the point that Canada had a single international personality and that the United Nations and its specialized agencies, as well as other international associations and international law, drew a very sharp line between jurisdictions which were sovereign states and those which were not. The general case was made that "foreign policy is indivisible" al-

> though in the Canadian circumstances this did not preclude the provinces, in cooperation with the federal government, from being involved in international affairs. (Smiley 1980, 48)

With some exceptions this has continued to be the status quo stance of the federal government.

This stance was given a new twist in the case of negotiation of international trade agreements; during the free trade negotiations in the late 1980s, federal spokespersons implied that their right to conclude the Free Trade Agreement rested on the federal trade and commerce power, and that provinces would be bound by the agreement (Canada 1988). The subliminal message in Ottawa's defence of its international role is that provinces have more than enough of an international presence. The Macdonald Royal Commission was a more explicit defence of federal predominance in international trade negotiations:

> Unless the negotiating parties in international negotiations can fully commit their own countries to abide by the agreements signed, they will have only limited ability to secure concessions. Informal undertakings made by provinces…to comply with negotiated international agreements will not solve the problem. (Macdonald 1985, 3:153)

The obverse to these lines of argument is that provinces both have and deserve a role in international arrangements. They have an implied role in the negotiating of treaties thanks to the silence of the Judicial Committee, at least until countermanded by the courts. Even the Macdonald Commission admitted this possibility, pointedly arguing only for a "predominant," but not exclusive, federal role in negotiating and ratifying treaties and in coordinating Canada's federal and provincial international activities (Canada 1985, 3:149, 155). It recommended a constitutional amendment to provide that, where treaties affecting provincial jurisdiction were negotiated, those sections placing obligations on provinces would only take effect on the passage of resolutions in two-thirds of provincial legislatures representing over half Canada's population. This would be a compromise between respecting the Constitution and effective international participation (Canada 1985, 3:154–5).

The Process of Constitutional Reform

A last cavil about provincial power being too broad on the constitutional : purported tendency of provinces to bring a narrow view to the process of constitutional reform. The increasing influence of the provinces in constitutional reform is said to have had a variety of negative effects. One is that the pursuance of constitutional renewal predominantly through "executive federalism"—that is, secretive and definitive bargaining by federal and provincial political élites upon which provinces have insisted as a modus operandi—has resulted in an unjustified appropriation of power by the provincial and federal authorities. As Alan Cairns has recounted, governments are recentralizing power that was not so long ago decentralized to popular groups. The federal government in the 1968 to 1982 rounds of constitutional negotiations successfully contrasted the rights of people (the Charter) with the provinces' "selfish pursuit of governmental advantage" (Cairns 1988, 257) and relegated the question of division of powers to a category of secondary importance. Referenda were suggested as deadlock-breakers in cases of constitutional impasse between governments. The citizens' voice in constitutional change began to be seen as a necessary supplement to the voices of governments, whose collective authority and legitimacy was definitely on the wane (Cairns 1988, 257).

Citizen groups established along non-territorial cleavages are also not likely to defer to government in matters of constitutional renewal.

> The Constitution is no longer an affair of governments. In addition to the governments' Constitution, which tends to focus on feder-alism, there is a citizens' Constitution which the Charter symbol-izes. A central task for the constitutional theory and practice of future decades is to find ways in which these two visions, warring in the bosom of the Canadian Constitution, can be reconciled. (Cairns 1988, 259)

Mr. Trudeau has given implicit approval to this distinction in his recent book, contrasting the "legal country" of Canada, namely a prime minister desirous of electoral victory and provincial premiers "all panting to increase their powers," and the "real country" of Canada, namely "the unorganized coalition of Canadian individuals and groups scattered across the country for whom Canada is more than a collection of provinces to be governed through wheeling and dealing" (Axworthy and Trudeau 1990, 383–4). Trudeau argues that the real country shared his antipathy to the values inherent in the Meech Lake accord.

It may be argued as well that the provinces have hindered constitutional modernization in Canada. Ontario and Québec jointly hindered agreement on amending formulae in the constitutional negotiations of 1927, 1936 and 1950. Claiming prerogatives arising from their sizable population and economic power, they demanded *de facto* or *de jure* veto powers through either unanimity provisions or provisions that accorded them special rights. Saskatchewan opposed the 1961 Fulton formula and Québec effectively torpedoed the Fulton-Favreau formula of 1964 and the 1971 Victoria Charter. The eight dissident provinces very nearly defeated the 1979–82 constitutional renewal process.

There are, of course, some effective parries to the thrust that provinces have harmed constitutional regeneration. The argument about participatory constitutional negotiations can be dismissed as oblivious to the lessons of Canadian history. The very characteristics of the bargaining process that have been criticized—its secretiveness, its resistance to legislative alteration, its elitism—are, in fact, its virtues. If one accepts the notion, as does S.J.R. Noel (Noel 1971, 15–18), that Canada is a "consociational democracy," a term inspired by Arend Lijphart (Lijphart 1969, 207–25), then the type of bargaining traditionally associated with constitutional negotiations begins to take on positive aspects. "Consociationalism" is both a descriptive and normative approach to the problems of limited identities and cultural fragmentation in stable democracies. It places the responsibility for the maintenance of the national political system with political élites. A process of "élite accommodation" overcomes cultural conflict and weak national consensus. The leaders of the various subcultures will be successful practitioners of consociational democracy

1. if they can accommodate the divergent interests of their own subcultures,

2. if they can transcend cleavages and engage in common efforts with the élites of rival subcultures,

3. if they are committed to maintaining the national system and, lastly

4. if they understand the perils of political fragmentation. (Lijphart 1969, 207–25)

Masses are expected to follow their élites. The élites in turn, discourage interaction between cultural fragments at the mass level as potentially destabilizing and counterproductive.

Noel has suggested some adjustments to the Lijphart model to make it applicable to Canada. The term "subculture" is expanded to include not only French- and English-speaking Canada, but also distinct regions of Canada (Maritimes, Québec, Ontario, the West) and even provinces. Élite accommodation therefore takes place at several levels: provincial representation on federal boards and commissions, interprovincial consultation among senior provincial bureaucrats, interprovincial ministerial bodies, federal–provincial conferences and especially the federal cabinet. One particularly relevant conclusion he draws is an answer to the Cairns argument:

> A decline of "élitism" in Canada and its replacement by a general acceptance of the Jacksonian myth of popular or "participatory" democracy may be detrimental to the maintenance of Canadian federalism if it leads to a situation in which the mass of the people are unwilling to accept the inter-élite accommodations made by their political leaders. If inter-élite accommodations must be popularly ratified they may be impossible to achieve. (Noel 1971, 17–18)

Of course, Cairns suggested melding the two traditions of the "citizen" and "government" constitutions, but the net effect of following Cairns would be to open up the process to dissension at the mass level. The tensions raised by legislative hearings on the Meech Lake accord is one example.

On the matter of provincial roadblocks to constitutional reform, one might retort that reform efforts in the modern era have been characterized by a remarkable degree of provincial consensus. In the Victoria Charter episode of 1971 only Québec demurred; this was again the case in 1981 as negotiations ended on the repatriation package. Ontario gave up its historical claim to veto as a way to clear a constitutional logjam in the early 1980s. Plus, as Gordon Robertson reminded us in the *Globe and Mail*, 13 March 1990, "the Meech Lake accord is the only arrangement since [constitutional] discussions began in 1968 to be approved by all 11 governments and so far by Parliament and eight legislatures." Even the dissident provinces in the Meech Lake process were relatively conciliatory, most wanting to save the "essence" of the accord (defined in various terms) and make clarifying amendments. Apparently provinces take the need for "élite accommodation" seriously.

International and Domestic Economic Factors
International and domestic economic factors are considered in another major argument against giving provinces increased powers. The federal government, it is argued, should have the predominant power to define economic strategy towards our increasingly influential international competitors and to minimize harmful economic competition between provinces. International trade and economic questions must therefore be considered in tandem with domestic industrial policy when contemplating who the major governmental actors should be.

Peter Leslie says that from about 1960 to 1984, the federal government operated on such a rationale, in what he called "a third national policy":

[Federal] initiatives were mainly aimed at strengthening and transforming the manufacturing sector to meet foreign competition in domestic and external markets, although (somewhat inconsistently), it [sic] frequently had recourse to various forms of protectionism to sustain failing industries and firms…. In one variant of the policy the government seemed ready to make the resource industries subservient to the needs of manufacturing; in another…the resource industries were to be the main motor of economic development, and manufacturing was to be built up by maximizing the linkages with primary production. Both variants called for an activist or interventionist federal government and required affirming and augmenting its powers over the economy. (Leslie 1987, 137)

This "interventionist-nationalist" approach as Leslie calls it was abandoned and replaced by the "liberal-continentalist" option of the Mulroney Conservatives.

During the interventionist period it was also clear that restrictions on foreign ownership were considered an important part of a federal economic role. A federal economic development statement of 1981 repeated with approval the preamble to the centralist *Foreign Investment Review Act* of 1974 that identified as a matter of "national concern" the extent to which foreign control of industry, trade and commerce had affected Canadians' control over their own economic environment (Canada 1981).

The Trudeau government of 1981 saw itself in a leading role in economic development, having "a special responsibility for preserving and strengthening the integrity of the economic union" (Canada 1981). This it interpreted as resisting balkanization of the Canadian market and promoting joint federal–provincial economic development planning. Joint planning did not imply joint implementation, however, and for the rest of its mandate the federal government was to focus increasingly on unilateral federal initiatives in major projects, regional development and the search for international markets. There were substantial advantages perceived in the federal approach, wrote an admiring Hugh Thorburn. It would promote efficiency by obviating the need for constant intergovernmental compromise, by favouring the provinces that were best located in respect to economic development opportunities and by encouraging internal population migration. Thus would Canada be better able to do economic battle with foreign unitary governments (Thorburn 1984, 202).

Other than a desire for coherence in international economic strategy, other factors may militate in favour of federal leadership in economic development. Michael Jenkin saw the need for comprehensiveness as the main reason for federal predominance. Provinces would miss opportunities that were not of immediate interest to them individually or collectively, and at any rate often lack the resources or capacity to seize opportunities quickly and effectively (Jenkin 1983, 172).

Federal leadership in development stems from the simple fact that federal development policies have the capacity to frustrate provincial policies. Provided, of course, that the federal government possesses the political will, its regulatory and taxation powers may be sufficient to counteract provincial economic and resource policies springing from constitutional heads of power, and even from the new Section 92A. This the National Energy Policy conclusively demonstrated, says Leslie (Leslie 1987, 176–77). As well, he says, political support may not always be forthcoming for provincially led development. It will not be attractive in resource-poor provinces. Boom-and-bust cycles may lead both public opinion and producers to welcome federal policies of stabilization. Even after prolonged periods of prosperity, when expected economic diversification promised by provincial governments does not materialize, public faith in provincial leadership may flag (Leslie 1987, 177).

Tom Kent says that contemporary provincial regional development should have only restricted, relatively modest components. These are the improvement of education and training, the offsetting of negative economic change on communities, and industrial intelligence assistance to small-scale enterprises that would engage in import substitution and export activity. The major hope for equality of opportunity across the nation, however, rests with the federal government. Only if it has the capacity to manage the economy for higher levels of employment are economic redistribution and a better regional balance of employment and income possible (Kent 1990).

International factors may, however, not always lead in the direction of greater economic policy centralization, argue opponents. Richard Simeon has stated that international constraints have diminished the advantages of belonging to a large, open-economy state like Canada. External market forces, not provinces, have limited the federal government's manoeuvrability in recent years, leading citizens to turn to subnational power centres (Simeon 1988, 375). David Milne says that Trudeau's unilateral, imposed federal industrial strategy was motivated more by a drive for federal power than by economic rationality; an international recession and acrimonious federal–provincial discord helped to lend such dirigisme a bad name and led to the market-oriented free trade agreement (Milne 1986, 161).

The Macdonald Commission Report noted in a similar vein that "while federalism does not entirely undermine, it certainly dilutes, our enthusiasm for a state-led, highly interventionist, industrial strategy" (Macdonald 1985, 1:71). However, in the particular area of regional economic development, it was willing to countenance provincial leadership and a merely supplemental federal role.

> The emphasis on place prosperity is both understandable and defensible when it comes from a provincial government. It should not, however, unduly concern the federal government. Commissioners believe that community preservation, to the extent that people want it, is ultimately the responsibility of citizens and of their local and provincial governments. (Macdonald 1985, 3:219)

The federal government would have no direct regional job creation role; it would only attend to overcoming regional productivity gaps and labour-market imperfections, as well as building complementary links between provincial economies. There would, however, be a federal commitment to regional economic development grants; these would increase in the next few years but provinces would make the primary decisions as to their use (Macdonald 1985, 3:219–20).

Many reasons have been suggested why provinces should play a lead role in regional and industrial development policies. The Macdonald Report itself argues that "the federal government has failed to form a satisfactory link between its regional development policies and its broader role in managing our national economy" (Macdonald 1985, 3:215). Constant reorganization of the federal regional development bureaucracy is a sign of the failure of the former type of policies. National economic management (as defined above) is said to have a better chance of serving the major aim that regional development seeks to serve in the first place: reducing regional disparities in wage gaps and employment-rate differences.

Another reason for provincial leadership may be simply that provinces have the tools to use in economic development and the disposition to use them. Various sections of the Constitution Act, 1867 (ss. 92(5), 92(13), 108, 109 and 117) give the provincial legislatures wide power over public property. This means that provinces can directly produce or can sell provincially owned natural resources, or grant leases for pr vate companies to do so; they can also control the rate of production, the degree of intra-provincial processing [the "manufacturing condition"] and the selling price within the province; and they collect fees, rents or royalties on such resources (Hogg 1985, 572–73). They can engage in commercial activities through provincial Crown corporations. Many of the powers complementary to actual industrial policy—over the environment, labour, financial institutions and land use—fall largely (though not exclusively) within provincial jurisdiction. In addition, of course, provincial spending and taxation powers have become potent instruments in the field of industrial policy. Not only are the powers available; they have been used aggressively, as a number of texts on provincial development policy have informed us (Richards and Pratt 1979).

The growing dependence on trade with the U.S., an international factor that Canada could not ignore, moved it to enter into free trade negotiations with the United States. Notably, the net result of the federal–provincial jockeying that preceded the Canada–U.S. trade negotiations was not political centralization but a form of joint national economic planning:

> In the end the provinces did not succeed in winning "seats at the table," [instructing the federal trade negotiator] although they were given assurances of consultation and regular monitoring of the process of negotiations every three months by the first ministers. Clearly the old federal claim to an exclusive role in defining the national interest in trade and economic matters and their simply projecting it onto the international scene was no longer tenable. (Milne 1986, 152)

Presumably future international trade and economic questions may see analogous monitoring structures established—or even extended—as a result of constitutional necessity and the free trade precedent.

Social Policy Considerations
Still another set of arguments against giving provinces increased powers in Canadian federalism centres around functional considerations. It is held by some that redistribution and citizenship rights are better performed by national rather than by subnational governments. Others resist slotting redistribution easily into a jurisdictional slot and deny that citizenship rights are the proper concern of constitution makers.

Redistribution
Many feel that redistribution is a federal function. A complex argument to this effect has been enunciated by Dan Usher (Usher 1980, 16–29). He feels that a "contractarian" (citizen-centred) approach to the question of division of redistributive powers reveals three principles: relative efficiency,

balance and harmony. Efficiency is understood to be maximization of real national income; balance is allowing linguistic, racial or religious minorities a certain area of self-determination; and harmony is the achievement of minimum conflict by means of a strict apportionment of rights. Usher summarizes the arguments, which seem weighted predominantly—although not exclusively—towards a federal role. Usher suggests that all arguments based on these principles are valid for all citizens, but that these same citizens will give different weights according to their own circumstances throughout the country. For example, consideration of balance would probably be foremost in the assignment of many redistributive responsibilities by French Canadians; in the case of English Canadians, considerations of harmony would probably predominate (Usher 1980, 26).

By and large, however, the weight of Usher's argumentation points towards federal administration. Direct federal redistribution links together all donors and recipients in Canada; redistribution authority limited to provinces would probably lead to limited concern by people in rich provinces for their brethren in poorer provinces (Usher 1980, 29). Choosing equalization grants as a surrogate for redistribution, in order to compromise between French and English Canadians, is no answer; equalization may not in fact always result in redistribution.

As might be imagined, the drive to place social policy functions predominantly under federal jurisdiction has raised some objections. Redistribution is not universally accepted as a federal responsibility (or even as a desirable policy). Public choice theorists of federalism, for example, are particularly consistent critics of watertight compartmentalization of constitutional responsibilities, social policy included.

West and Winer have written what they call "a defence of decentralization." Decentralization can be viewed in two senses: "decentralization in the narrow sense of moving toward more scope and autonomy for subcentral jurisdictions; and decentralization in the broad sense, which also includes movement to a system of competing regimes" (West and Winer 1980, 3–15. See also Sproule–Jones 1975). The narrower sense of decentralization is preferred, but West and Winer's preference lies with the broader option. Broad decentralization reflects the authors' philosophic preference for James Madison's "compound republic," under which there is a need for "*overlapping* sets of political regimes operating *concurrently* upon the same constituencies" (West and Winer 1980, 7: emphasis in original). A choice among political authorities replaces a monopoly of political authority, allowing citizens to establish sets of countervailing power.

In terms of redistributive policies, what once seemed vices are now deemed virtues. Usher argues against provincial jurisdiction over redistribution to prevent people migrating to generous programs in specific provinces; West and Winer say that such migration would act as a healthy deterrent to provinces establishing divergent programs (West and Winer 1980, 8). Whereas Usher argues for federal jurisdiction over redistribution to reduce conflict, West and Winer suggest that some "optional" tension emerging from a system of checks and balances is necessary to protect citizens from government power (West and Winer 1980, 9).

Social Policy and The Job of Constitutions
A.W. Johnson perceives citizenship rights to be the appropriate purview of the federal government (Johnson 1988, 145–53). Constitutions, he says, should do three things: define rights and freedoms, establish a system of governance and strengthen the bonds of nationhood. The third objective depends on the strength of feeling that a people feels for the nation, which in part depends on the degree of commonality of benefits enjoyed by all members of the nation and in part on a sense of association with national institutions. The historical benefits of Canadian citizenship have, for example, been programs like medicare, hospital care, old age pensions, disability allowances, access to higher education and the Trans-Canada Highway. Most of these programs were established either by a shared-cost federal–provincial program operating under federal standards or by constitutional amendment to allow federal assumption of a previous provincial responsibility. An initiative like the Meech Lake accord threatened both the commonality of benefits and Canadians' affinity for national institutions. Meech's endowing of provincial governments with the right to "opt-out" of nationalizing amendments, or of new shared-cost programs, with federal compensation, would have seriously attenuated the possibility for national "sharing" or commonality of benefits (Johnson 1988, 147–48). In other words, provincial efforts to seek more power over social programs, by deviating from national norms, should be resisted.

The contention that the job of the constitution is to strengthen the bonds of nationhood by assuring the federal provision of common benefits does not pass unchallenged. One could look to Andrew Petter, now a British Columbia cabinet minister, for a different view (Petter 1988, 187–201). There are, he says, two predominant values to be served by the Canadian Constitution: federalism and responsible government. The federal spending power violates the political purposes of federalism by allowing national majorities to invade areas allocated to regional majorities under the Constitution. It also violates responsible government by allowing the federal government to influence provincial policies, making the electors unable to determine what level of government is in effective control of various programs (Petter 1988, 188–91).

Petter has also challenged the assumption behind unconstrained use of the federal spending power: that national politics is inherently more progressive than provincial politics. As reported in the *Globe and Mail*, 30 June 1987, he said provinces have been catalysts for reform during the past 40 years in a number of social areas: hospital insurance, medicare, human rights codes and public automobile insurance, to name but a few. Success in one province inevitably leads other provinces to implement the reform in question. As well, provincial governments have acted as spurs to expand and improve social programs that have eventually been adopted by the federal government. Petter admits that opting-out with compensation from federal shared-cost programs has some risks attached; but he feels that on balance there are compensating benefits likely in the areas of provincial experimentation and innovation. The national government by its very nature is preoccupied with mediating between regional, cultural and linguistic interests; however, in the provincial context social and economic matters are the focus. Despite the appearance in our day of conservative administrations and retrenchment, the general trend has been towards social progress. Certainly succeeding administrations find it unwise to dislodge major social programs instituted by their predecessors. As he further noted

> The lesson of Canadian history is that social progress is seldom attained all at once. It evolves from the small to the large. It must be fought for one piece at a time.

Canadian Decentralization in a Comparative Context
Another argument against giving provinces more power is that Canada, in terms of comparative politics, is already a highly decentralized federation. The general line of reasoning is as follows: 1. provinces have more power in Canada than do other subnational units, 2. they should thus be satisfied with this state of affairs and 3. even if they are not, we have something to learn from the political stability of the more centralized federations.

Riker has argued that "among the more or less centralized federations of the modern world, most writers would agree that Canada is about as decentralized as one can get.* "Political centralization" for him means shifting the locus of decision-making to the central government from

---

* The Canadian Bar Association used the argument about Canada's relative decentralization in its 1978 report *Towards a New Canada*.

constituent units; "partially centralized federalism"—the case in Canada—means constituent governments making many significant political decisions and operating according to a meaningful "provincial rights" doctrine (Riker 1975, 132–33). Of course the main correlate of political centralization/decentralization is the party system. "The Canadian party system as a whole is just about as decentralized as it can be to match a federal union that is increasingly decentralized in order to keep Quebec content" (Riker 1975, 135–36).

Others see Canada's comparative decentralization largely in fiscal terms. Albinski noted some years ago that constitutional and political factors had rendered Canadian federalism far more devolutionary that Australian federalism, requiring substantial transfers from Ottawa to the provinces (Albinski 1973, 382–83). Canadian provinces, in contrast to Australian states, had wider tax bases that were also more stable and more accessible, and they were not as subject to federal priorities in their borrowing activities. A contemporary analyst of Canadian and Australian fiscal federalism says that there is significance in the fact that in the early 1950s Australian states declined the return of income tax powers originally taken from them during the Second World War, whereas Canadian provinces pressed the federal authorities to allow them a greater share of direct tax fields. The struggle for fiscal independence is the ultimate symbol of sovereignty (Wiltshire 1989, 193).

Of course, there is a counterargument, also drawn from comparative politics. Hueglin suggests that whereas Canadian federalism is indeed more decentralized than that of the United States and the former West Germany, the Canadian situation should be considered a strength instead of a liability (Hueglin, 1988, 29). To be sure, there are in America and Germany substantial elements of "intrastate federalism"—that is, state involvement in the national political substructures. German *Laender* instruct their delegates in the *Bundesrat* (Federal Council, or Upper House) who must vote unanimously. The American Senate has two members from each state, thus offering a measure of representation for regional minority interests. Yet in Germany "unitary federalism" (highly centralized federalism) has come to dominate since the late sixties due to joint economic and financial planning, more integrated law-and-order forces and finally the conflict-avoidance governing style inherent in a centralized party system where the adoption of major policies requires all three parties to agree (Hueglin 1988, 23–24). The U.S. style of "permissive federalism," which subordinates state power in a dominating federal grant system, achieves a centralizing dynamic as well. The Canadian system by contrast features strong intergovernmental conflict with substantial provincial autonomy in the grant system.

In addition to political substructures, the economic and cultural substructures also reveal that Canada is less centralized than the other two countries; and all three substructures are at once interdependent and relatively autonomous, says Hueglin. In the economic sphere, the U.S. federal government dominates because it collects most of the revenue and states spend most of it. A full 75 percent of all federal grants are categorical [conditional]; neither liberals nor conservatives have a meaningful agenda for shifting power to the states; and Congress is loath to let control over the purse slip from its grip. In Germany, economic interests—the interconnected financial and industrial sectors—are closely allied with the CDU and FDP political parties and with government and labour in a system of corporatist planning. The result is a focus on national, rather than regional economic strategy. By contrast, Canada's tax sharing, cost sharing and equalization are sensitive to provincial needs. "As long as the commitment to equalization remains intact, the Canadian polity can be regarded as living up to the federal yardstick for sharing and balancing regional group liberty with national individual liberty" (Hueglin 1988, 27).

In the cultural sphere, the institutions of federalism in general channel conflicts between capitalist factions and between classes in ways that accommodate or deny regional identities. Hueglin says U.S. and German federalism deny regional identities, the former by suppressing class conflict and promoting mass culture, and the latter by interlocking (or "cartelizing") ideological blocks in the institutions of intrastate federalism. In both cases, potential legitimation crises loom as regional interests bypass national institutions and seek solutions elsewhere. However, because Canadians have "dual loyalties" both to the centre and to regional differences, the Canadian system is not as inherently unstable.

> When compared to the potentially delegitimizing conflicts between the economic centralism and societal bifurcation in West Germany or between federal supremacy and regional decline in the United States, the relative congruence of politics, economy and culture in Canada ought to be considered a strength and not a liability. (Hueglin 1988, 29)

Reconciliation

The arguments for and against increasing provincial powers in many respects seem to cancel each other out. The whole process of arguing the distribution of powers question in such terms is, moreover, inherently unsatisfactory. The terms of the debate mean different things to different commentators. The objectives to be maximized differ also. Some seek innovation, others stability; some, self-harmony, others, creative tension; some seek coherence, others equality.

However, the major flaw in the process of debate revolves around the lack of nuance. Reality is seldom an either-or proposition. Yet the debate about the extent of provincial power is phrased in terms of strong provinces versus a strong central government. Most Canadians instinctively shy away from having to make such a Hobson's choice. This paper joins a growing literature that rejects the necessity for such a choice. It suggests that a realistic approach to the division of powers would take into consideration differences between provinces in terms of wealth, population and aspirations. It would also aim for something other than zero-sum solutions in structural and jurisdictional arrangements. As well, it would admit the relative impact of different types of issues.

The Mintz-Simeon Approach

There are several commentators who have resisted the temptation to dichotomize questions of jurisdiction. One of the most fruitful approaches of recent years has been the famous essay by Jack Mintz and Richard Simeon (Mintz and Simeon 1982). The authors refuse to make generalized statements; instead, they discuss the relative impact of different types of issues, different sizes of province and different states of provincial wealth.

Mintz and Simeon distinguish between two types of interregional conflict. The first is "conflict of taste," which refers to the extent to which regional majorities have preferences about public policies that are different from, or incompatible with, those of other regional or national majorities because of different social or cultural values (Mintz and Simeon 1982, 2–4). The second is "conflict of claim," which refers to the competition between regions (provinces) that share certain values but disagree on the distribution of wealth between them; in order for one region to get what it wants, it must obtain it, or its equivalent, from other regions that want the same things (Mintz and Simeon 1982, 4–5). There are "efficient" solutions to "conflicts of taste" in the sense that in federalism, responsibilities (like health, welfare and education) can be allocated so as to respond to the desires of regional majorities and to minimize interference or vetoes from other majorities. There are no "efficient" solutions possible in "conflicts of claim" since the usual objective is the maximization of regional welfare rather than national welfare. Conflicts of claim may take the form of competition for investment, interprovincial trade barriers, arguments over relative shares of resource wealth, or hostility to central government policies that discriminate against the region in question in favour of other regions. Although conflicts of claim have existed since Confederation they are becoming increasingly salient. Many disputes supposedly about conflicts of taste may in fact be conflicts of claim in disguise.

Conflicts of taste and claim make simple statements about such centralization or decentralization hard to formulate. In regard to the conflicts of taste category, patterns differ. Centralized (federal) provision of the public good is appropriate if there are only small regional differences. Decentralization is generally appropriate, therefore, where centralization is counterindicated, save for those federal equalization and factor mobility policies that complement provincial policies. Intergovernmental arrangements are appropriate where there are deficiencies in provincial provision of services or where it is necessary to provide joint support for provinces to pursue their own preferences (Mintz and Simeon 1982, 23–27).

Conflicts of claim are even less susceptible to generalizations about centralized, decentralized and intergovernmental arrangements. Centralization allows the poorer provinces to lay claim to the wealth of richer provinces and to have the federal government regulate the competition between regions. Size makes a difference as well. Presuming that the centre honours majority rule, large provinces (be they rich or poor) will *generally* find centralization attractive because their population will be able to influence redistribution policies of the federal government. Yet a large, rich province is likely to be more ambivalent about centralization than a large, poor one, since its resources form the core of what is to be redistributed in the federation. A small, poor province will favour centralization because Ottawa is its main hope for redistribution. However, a small, rich province will find centralization threatening because of its limited bargaining power, especially when it has no provincial allies with similar interests. Small, rich provinces may therefore find decentralization appealing but both large and small poor provinces will not stand to gain much by it. Intergovernmental or "confederal" approaches to redistribution will work where each member feels it has something to gain, but confederal bargaining raises the possibility that general welfare will be ignored.

Thus each major institutional mechanism for dealing with conflicts of claim seems to have serious weaknesses. Central authority raises the possibility of large dominant regions exercising control over the smaller ones without providing compensating or proportional benefits. Decentralization and confederalism protect the small and privileged. (Mintz and Simeon 1982, 33)

There are therefore few clear rules for defining when national or regional majorities should carry the day. Mintz and Simeon offer as guidance only that federal and provincial bargainers should all aim at system maintenance. They should avoid systematic coercion of specific regions and attempt to balance regional wins and losses even when this means departing from majority rule. National integration in the final analysis depends on the principle of mutual advantage.

The Pépin-Robarts and Macdonald Approaches

However, it is natural to query the relative validity of principles and values other than mutual advantage and system maintenance. There have been many investigations of the question of division of powers and related matters; they have employed a wide variety of values in their attempts to chart the future of the Canadian federation.* However for the sake of simplicity, it is convenient to mention only two categories of approach: on the one hand, those that are elaborate as to the values to be sought in federalism and that outline detailed changes to the division of powers, and those that posit relatively few values and do not advocate detailed changes to the division of powers. We call the first the "Pépin-Robarts Model" and the second the "Macdonald Commission Model."

The two major governmental reports that have examined the question of Canadian federalism recently are the Pépin-Robarts Task Force, 1979 (Pépin-Robarts 1979) and the Macdonald Royal Commission on the Economy (Macdonald 1985). The Pépin-Robarts Report posited several "objectives" for constitutional reform (Pépin-Robarts 1979, 81)

---

*A few are as follows: Canada, 28th Parliament, 4th Session, Special Joint Committee on the Constitution of Canada, *Final Report* (Ottawa, 1972); Canadian Bar Association, Committee on the Constitution, *Towards a New Canada* (Montréal: Canadian Bar Foundation, 1978); Quebec Liberal Party, Constitutional Committee, *A New Canadian Federation* (Montréal: January 9, 1980) ("The Beige Paper"); Garth Stevenson. The Division of Powers. In *Division of Powers and Public Policy* edited by Richard Simeon. (Toronto: University of Toronto Press, 1985); M.H. Sproule-Jones, *Public Choice and Federalism in Australia and Canada* (Canberra: Centre for Research on Federal Financial relations, Australian National University, Research Monograph No. 11, 1975); Anthony Scott. An Economic Approach to the Federal Structure. In *Options*, Proceedings of the Conference on the Future of the Canadian Federation, University of Toronto (Toronto: University of Toronto, 1977).

(reinforce central institutions; respond to provincial self-confidence; reflect Canadian duality, accountability, effectiveness and efficiency)—and outlined several "criteria" for distribution of powers (Pépin-Robarts 1979, 88) (national and provincial concerns, efficiency and effectiveness, consensus, continuity and balance). It seemed to give special emphasis to the value of accommodation (or, alternately, cooperation) over that of conflict in intergovernmental matters (Pépin-Robarts 1979, 81, 85, 86, 89). It saw the federal government's responsibilities—other than defence, foreign policy and trade—as "combating regional disparities, establishing appropriate minimum standards of living for all Canadians where appropriate, and redistributing income between individuals and between provinces" (Pépin-Robarts 1979, 85). Provinces were to take "the main responsibility for the social and cultural well-being and development of their communities, for the development of their economies and the exploitation of their natural resources, and for property and civil rights" (Pépin-Robarts 1979, 85). It suggested a vague list of exclusive (and occasionally concurrent) powers in a number of areas. Québec was to be given powers necessary for the preservation and expansion of its distinct heritage—assigned to it alone or, preferably, to the provinces in general (Pépin-Robarts 1979, 85–86).

The main implication (for the division of powers) of the Pépin–Robarts emphasis on accommodation and cooperation was a high degree of categorization and specificity. There was to be a "full enumeration" of federal and provincial powers under seven categories: exclusive central powers, exclusive provincial powers, concurrent powers with central paramountcy, concurrent powers with provincial paramountcy, provincially administered central laws (a limited list), powers requiring joint action (also a limited list) and overriding central powers with specific limitations (Pépin-Robarts 1979, 88–89). The enumerated powers of Sections 91 and 92 of the 1867 Constitution, lacking a coherent theme to their arrangement, were to be rearranged into general domains of public activity, with more specific subject matters listed under them that could be then distributed exclusively or concurrently to the most appropriate level of government. The implications of Québec's "distinctive culture" were that it should achieve powers in areas needed for its cultural survival, but that these powers should be generalized to other provinces as well. This would be done both by allowing intergovernmental delegation of powers as well as by placing the powers under concurrent jurisdiction with provincial paramountcy. The unstated implication of Pépin-Robarts was that the provinces would get more powers in a renewed federalism.

The Macdonald Royal Commission took a different approach than did
Pépin-Robarts to the philosophy of federalism and this yielded a different
set of prescriptions for the division of powers. In actual fact, the Commission offers a somewhat conflicting theory of federalism. In Volume One of
its Report it seems to promote the value of "competition" over cooperation
(Macdonald 1985, 1:68). However in Volume Three, the Commission
argues for "balance":

> We Canadians must seek to establish balance in our federal insti-
> tutions. We must try to find a middle ground between unregulated
> competition and implausible harmony, and between accountabil-
> ity of governments to citizens and collaboration among govern-
> ments. (Macdonald 1985, 3:252)

This balance is to be exercised within the "spirit of the Constitution," which
is said to be self-restraint by both orders of government.

The Commission, evidently using the notions of balance and self-
restraint as its operative guides, resisted the urge to modernize or specify
aspects of the division of powers (other than in the area of regional
development). It noted that the present Constitution is a useful record of
the collective experience of Canadian society, that any attempt to codify the
division of powers would be a dauntingly controversial topic in an era of
interwoven policy areas and, finally, that any specific reallocation of
powers, rather than clarifying matters of jurisdiction, would run the
distinct risk of obsolescence (Macdonald 1985, 3:254–55).

The Commission could see no outstanding case for either increasing
centralization or advocating decentralization. "Disentanglement" or re-
turning to "watertight compartments" might reduce the costs of decision-
making; but overlapping authority and *de facto* concurrence were, on
balance, more attractive. Governments would "compete" to respond to the
needs of citizens. However, some mechanisms allowing flexibility would
be valuable: delegation, establishing First Minister's Conferences in the
Constitution, creating "third-party bodies" to facilitate intergovernmental
relations and establishing three ongoing federal–provincial "Ministerial
Councils" in the fields of Finance, Economic Development and Social
Policy (Macdonald 1985, 3:399–400).

Directions
The Macdonald model comes closest to meeting the objectives of mutual
advantage and system survival. Basically, these objectives are the condi-

tions that bargainers and negotiators usually seek. If bargainers are hemmed in by a multiplicity of objectives—à la Pépin-Robarts—their freedom to accommodate each other may be restricted. If they are given free rein to be flexible—à la Macdonald—they may be more likely to come up with mutually satisfactory results.

Of course the Mintz-Simeon approach should not be considered as totally amenable to the "stripped-down federalism" of Macdonald. The Commission's approach to federalism, like its approaches to many other aspects of Canadian public life, is coloured by a belief in the beneficial effects of competition (despite its occasional discussion of "balance"). Competition however is not always compatible with the notions of mutual advantage and system maintenance. It is significant, for example, that the Commission resorts to an emphasis on Canada-Québec "cooperation" in its section on the "place of Quebec in Confederation" (Macdonald 1985, 3:329–44). Another reason to finesse the Macdonald approach is that the new constitutional specificity on some aspects of the division of powers question is unavoidable. Québec political culture emphasizes codification and completeness in legal and constitutional matters; Québec is unlikely to be satisfied with continued emphasis on unwritten understandings the moorings of which are loosened by constitutional drift. And Québec is not without bargaining chips in any process of constitutional renewal.

There are a number of directions that may follow from a reliance on mutual advantage and system maintenance. They will be discussed at the level of generalities rather than of detail; if agreement cannot be reached on the former it is unlikely to be sought on the latter.

Constitutional Minimalism

A general reflex must be to resist the trend towards rendering intergovernmental understandings into constitutional form. It has been repeatedly demonstrated in Canadian history that governments intent on achieving certain public policy aims often do so in spite of, rather than because of, the Constitution. If Meech Lake has taught us one thing, it is this: the more that we constitutionalize—or more precisely, *attempt* to constitutionalize—the more divisions result. Canadians now have disputes about arcane legal and institutional subjects that were unknown to them a few years ago. It is the consociationalist's nightmare come true. If constitutional reforms are deemed absolutely necessary, it is better to do them *ad seriatim* rather than in complex, comprehensive constitutional packages. Such comprehensiveness leads to instability and divisiveness. We should deal with individual problems individually.

There is a need for a general theory of constitutional reform that de-emphasizes formal constitutional change. I call this "constitutional minimalism." Constitutional minimalism consists of doing the least possible in a strict constitutional sense; however, it also consists of an openness to constitutional renewal by a mixture of existing pragmatic approaches. Constitutional renewal is not synonymous with constitutional amendment. There should be a system of organic and experimental growth in constitutional matters. In short, we should see constitutional renewal as occurring along a continuum ranging from what is currently available in the constitution all the way to formal change by amendment, with much imagination used to fill in the middle of the continuum. This may have particular relevance to the division of powers question.

Constitutional minimalism has some advantages. The first is that it would avoid the "Reformer's Fallacy"—that it is possible to predict accurately the results of institutional and jurisdictional reforms. It is not: these are essential matters for empirical research.

A second advantage is that it offers a stabilizing tendency in constitutional renewal. We can get to this stabilization by dealing with smaller constitutional packages and in more staggered series of reforms. There should be fewer targets and fewer threats in constitutional matters. By concentrating on renewal other than by amendment, constitutional minimalism offers one way of achieving smaller packages.

A third advantage of minimalism is that it is the procedure most likely to accommodate constitutional experimentalism and even reversibility, if some reform "fails."

Alternatives to Formal Amendment of the Division of Powers
One way of putting constitutional minimalism into practice is to resist formal amendments to the division of powers. The myriad of provincial citizen consultation exercises that followed the demise of the Meech Lake accord were, perhaps ironically, virtually unanimous in their discovery of Canadian reluctance to weaken the federal government by a substantial decentralization of powers. (Québec, of course, was a notable exception.) Even the federal government's 1991 position paper *Shaping Canada's Future Together* concentrates on a variety of mechanisms for affecting the federal–provincial power balance. It raised the possibility of legislative and administrative delegation between governments, program review to see which level of government is appropriate to deliver selected programs and services, reform of concurrent powers and, finally, recognition of areas of exclusive provincial jurisdiction (where now there is considerable jurisdictional overlap).

Changes in the division of powers should be avoided, if possible, for a panoply of reasons: the potential of divided public opinion, potential obsolescence, lack of flexibility and, lastly, the general workability of present arrangements. At any rate, consistent with constitutional minimalism, such changes should be placed on a continuum of choice, with proponents of formal power shifts forced to justify their stand in the court of public opinion. What such a continuum should look like is open to debate, but the following is perhaps useful: using opting-out or opting-in that presently exist in the Constitution, federal–provincial agreements, federal–provincial accords, administrative delegation, legislative delegation, concurrent powers with paramountcy assigned, asymmetrical jurisdictions and formal amendment of the division of powers (*see* Meekison 1991; Milne 1991).

The principle of delegation of powers might be profitably expanded in Canadian federalism. It offers an alternative to once-and-for-all changes in the general division of powers. It also offers the opportunity of specific rather than general application. The expansion of the number of concurrent federal and provincial powers could be considered a more expensive and complex alternative to delegation of powers. It is a "half-way house" between delegation and changes to the division of powers.

Asymmetrical federalism
A workable Canadian federalism would depart from the notion of "provincial equality." International organizations give special roles to large, powerful and rich nations and in doing so ensure the organization's viability as a working union. Analogous arrangements should be made in Canadian federalism. We do not begrudge the kind of equality that is implied in the equalization provisions of the Constitution Act, 1982. However, when provincial equality in constitutional amendment powers threatens national unity—as was the case with Meech Lake—this cannot be right. If power is to be sought by the smaller provinces in amendments and in public policy matters generally, it should be sought through regional power blocks of voters or governments.

This is where a discussion of Québec's aspirations seems relevant. Québec has the power to destabilize or even destroy the Canadian federation. Québec's bargaining chips should have been recognized by according it much of the content of the original "five demands" it sought in the pre-Meech period. But the achievements of Québec should n(t have been generalized to all the provinces, unless a convincing case can oe made that a blanket concurrency with provincial paramountcy will not result in the provinces other than Québec making much use of this arrangement (Milne 1991).

The powerful provinces of Canada must, for the sake of national unity, be accorded special powers in a new amending formula; but not all provinces need be so recognized. An amending formula that combines "provincial vetoes" for large provinces and "regional vetoes" for small provinces seems preferable.

The Spending Power

The federal package suggests a "Council of the Federation" applying a rough equivalent of the general amending formula to the use of the federal spending power. This suggestion has received a less than lukewarm response. If one remembers the Meech debate, he or she will recall that Premier Wells made an excellent suggestion about modification of the Meech Lake spending power provisions. With some adjustments to remove a centralist bias, it could be a true compromise between centralization and decentralization. It allows provincial opting-out with compensation from new national shared cost programs, but not in the case of new national programs meant to honour the intent of Section 36(1) of the Constitution Act, 1982. This allows a residual nationalizing role for the federal Parliament, while providing for the more activist, progressive provinces to innovate and improve the delivery of public services.

Constitutional Councils

One possible mechanism for seeking mutual advantage is an independent third-party assemblage to advise on matters of federalism. Constitutional councils—or national intergovernmental advisory councils—could at regular intervals recommend on approaches to division-of-powers questions; they could analyze systematic cases of discrimination against regions and provinces; they could investigate the cost efficiency of the existing division of powers. In short, their job would be to promote compromise and mutual advantage. Now that there has been a tentative commitment by the first ministers to the notion of recognizing Native people as a "third order of government"—thus complicating the division-of-powers question even more—there is an increased need for technical advice.

Conclusion

The tendency to dichotomize questions of federal and provincial power has become a characteristic of the last few decades in Canada. Perhaps this tendency makes sense at the level of executive federalism or in certain academic circles, but it does not at the level of citizens with allegiances to both federal and provincial governments. We have suggested that a new dedication to the notion of mutual advantage and system maintenance may be warranted—at least at this particular juncture of Canadian history. Our review has applied the principle to some areas of federalism but not to others due to the constraints of length—for example international relations, intrastate federalism, as well as the residual, declaratory and reservation and disallowance powers have not been discussed. Enough has been revealed, however, to indicate some practical effects of the Mints-Simeon approach. One may or may not disavow the results, but that is another chapter.

References

Albinski, Henry S. 1973. *Canadian and Australian Politics in Comparative Perspective.* New York: Oxford University Press.

Axworthy, Thomas S. and Pierre Elliott Trudeau, eds. 1990. *Towards a Just Society: The Trudeau Years.* Toronto: Viking.

Cairns, Alan C. 1988. The Limited Constitutional Visions of Meech Lake. In *Competing Constitutional Vision: The Meech Lake Accord,* edited by Katherine E. Swinton and Carol J. Rogerson. Toronto: Carswell.

Canada. 1979. Task Force on Canadian Unity. *Report.* 3 vols. Ottawa: Minister of Supply and Services. The main report, *A Future Together: Observations and Recommendations* (January) is cited as "Pépin-Robarts Report."

———. 1981. *Economic Development for Canada in the 1980s.* Ottawa, November.

———. 1985. *Report of the Royal Commission on the Economic Union and Development Prospects for Canada* ("Macdonald Commission Report"). 3 vols. Ottawa: Minister of Supply and Services.

———. 1988. Standing Senate Committee on Foreign Affairs. *Constitutional Jurisdiction Pertaining to Certain Aspects of the Free Trade Agreement.* Ottawa.

———. 1991. *Shaping Canada's Future Together.* Ottawa: Minister of Supply and Services.

Hogg, P.W. 1985. *Constitutional Law of Canada,* 2d ed. Toronto: Carswell.

Hueglin, Thomas O. 1988. Federalism in Comparative Perspective. In *Perspectives on Canadian Federalism,* edited by R.D. Olling and W.W. Westmacott. Scarborough: Prentice-Hall Canada.

Jenkin, Michael. 1983. *The Challenge of Diversity: Industrial Policy in the Canadian Federation.* Ottawa: Science Council of Canada.

Johnson, A.W. 1988. The Meech Lake Accord and the Bonds of Nationhood. In *Competing Constitutional Vision: The Meech Lake Accord,* edited by Katherine E. Swinton and Carol J. Rogerson. Toronto: Carswell.

Kent, Tom. 1990. Regional Development in Hard Times. Lecture delivered to Department of Political Science, Memorial University, St. John's, February 16.

Leslie, Peter M. 1987. *Federal State, National Economy*. Toronto: University of Toronto Press.

Lijphart, Arend. 1969. Consociational Democracy. *World Politics* XXI:2(January):207–25.

Macdonald [Commision Report]. *See* Canada 1985.

Meekison, J. Peter. 1991. Distribution of Functions and Jurisdiction: A Political Scientist's Analysis. In *Options for a New Canada*, edited by Ronald Watts and Douglas M. Brown. Toronto: University of Toronto Press.

Milne, David. 1986. *Tug of War: Ottawa and the Provinces under Trudeau and Mulroney*. Toronto: James Lorimer and Company.

———. 1991. A Quality of Symmetry: Why Choose? In *Options for a New Canada*, edited by Ronald Watts and Douglas M. Brown. Toronto: University of Toronto Press.

Mintz, Jack, and Richard Simeon. 1982. *Conflict of Taste and Conflict of Claim in Federal Countries*. Discussion Paper No. 13. Kingston, Ont.: Institute of Intergovernmental Relations, Queen's University.

Noel, S.J.R. 1971. Consociational Democracy and Canadian Federalism. *Canadian Journal of Political Science* 4:1(March):15–18.

Pépin-Robarts Report. *See* Canada 1979.

Petter, Andrew. 1988. Meech Ado About Nothing? Federalism, Democracy and the Spending Power. In *Competing Constitutional Vision: The Meech Lake Accord*, edited by Katherine E. Swinton and Carol J. Rogerson. Toronto: Carswell.

Richards, John, and Larry Pratt. 1979. *Prairie Capitalism: Power and Influence in the New West*. Toronto: McClelland & Stewart.

Riker, W.H. 1975. Federalism. In *Handbook of Political Science*, edited by F.L. Greenstein and N.W. Polsby. Reading, Massachusetts: Addison-Wesley Publishing Company.

Simeon, Richard. 1988. Considerations on Centralization and Decentralization. In *Perspectives on Canadian Federalism*, edited by R.D. Olling and M.W. Westmacott. Scarborough: Prentice-Hall Canada.

Smiley, Donald V. 1980. *Canada in Question: Federalism in the Eighties*, 3d ed. Toronto: McGraw-Hill Ryerson Limited.

Sproule-Jones, Mark. 1975. *Public Choice and Federalism in Australia and Canada*. Research Monograph No. 11. Canberra: Centre for Research on Federal Financial Relations, the Australian National University.

Thorburn, H.G. 1984. *Planning and the Economy: Building Federal–Provincial Consensus*. Ottawa: Canadian Institute for Economic Policy.

Usher, D. 1980. How Should the Redistributive Power of the State be Divided between Federal and Provincial Governments? *Canadian Public Policy*. VI:1(Winter):16–29.

West, Edwin G., and Stanley L. Winer. 1980. The Individual, Political Tension and Canada's Quest for a New Constitution. *Canadian Public Policy* VI:1(Winter):3–15.

Wiltshire, Kenneth. 1989. Federal State/Provincial Relations. In *Federalism in Canada and Australia: Historical Perspectives 1920–1988,* edited by Bruce W. Hodgins. Peterborough: The Frost Centre for Canadian Heritage and Development Studies, Trent University.

MILDRED A. SCHWARTZ

Regionalism and Canadian Constitution-Building

Canada's regionally divided nature is an uncomfortable reality for those who study Canada and for those who attempt to shape its policies. What is uncomfortable is often downplayed, as Marshak has observed in the tendency of social scientists to "focus on class divisions [which] has obscured the fact that populations are geographically situated. Neo-Marxists, together with classical economists, tend to treat not only the ideology of nationalism but also the reality of common territorial interests as unimportant" (Marshak 1980, 95). Brodie makes a similar assessment about the failures by the dominant schools of Canadian political science to adequately account for the spatial dimension underlying the political economy (Brodie 1980, 33. *See also* Boismenu 1989).

To the extent that political leaders have been concerned with regionally based issues, most of the focus has been on Québec and the split between French and English language interests. Overwhelming attention to this reality had served to draw attention away from the broader nature of regional cleavages and the fissures they create. But as Canada has become engaged in constitution-building, a reluctant recognition of regionalism has come to the fore.

My argument begins by defining regionalism as distinct from federalism and regions as analytically separate from provinces. These definitions rest on a theory, pioneered by Juan Linz in relation to Spain, that regional variations in a country's characteristics create the contexts out of which social behaviours take place (Linz and Miguel 1966, 267–319). Although particular patterns of economic development, political power, and cultural expressions arise from historical conditions, once regions are delineated they continue to have repercussions for contemporary outcomes (Schwartz 1993).

The evolving character of regionalism is paralleled by the evolving process through which constitutions are built. For example, even though we associate the British North America Act (now the Constitution Act, 1867) with a specific date, in reality it was created in a process that began years before and it has continued to change its meaning under new circumstances and challenges to its application. That is one kind of evolution; another has characterized recent Canadian politics. Most commentators would agree that only in the past 30 years has the Constitution become the focus of intense scrutiny and the subject of impassioned political activity. Peter Russell refers to this period as one of "macro-constitutional politics," by which he means a form of politics that "is concerned with reaching agreement on the identity and fundamental principles of justice of the body politic on which the constitution is to be based" and consequently "is exceptionally emotional and intense" (Russell 1991, 699–700). The purpose of this paper is to show the extent to which regionalism has been a prominent factor during this era of macro-constitutional politics.

Defining Regions and Regionalism

The regionally divided nature of Canada has been institutionalized since the beginning of Canadian statehood through a federal system of government. Federalism was initially adopted as an accommodation to existing sectional interests represented by the colonies that were to make up modern Canada and it has continued to express and reinforce regional divisions. As a system of government, federalism rests between the polarities of centralization and decentralization, depending on the powers and resources allocated to the central government compared to its constituent parts. One form of decentralization is "provincialization," in which provincial authorities and institutions have a direct say in the representation of provinces within the federal level of government, as in the appointment of senators. In contrast, a centralized form of federalism can bypass provincial institutions and still take account of regional concerns by creating its own, centrally coordinated organizations with a regional focus (Cairns 1979, 11–12).

Regionalism is located along a different axis of organization, one that pulls regions between *autonomy* and *dependence*. Distinctions between greater autonomy through "regionalization" and greater decentralization as a form of federalism are clearly implied, even if they are not spelled out in the same way I do, by Arthur Benz (1987, 128–29). Both the drive for autonomy and the conditions that create dependence can exist independently of a federal system of government and may often, as in the case of Canada, precede the creation of formal federal structures. Where regionalism and federalism coexist, their relations are often tense. For example, the federal government can decentralize by devolving responsibilities to the regions without, at the same time, making them more autonomous. Conversely, the federal government can centralize by assuming responsibility for the reduction of regional economic inequities and still foster dependency.

Federalism determines the form by which a country is governed; regionalism determines how its interests are divided. Those interests may arise out of any of the three components of regionalism—economic opportunity, power and culture. I describe how this may occur for each component in turn.

Regions are structures of opportunity, shaped by past conditions. Those structures will change over time, whether through technological discoveries, political policies or market forces, but rarely in ways that remove all differences. At any particular time, residents are constrained in their economic activities by what they find available to them. The outcomes are differences in wealth that then colour relations among regions. Tocqueville's observation about the United States in the 1830s remains generally applicable to all such situations. "The weak seldom have confidence in the justice and reasonableness of the strong. States which are growing comparatively slowly therefore look with jealous distrust on fortune's favourites" (Tocqueville [1839] 1988, 381).

Throughout its history, Canada has had a regionally uneven economy (Economic Council of Canada 1978; Norrie 1986, vol. 64). What has changed over time are the sources and sites of inequalities, not the inequalities themselves (Lithwick 1980, 62–73). The Atlantic region alone has retained its status as the one with the longest standing disadvantages. This is true as well of the component provinces—their recurring interest in an Atlantic economic union reflects their concern with regional economic prospects (Clancy 1994). The four western provinces are often described as two regions—the prairies and British Columbia. Compared to the Atlantic region, they are internally much more differentiated, enjoying both great wealth but also great economic instability (Chambers and Schneck 1990, 74–78). Historically, Ontario has been the economic leader, although not without challenges from the West (Simeon and Robinson 1990, 71:306). Québec, meanwhile, has moved from an area with low levels of development to one with a dynamic business class (McRoberts 1988, 427–30) and declining income disparities (Shapiro and Stelcner 1987, 97–104).

Regions are also systems of power, whether or not they are formally recognized as such under a federal system of government. Politics by its very nature is inherent in regionalism because competing interests are defined in spatial terms (Breton 1981, 59). Regional power differences are manifested in the ways in which regions affect the recruitment of élites, the mobilization of citizens and the political alignments that endure over time.

The political expression of regionalism in Canada arising from dissatisfaction with conventional political outlets for expressing grievances, has found a unique voice in minor parties. While conditions associated with the rise of minor parties are not restricted to any single province, historically the consequences of regional existence have meant that minor parties, whether provincial or national, have had both greatest stimulus and greatest scope in Québec and in the West. That is, they reflect a sense of less power in relation to the central government or to the central provinces.

In earlier research, I explored the relative power of regions from 1921 through 1965 by taking into account trends in partisanship, the composition of the federal Cabinet and trends in popular support. During that time, Liberal governments were made up of ministries that overrepresented Québec and underrepresented the West; Conservative governments underrepresented Québec. By all the measures used, Ontario was the most powerful province (Schwartz 1974, 51–82).

The attention I gave to Cabinet was determined by the importance of that body in the Canadian parliamentary system and the role it has played in representing regional interests (see Bakvis 1991, especially 202–37, 238–82). Although there are predictions that Cabinet will become less important as a source of regional power differentials, I believe there are limits to this possibility (see Smiley 1980; Simeon 1972; Gibbins 1982). As long as Cabinet functions, we can expect that "this body will continue to be thoroughly alive to the myriad pressures and nuances involved in the representation of regional interests" (Bakvis 1991, 302).

As a third component, regions have the character of bounded cultures, in which traditions and values persist over time through the socialization of residents. Counter to the expectation that geographic mobility and the nationalizing effects of industrialism and the mass media will smooth out differences among regions, uniqueness is evidence of the tenacity of regional cultures, defying too easy smoothing out of local differences. The "feel" of life in different parts of Canada remains palpably different (see Brook 1987).

The existence of regional differences may, surprisingly, go along with the absence of clearly delineated boundaries setting regions apart from each other. This is because the establishment of boundaries depends on the kind of gradations one looks for, not just in the sense of a particular research agenda, although that is certainly relevant, but with respect to the political and ideological meanings underlying boundary definition. So, when political scientist Donald Smiley urged his colleagues to "banish the term region from our vocabulary and speak instead of province," he was speaking as a student of federalism who found, in the unambiguity of provincial boundaries, the institutional milieu out of which to recognize political actors (Smiley 1987, 23). But region conveys a different meaning, one analytically distinct from the political concept of province, just as regionalism is distinct from federalism. Brodie's argument for distinguishing between regions and provinces makes this clear when she states that "Regions in Canada have concrete political and social dimensions which are deeply imbedded in our collective historical experience: they are much more than arbitrary intellectual constructs" (Brodie 1989, 36).

At times, regional and provincial boundaries coincide, hardly an accident since provinces have the institutional means to speak for territorial interests. But there are also times when other groupings are needed to capture either historical or current alignments. History is captured in the designation of the Maritime and prairie provinces. Brodie advocates a relational method for recognizing when provinces form competing groups defined by issues, as they have over energy resources (Brodie 1990). Progressive Conservative politician David Kilgour relies on his perception of power differences to define Inside and Outside Canada. Kilgour presents the alienation of Outside Canada from the perspective of one who has opposed his own party's policies and suffered rejection from its caucus. He confines Inside Canada to a nexus made up of Toronto-Ontario-Montréal— "those who by means of private wealth, position, and political clout have called most of the shots on national policy since Confederation" (Kilgour 1990, 11). All these approaches pick up some of the cultural residues associated with regionalism.

It may come as a surprise that, today, I do not place much weight on the existence of regional self-identification as a necessary precondition for attributing the existence of regional cultures. In writing *Politics and Territory* two decades ago, I did include collective identification as members of privileged or oppressed regions in the concept of regionalism (Schwartz 1974, 309) and I still agree that such self-identifications remain a strong link with the concept of regional cultures, but their expression cannot be taken as a *sine qua non* of regionalism. Giving primacy to self-identification can be misleading whenever those who cannot perceive such identity then rationalize rejecting the significance of regionalism itself. This was the case, for example, for one of the best-known Canadian sociologists, John Porter, who stated that "it has never struck me that regions provide basic group identities in Canada" (Porter 1975. *See also* Cook 1977, 110). But a culture exists in the behavioural manifestations of common norms and values; it does not require that they be consciously articulated.

My rationale for arguing the importance of regionalism in Canada rests on the historical and contemporary existence of regionally based economic constraints and opportunities, power differences and cultural uniqueness. It has been necessary to take this much space to establish my position because it is not one widely shared in Canada. Regionalism is a reality, no matter how unappealing to some, that has found its way into the constitution-building process of the last three decades.

The Onset of Macro-Constitutional Politics

My interest is in how regionalism was treated during the rounds of macro-constitutional politics that are delineated by Russell (Russell 1993). How did political actors involved in the process, particularly those in the federal government, acknowledge the regional roots of economic opportunity, political power and cultural identity? Although we can be sure that the answers will reflect on the evolving nature of Canadian federalism, for my purposes the more relevant question is the impact that the treatment of regionalism had on the ongoing tension between regional dependency and autonomy.

Russell dates the beginning round of macro-constitutional politics to 1964, when E. Davie Fulton, justice minister in the Diefenbaker government, and Guy Favreau, his successor in the Pearson government, prepared an amending formula for the constitution that would allow its patriation. It required unanimous provincial approval, denied when Premier Jean Lésage of Québec rejected it. This first round continued to 1971 and included Ontario Premier John Robarts' Conference on Confederation for Tomorrow in 1967; a constitutional conference the following year in which Pierre Elliott Trudeau, then justice minister in the Pearson government, took the lead; and a first ministers conference that drew up the amending formula, called the Victoria Charter, June 1971. Its end was like its beginning: Québec Premier Robert Bourassa withdrew his support for the Victoria Charter once he returned to Québec and faced pressure from his constituents.

Russell allows a hiatus between the end of the first round and the beginning of the second in 1976. This new round was centred in Québec, where the *indépendantiste* Parti Québécois had just attained office. As the federal government and the premiers of other provinces confronted the urgency of finding a solution to the constitutional impasse, the Québec government delivered on its election pledge to hold a referendum on whether to change Québec's relations with Canada to those of sovereignty–association. Round two ended with the May 1980 referendum, in which Québec voters rejected sovereignty–association (McRoberts 1988, 300–40).

In round one, the chief actors were in the federal government. They had recognized, at least since the early 1960s, the severity of territorially based economic and cultural inequities, but the solutions they presented were part of the normal business of government, not constitutional issues. Any economic unevenness would be dealt with through legislation by the federal government or through bargaining between the federal government and one or more provinces. Problems of cultural identity were conceived in Canada-wide terms, most notably in the Official Languages Act of 1969. Through it, French would be protected across the nation and the growing practice of bilingualism would foster a sense of nationhood unfettered by older, more parochial loyalties. Constitutional issues addressed by the Victoria Charter recognized power differences associated with population and with Canada's dualism by giving Québec and Ontario veto authority over constitutional changes. My assessment of round one is that regionalism had a relatively small place in the prevalent constitutional thinking. To the extent that a more centralized form of federalism was advocated, one could expect continued regional dependency.

If we shift our focus to regional forces over the period covering the end of round one through round two, we find at least three developments that began outside the confines of constitutional debate but that were eventually bound to penetrate it. They dealt with issues of energy development and pricing, multiculturalism, and separatism in Québec. These were all issues that represented pressure for greater regional autonomy.

The Constitution Act, 1867 gave the federal government control over resources in what were to be the three prairie provinces and parts of British Columbia, a condition altered by a constitutional amendment in 1930 but not before laying the groundwork for a legacy of western alienation from central Canada and the paternalistic federal government (Richards and Pratt 1979, 14–42). The discovery of oil and gas reserves, especially large ones in Alberta, opened opportunities for development. But, as Norrie has argued, a small, resource-rich economy remains vulnerable in a state where population centres and, hence, potential consumers, remain concentrated in areas away from more natural markets to the south (Norrie 1992, 697–714). The creation of a National Energy Policy (NEP) about 1960 was viewed by some critics as a means to keep out cheap foreign oil. But the aftermath of the sharp rise in oil prices on the world market in 1973 led the federal government to alternately freeze and unfreeze domestic prices over the ensuing years (Bothwell et al. 1981, 417–23). For westerners, perceptions remained that it was Ontario's interests that the NEP furthered (Leslie 1987, 14). Simeon and Robinson's assertion, that between 1973 and 1983, "Energy divided Canada regionally as did no other issue," predicts the combination of regional economic opportunity and grievance that would march the West to the constitutional table (Simeon and Robinson 1990, 71:236).

Multiculturalism became a potentially volatile issue as a result of the narrow terms of reference originally given to the Royal Commission on Biculturalism and Bilingualism. It is important to note that the advocates of multiculturalism had a demographic base in western Canada, where, at that time, half the population reported it was of neither French nor British origin. Abandoning the possibility of an official biculturalism, the Liberal government under Prime Minister Trudeau adopted a policy of multiculturalism in 1971. According to McRoberts, it may be that Trudeau was always suspicious of biculturalism. "By recognizing a multitude of cultures, multiculturalism could rein in the notion of duality and nullify Québec's claim to distinctiveness on the basis of culture" (McRoberts 1991, 13). Once again, the grounds were laid for an emotional issue with a regional base to find its way into constitutional negotiations.

Expectations generated by the Quiet Revolution in Québec had also led to disappointment. For some, the pace of change was too slow; for others, the parliamentary manoeuvring and bargaining with the central government were demeaning. Separatist movements arose, most espousing peaceful change, but the most extreme, the Front de Libération du Québec (FLQ), engaged in terrorist acts that culminated in kidnappings and the violent death of a Québec cabinet minister (Laurendeau 1974). The federal government's use of the War Measures Act to suspend basic rights and bring armoured troops into the streets of Montréal reinforced the perception of a powerful central government and the dependency of Québec society. The sense of urgency about the need for constitutional repair increased with the election of the separatist Parti Québécois government.

Round two was not simply conceded by the federal government to Québec. On 5 July 1977, it appointed a Task Force on Canadian Unity, chaired by Jean-Luc Pépin, a former Liberal cabinet minister, and John Robarts, the former Progressive Conservative premier of Ontario. When the Pépin-Robarts Task Force issued its final report in 1979, it was explicit in accepting the essential cultural duality of Canada and its regional makeup. But its recommendations were more or less ignored by Prime Minister Trudeau, to whom it came as a rejection of his comprehensive national vision. David Cameron, who was a member of the Task Force, gives a retrospective evaluation that emphasizes its courage and foresight.

> The Pépin-Robarts Report recognized, accepted and sought to accommodate the very forces in Canadian life and politics that Trudeau was combating. It accepted and celebrated diversity, and in its development of the concepts of duality and regionalism, the Task Force fashioned a view of Canada and Confederation that comfortably acknowledged the communitarian foundation of much of what was most valuable and most strongly cherished in our national existence. What is more, the Report frankly accepted the structural role of the Province of Quebec as the "foyer" of the Francophone community in North America and the role of the other provinces in expressing the regional loyalties of Canadians in other parts of the country. (Cameron 1993, 333–45)

From the Charter to Meech Lake

No breathing space was possible at the end of round two and round three began at once. Now, Prime Minister Trudeau's vision of Canada dominated, including a patriated constitution, an entrenched Charter of Rights and Freedoms, equal rights for francophones everywhere in the country, but no special status for Québec (*see* Trudeau 1968; Canada 1968; Canada 1969). Without the consent of Québec it produced the Constitution Act, 1982, to which the Québec National Assembly responded with a symbolic repudiation.

Round four began five years later with the Meech Lake accord signed by Prime Minster Brian Mulroney and the ten provincial premiers. Its intent was to include Québec in the 1982 constitutional agreement by extending veto power over constitutional amendments, entrenching bilateral immigration agreements, giving the provinces a role in Supreme Court appointments and protecting them against unwanted federal spending powers. Russell notes that the recognition of Québec's claim to be a "distinct society," although present in the accord, "was hedged in by clauses ensuring that this recognition was not at the expense of federal power, aboriginal peoples or multiculturalism" (Russell 1993, 705). The end blow to round four this time was delivered from outside Québec, by the failure of Manitoba and Newfoundland to ratify the accord in time for the June 1990 deadline.

Without falling into the trap of attributing unlimited influence to the persuasiveness of one person, even one with the intellectual and charismatic qualities and the great political power accorded Prime Minister Trudeau, we still must acknowledge the way his own agenda for Canada encouraged other, like-minded politicians in shaping the patriated constitution. His agenda grew out of a longstanding conception about what should be the nature of the Canadian polity and a deliberate effort to strengthen a centralized federalism (Doern 1982, 1–2; Smiley 1983, 75–76). It was an agenda designed, not so much to increase regional dependency, but to make regionalism itself irrelevant.

The Charter of Rights and Freedoms recognized and gave legitimacy to a new set of political actors. Alan Cairns enumerates these as "women, aboriginals, official-language minority populations, ethnic groups through the vehicle of multiculturalism, and…those social categories explicitly listed in the equality rights section of the Charter" (Cairns 1993, 109). What is especially relevant for the present argument is the way these new Charter groups cut across the usual understandings about the territorial basis of subnational communities (see Elkins 1992). Although Aboriginal peoples, through land claims settlements with both provincial and federal governments and the promise of self-government, would introduce an additional element to the practice of federalism, the others were expected to transcend regional identities by limiting provincial governments. According to Cairns, "The Charter is a federal government instrument to limit the balkanization of Canada as a moral community by the differential and inconsistent impacts of ten provincial governments on the Canadian citizenry" (Cairns 1993, 97).

One region where the patriated constitution and the Charter were insufficient to displace existing loyalties and power relations was Québec. That reality was present during round two and led inevitably to round three. It required recognition that Québec was not a province like all the others and that the French language in Québec required protection that placed it above other commitments to individual rights and the Charter (McRoberts 1991, 25).

Elsewhere, as well, regional fires were not quenched. They were kept alive by economic grievances, like those concerning resources in Saskatchewan and Alberta or inequalities generally in the Atlantic provinces (Savoie 1988, 295–99). They also had a political focus, with British Columbia initially in the forefront of those advocating constitutional changes that would lead to reallocations of power. By 1978, Senate reform was uppermost in British Columbia's agenda for change. If the province would be recognized as a distinct region within a reformed Senate, then there would be a means to compensate for federal inattention to regional needs (Elton 1988, 357). The attractions of Senate reform spread to Alberta through a proposal of the Canada West Foundation and a special legislative committee, set up in 1983, that recommended a Triple E Senate—elected, effective and equal (Elton 1988, 358–59; Alberta 1985).

The Conservative government, elected in 1984 under the leadership of Brian Mulroney, had pledged during the campaign to foster a new sense of harmony with the provinces; in particular, to reconcile Québec to the Constitution. The following year in Québec a Liberal government was elected, apparently willing to encourage new relations. It would do so, it indicated, if the following conditions were met:

> ...constitutional recognition of Quebec as a 'distinct society,' a constitutionally secured provincial role in immigration, a provincial role in Supreme Court appointments, limitations on the federal power to spend in areas of provincial jurisdiction, and an assured veto for Quebec in any future constitutional amendments. (Simeon 1988, S9)

Through the 1986 Premiers' Conference and continuing private negotiations between the federal government and individual provinces, a conciliatory document was agreed to in 1987—the Meech Lake accord. All that was required was ratification by Parliament and the ten provincial legislatures. But that would not happen. The failure of Manitoba and Newfoundland to ratify the Meech Lake accord by the 1990 deadline highlighted the complexity of regional discord. Certainly there are other, even more immediate, ways of explaining those failures, including the mobilization of Native grievances in Manitoba and partisan ones in Newfoundland. But the enduring legacy of regional divisions, in which one region's autonomy was another's dependency, was also clearly at work in bringing round four to an end.

Regionalism to the Fore

In what by now must seem like a clichéd analogy, a constitution-drunk Canada rose on its shaky knees to fight on in round five. Known as the Canada round, it began with broad public consultation. The Conservative government under Prime Minister Mulroney set out an agenda for change in its 1991 proposals for constitutional reform (referred to as *Proposals*) (Canada 1991a). Working within that framework, the Beaudoin-Dobbie joint parliamentary committee tabled its report in February 1992 (Canada 1992). First ministers (initially without the participation of Premier Bourassa of Québec), Aboriginal leaders and representatives from the two northern territories then had their say in working out compromises. The result was the Charlottetown accord (the text of which can be found in Russell 1993) which voters in October 1992 were asked to accept in an advisory referendum. They gave their answer with a majority "no" vote.

Round five is unique in the attention that the federal government actors gave to regionalism. The *Proposals* placed regionalism, in all its complexity, on the political agenda with language explicitly steeped in conciliatory efforts at healing. By the time the Beaudoin-Dobbie report was modified in the Charlottetown accord, a different version of regional interests would prevail, one in which provincialization, not autonomy, was the objective. To trace that journey, I use examples dealing with the economy, power and culture in all three documents.

Regional differences in economic opportunities were confronted in the *Proposals* with policies to eliminate barriers to the free flow of people, goods, services and capital across provincial borders. That such impediments presently exist is, by itself, one of the strongest indicators of the regionalization of the country. In a separate publication accompanying the *Proposals* the government made its case for economic changes (Canada 1991b). Presented were examples of internal discriminatory practices in governmental procurement preferences for locally produced goods and services, the operation of similar preferences in the wire and cable manufacturing industry and restrictions on beer marketing (Canada 1991a, 43-45). One could satisfy the urge for good Canadian beer in Chicago by buying Moosehead beer; because it is brewed in Nova Scotia, the same purchase could not be made in Toronto.

Some signs of the difficulties entailed in fostering an internal market and curtailing discriminatory practices appeared in the Beaudoin-Dobbie committee's proposals for "ensuring the well-being of Canadians and managing interdependence." Although the committee agreed on the need for an internal common market that would remove interprovincial trade barriers, it apparently responded to regional pressures by qualifying the extent to which restrictions would be eliminated (Canada 1992).

The amendment of section 121 of the Constitution Act, 1867 that would be required for ensuring a common market in Canada was able to generate even less support in the Charlottetown accord (Russell 1993, 241–42). Trade barriers actually reappeared in the draft version but when Prime Minister Mulroney made it clear that these were unacceptable, they were dropped from the final version. In Russell's assessment,

> The guarantee of free trade across the federation was to be included, but hedged in by thirteen qualifications protecting virtually every conceivable form of government intervention in the economy. The provincial premiers had accepted the federal government's priority proposal by making a mockery of it. (Russell 1993, 211)

The 1991 Senate reforms responded most explicitly to regional demands emerging outside the federal government. The *Proposals* advocated an "elected, effective, and more equitable Senate." The government justified its unwillingness to promote equal as opposed to equitable representation on the grounds that equity reflected a consensus among the federal and provincial premiers in the 1990 First Ministers' Conference and recommendations from the Royal Commission on the Economic Union and Development Prospects for Canada. It might also have referred to the Confederation agreements, originally based on equal representation for the three regions that entered Confederation—the Maritimes, Ontario and Québec. Still, the possibility was left open that equal representation might be worth considering (Canada 1991a, 19).

The Beaudoin-Dobbie report considered Senate reform as a direct response to the "challenge of inclusion of Western and Atlantic Canada" (Canada 1992, xv). It too opted for "equitable" representation for provinces and territories.

The Charlottetown accord was unequivocal in opting for equality (Russell 1993, 243). Although there was considerable resistance from the federal government because of anticipated objections from Québec, it was Ontario Premier Rae who carried the banner opposing equality. In so doing, he was also recognizing how the provinces most committed to Triple-E—the prairies, Newfoundland and Nova Scotia—were attempting to limit the power of central Canada (Russell 1993, 205). The final compromises placed some limits on the new Senate's effectiveness and added guarantees to the size of Québec's representation in the House of Commons. They also allowed Senators to be elected either by population or by members of the legislative assembly in the respective provinces, the latter a concession to Québec.

Of the many elements with cultural implications in all three documents, the one with greatest symbolic significance attached to the designation of Québec as a distinct society. It was the bottom line for Québec and it remained in the Charlottetown accord, even if it was followed by the commitment of "Canadians and their governments...to the vitality and development of official language minority communities throughout Canada" (Russell 1993, 240). When Premier Bourassa refused to include the same language of government commitment to other rights, there was an outcry during the referendum campaign that the accord had established a hierarchy of rights (Russell 1993, 216–17).

The referendum on the Charlottetown accord failed to obtain majorities except in three of the four Atlantic provinces and, barely, in Ontario. These results are relevant to my general argument even if commentators are not able to agree on why they occurred. It is enough that they exhibit their regional contours.

The Impact of Regionalism

This review indicates the brevity of those periods when regionalism was cultivated by the federal government as a critical component of constitution-building. Almost alone among federal political actors during these decades of macro-constitutional politics was the Mulroney government. All complainants identified in its *Proposals*, either in the introductory passages, which set out what were seen as the most pressing problems, or in the conclusions, which presented future objectives, had a spatial location. But in the end, its efforts to grapple with problems of Canada's future by harnessing regional complaints failed. Why should it be so difficult to utilize regionalism as a positive, creative force?

One answer lies in the lack of legitimacy accorded to regionalism. Even in the midst of its most positive evocation in the *Proposals*, we find the statement that "the reality of contemporary Canadian politics is that *provinces and territories, and not regions,* are basic to our sense of community and identity" (Canada 1991a, 18: emphasis in original). To the extent that this implies that region means nothing unless it is equated with province, it devalues any separate status associated with region, whether or not its boundaries are identical with those of a province.

Regionalism is also devalued because it is perceived as an obstacle to the creation of an active central government. This was manifested during Trudeau's leadership. As seen from the left, regionalism is one of the forces that endangers the continuity of the Canadian state (*see* Stevenson 1980, 16–28).

Regionalism is also an obstacle to clear jurisdictional division of powers under federalism, in the sense that it raises the possibility of alternatives to provincial authority. Provincial governments then opt for provincialization rather than regional autonomy. This process was manifest during the negotiations creating the Charlottetown accord, where meetings were dominated by provincial governments with the exception of Québec. The outcome was conceived as a bargaining among governments and the major issue appeared to be provincial equality in relations with the federal government (Russell 1993, 195, 198–200).

Regionalism, as it presently exists, evokes competing, and probably irreconcilable, conceptions of Canada. For example, the centrality of Ontario—as the site of the federal government in Ottawa, the locus of industrial wealth and the concentration of intellectual and cultural élites—has given much of the perspective on Canada an Ontario focus. In previous references to those who did not perceive regional identities I could have pointed out that the authors were from Ontario, just as previous references to national energy policy noted how it served Ontario's interests. Similarly, Québec's relations with Canadian federalism have been largely in terms of its dealings with Ontario (McRoberts 1988, 353–54). A recent review of the role of cultural diversity in Canadian literary criticism points out how Francophone writers in Québec have tended to view the world as bifurcated between French and English, ignoring the multiple ways in which Canada is divided ethnically and regionally (Padolsky 1991, 120). Although there is no question that the duality of Canada remains its most dramatic characteristic, both to those who live in Canada and to outside observers, that dualism is not sufficient to explain the essence of Canada or to encapsulate its national agony. It has been left to those outside central Canada to lament their peripheral status. But when they speak, it is often to those who do not understand their grievances.

I have argued that regions are collective political actors and cultural systems, and hence sources of social action. This makes regions more than simply the political manifestation of federalism. They existed prior to the federal state; they interact with, shape and are shaped by federal structures. This is not to say that all of Canada's problems are encompassed by region. Regionalism, in fact, has helped generate other problems that cut across territorial lines. One example is the existence of francophones outside of Québec. Another is the dramatic increase in the political mobilization of Aboriginal peoples. To the extent that these groups are able to seek protection for their interests, they will inevitably do so in ways that limit the independence of regionally based actors.

In light of the persistence of regionalism, what does this say for the future of Canada's constitutional problems? Prognosis is a dangerous game. But I will not follow in the footsteps of those who have predicted the decline or disappearance of regionalism and now must prefer to remain uncited. However Canada may constitute itself in the future, and no matter how it may be drawn into larger alliances and federations, its own regional components will live on.

References

Alberta. 1985. Report of the Alberta Select Special Committee on Upper House Reform. *Strengthening Canada: Reform of Canada's Senate*. Edmonton: Queen's Printer.

Bakvis, Herman. 1991. *Regional Ministers. Power and Influence in the Canadian Cabinet*. Toronto: University of Toronto Press.

Beaudoin-Dobie [Report]. *See* Canada 1992.

Benz, Arthur. 1987. Regionalism and Decentralization. In *Federalism and the Role of the State*, edited by Herman Bakvis and William M. Chandler. Toronto: University of Toronto Press.

Boismenu, Gérard. 1989. The Federated State and the Heterogeneity of Space. In *Federalism in Canada: Selected Readings*, edited by Garth Stevenson. Toronto: McClelland & Stewart.

Bothwell, Robert, Ian Drummond and John English. 1981. *Canada Since 1945: Power, Politics and Provincialism*. Toronto: University of Toronto Press.

Breton, Raymond. 1981. Regionalism in Canada. In *Regionalism and Supraregionalism*, edited by David Cameron. Montréal: Institute for Research on Public Policy.

Brodie, Janine. 1980. The Concept of Region in Canadian Politics. In *Federalism and Political Community. Essays in Honour of Donald Smiley*, edited by David P. Shugarman and Reg Whitaker. Peterborough Ont.: Broadview Press.

———. 1990. *The Political Economy of Canadian Regionalism*. Toronto: Harcourt Brace Jovanovich.

Brook, Stephen. 1987. *The Maple Leaf Rag. Travels Across Canada*. Don Mills, Ont: Collins.

Cairns, Alan. 1993. *Disruptions: Constitutional Struggles from the Charter to Meech Lake*, edited by Douglas E. Williams. Toronto: McClelland & Stewart.

———. 1979. *From Interstate to Intrastate Federalism in Canada*. Kingston, Ont.: Institute of Intergovernmental Relations, Queen's University.

Cameron, David R. 1993. Not Spicer and Not the B & B: Reflections of an Insider on the Workings of the Pepin-Robarts Task Force on Canadian Unity. *International Journal of Canadian Studies* 7–8(Spring-Fall):333–45.

Canada. 1968. *Federalism for the Future*. Ottawa: Queen's Printer for Canada.

———. 1969. *The Constitution and the People of Canada*. Ottawa: Queen's Printer for Canada.

———. 1979. Task Force on Canadian Unity. *Report*. 3 vols. Ottawa: Minister of Supply and Services. Main volume is *A Future Together: Observations and Recommendations*. ("Pépin-Robarts Report") (January).

———. 1991a. *Shaping Canada's Future Together: Proposals*. Ottawa: Supply and Services Canada.

———. 1991b. *Canadian Federalism and Economic Union: Partnership for Prosperity*. Ottawa: Supply and Services Canada.

———. 1992. *Report of the Special Joint Committee of the Senate and the House of Commons on a Renewed Canada* ("Beaudoin-Dobbie Report"). Ottawa: Queen's Printer for Canada.

Chambers, Edward J. and Rodney E. Schneck. 1990. The Political Economy of Western Canada. *Business in the Contemporary World* 3(Autumn):74–78.

Clancy, Peter. 1994. The Political Significance of Maritime Economic Union: A Case Study from the Forest Industry. In *Change and Impact: Essays in Canadian Social Sciences*, edited by Sally F. Zerker. Jerusalem: The Magnes Press.

Cook, Ramsay. 1977. The Burden of Regionalism. *Acadiensis*. (Autumn):110.

Doern, G. Bruce. 1982. Liberal Priorities 1982: The Limits of Scheming Virtuously. In *How Ottawa Spends Your Tax Dollars: National Policy and Economic Development, 1982*, edited by G. Bruce Doern. Toronto: Lorimer.

Economic Council of Canada. 1978. *Living Together: A Study of Regional Disparities*. Ottawa: Supply and Services Canada.

Elkins, David J. 1992. Where Should the Majority Rule: Reflections on Non-Territorial Provinces and Other Constitutional Proposals. *Points of View* 1, Occasional Papers of the Centre for Constitutional Studies, Faculty of Law, University of Alberta, Edmonton.

Elton, David. 1988. Federalism and the Canadian West. In *Perspectives on Canadian Federalism*, edited by R.D. Olling and M.W. Westmacott. Scarborough.: Prentice-Hall Canada.

Gibbins, Roger. 1982. *Regionalism: Territorial Politics in Canada and the United States*. Toronto: Butterworths.

Kilgour, David. 1990. *Inside Outside Canada*. Edmonton: Lone Pine Publishing.

Laurendeau, Marc. 1974. *Les Québécois violents*. Montréal: Les Editions du Boréal.

Leslie, Peter M. 1987. *Federal State, National Economy*. Toronto: University of Toronto Press.

Linz, Juan J., and Amando de Miguel. 1966. Within-Nation Differences and Comparisons: The Eight Spains. In *Comparing Nations. The Use of Quantitative Data in Cross-National Research*, edited by Richard L. Merritt and Stein Rokkan. New Haven: Yale University Press.

Lithwick, H. 1980. Is Federalism Good for Regionalism? *Journal of Canadian Studies* 15(Summer):62–73.

Marshak, Patricia. 1980. The Two Dimensions of Canadian Regionalism. *Journal of Canadian Studies* 15(Summer):95.

McRoberts, Kenneth. 1988. *Quebec: Social Change and Political Crisis* 3d ed. Toronto: McClelland & Stewart.

———. 1991. English Canada and Quebec: Avoiding the Issue. Sixth annual Robarts lecture, York University.

Norrie, Kenneth H. 1992. A Regional Economic Overview of the West Since 1945. In *The Prairie West: Historical Readings* 2d ed., edited by R. Douglas Francis and Howard Palmer. Edmonton: Pica Pica.

———, ed. 1986. *Disparities and Interregional Adjustment*. Research Studies of the Royal Commission on the Economic Union and Development Prospects for Canada, no. 64. Toronto: University of Toronto Press.

Padolsky, Enoch. 1991. Cultural Diversity and Canadian Literature: A Pluralistic Approach to Majority and Minority Writing In Canada. *International Journal of Canadian Studies* 3(Spring):120.

Pépin-Robarts [Report]. *See* Canada 1979.

Porter, John. 1975. Plenary Address, Annual meeting of the Canadian Sociology and Anthropology Association, Edmonton.

Richards, John, and Larry Pratt. 1979. *Prairie Capitalism: Power and Influence in the New West*. Toronto: McClelland & Stewart.

Russell, Peter H. 1991. Can the Canadians be a Sovereign People? In *Canadian Journal of Political Science* 24(December):699–700.

———. 1993. *Constitutional Odyssey: Can Canadians Become a Sovereign People?* 2d. ed. Toronto: University of Toronto Press.

Savoie, Donald J. 1988. The Atlantic Region: The Politics of Dependency. In *Perspectives on Canadian Federalism*, edited by R.D. Olling and M.W. Westmacott. Scarborough: Prentice-Hall Canada.

Schwartz, Mildred A. 1974. *Politics and Territory: The Sociology of Regional Persistence in Canada*. Montréal: McGill–Queen's University Press.

———. 1993. Regions and Regionalism in Canada. In *Politics, Society, and Democracy: Comparative Studies*, edited by H.E. Chalabi and Alfred Stepan. Boulder, Colo: Westview.

Shapiro, D.M., and M. Stelcner. 1987. Income Disparities and Linguistic Groups in Quebec, 1970–1980. *Canadian Public Policy* 13:1:97–104.

Simeon, Richard. 1972. *Federal–Provincial Diplomacy: The Making of Recent Policy in Canada*. Toronto: University of Toronto Press.

———. 1988. Meech Lake and Shifting Conceptions of Canadian Federalism. *Canadian Public Policy* 14 supplement (September):S9.

Simeon, Richard, and Ian Robertson. 1990. *State, Society, and the Development of Canadian Federalism*. Research Studies for the Royal Commission on the Economic Union and Development Prospects for Canada, no. 71. Toronto: University of Toronto Press.

Smiley, Donald V. 1980. *Canada in Question: Federalism in the Eighties*. Toronto: McGraw-Hill Ryerson.

———. 1983. A Dangerous Deed: The Constitution Act, 1982. In *And No One Cheered: Federalism, Democracy and the Constitution Act*, edited by Keith Banting and Richard Simeon. Toronto: Methuen.

———. 1987. *The Federal Condition in Canada*. Toronto: McGraw-Hill Ryerson.

Stevenson, Garth. 1980. Canadian Regionalism in Continental Perspective. *Journal of Canadian Studies* 15(2):16–28.

Tocqueville, Alexis de. [1835–39] 1988. *Democracy in America*. Edited by J.P. Mayer. Translated by George Lawrence. New York: Harper and Row.

Trudeau, Pierre Elliott. 1968. *Federalism and the French Canadians*. Toronto: Macmillan.

H. PETER OBERLANDER

A National Urban Policy: A "Hiccup" on Canada's Constitutional Horizon

Canada's territory is 10 percent larger than the area of the United States and remains, even with the dismemberment of the USSR, the second largest spatially unified nation state in the world. However, in relation to its immense territory its population of 27 million is among the smallest.

Constitutionally, Canada consists of one federal government, 10 provincial governments and two federal territories. The federal–provincial structure operates under the aegis of federalism and it is this aegis that is currently under siege by the 10 provinces and Canada's Aboriginal population. Nowhere is this challenge more vigorously felt than in the public policy sector of urban affairs.

Canada moved towards national independence when the British Parliament passed the British North America Act on July 1, 1867 designating Canada a Dominion within the British Empire. Under this statute the power to govern Canada was divided between the provinces and the federal government, based on an unequal and tenuous balance of strength, resources and political will. During the nineteenth century, Canada was a rural society with an agrarian economy. Geographically it had a dispersed settlement pattern, self-sufficient within its rural needs and agrarian resources.

This dispersed population and its agrarian production and trade required only a modest governing structure, and history records that "the least government was the best government"(Oberlander 1986, 33). Neighbours helped neighbours, and rural communities governed themselves on the principle of town-hall meetings. Potential conflicts were resolved by compromise, without either conceding or demanding policy choices or their implementation.

Since then, Canada has developed into a highly urbanized society based on a competitive industrial economy. Urban problems have intensified and multiplied during the post-World War II decades, demanding administrative and political solutions well beyond the historical constitutional framework, within which concerns for "property and civil rights" and matters of "local concern" were allocated to the provinces (Rowat 1975, 12). They in turn have delegated certain limited administrative processes and responsibilities to their municipalities. Local self-government operates at the whim of the provinces and has no constitutional anchor, either now or, apparently, in the future.

The current reality is reflected in the often quoted conundrum, "The Feds have the money, the Provinces have the jurisdiction, and the municipalities have the problems!" (Rowat 1975, 23).

What constitutes a national urban policy for Canada? It must be based on the recognition that urbanization is the single most significant force shaping Canada and the current and future life of all Canadians, socially, economically and politically. While nearly 80 percent of all Canadians live in cities of significant size, all Canadians owe their living to the cities as centres of employment, production and distribution of goods and services, and as a system of Canada-wide governing of all Canadians, whether they live close to the U.S. border or in the Arctic. Wherever Canadians live—in downtown Toronto or Montréal, among the fruit orchards of the Okanagan, the wheat fields of the prairies or the fishing villages of Newfoundland—all are urban, bound by their common value system and the way of life they pursue, through their means of consumption, production and employment. While urbanization in Canada has generated a seamless web of industrialization and continuing urbanization, changing public policies dealing with economic, social or environmental issues have remained segmented and issue-oriented.

These segmented policies reflect their separation by function, population, age or gender characteristics. They fail to reflect two essential Canadian characteristics. First, life in Canada is highly interactive because most of its aspects are interdependent. Second, life is spatially specific and location focused. Segmented policies result in the partitioning of social, economic and environmental activities and deny the interdependence of human activity and the spatial context in which these activities are to be measured, assessed, supported, and ought to become the bases for governmental action. Acceptance of urbanization as a country-wide phenomenon ought to underlie all public policies that deal with the economic, social and environmental needs of Canada.

Reflecting the constitutional heritage of 1867, politically Canada is partitioned among the 10 provinces and has assigned to them the management of the municipalities, which is often equated with managing urban affairs. The current governance of municipal administration in no way reflects the reality of urban linkage and interaction between Vancouver and Toronto, or Winnipeg and Regina, or St John's and St. John. It does not account for the vibrant reality of Vancouver/Seattle, or Winnipeg/ Minneapolis, or Montréal/New York. Cross-border shopping recently revealed these dynamic relationships even to the most somnolent politician in Ottawa or in any respective provincial capital. Significantly, the government solution was to prohibit cross-border shopping and legislate against it administratively or economically. Another urban habit is the convenience of Sunday shopping, which Ontario has legalized as recently as 1993. Even then, the exact details of hours of operation and location to be open have been left to the municipalities, which can enact whatever by-laws they choose.

Throughout the 1960s as urbanization transformed Canada from sea to sea, the need for some concerted national action seemed urgent and even self-evident to some.

Twenty years ago a determined federal government, during the first Trudeau administration of 1968–72, asserted itself in urban affairs by creating an important initiative based on its "superior power of the purse"(Oberlander 1987, 19). As a courageous experiment in public administration, it established the Ministry of State for Urban Affairs (MSUA), with its primary mandate to formulate, negotiate and initiate a national urban policy.

In order to overcome the deeply ingrained impediment to federal action on a national urban agenda, considered a provincial responsibility, MSUA was initially created because:

- the federal government was a major actor in urban Canada through its direct land ownership and staff employment, notwithstanding the constitutional primacy of provincial and municipal governments in municipal affairs;

- the local urban implications of federal activities needed to be understood more precisely;

- the national urban linkages emerged as highly interactive and responsive to policies at the national level;

- interdependent urban problems (housing, transportation, land use, environmental deterioration, fiscal pressures and financial demands, among others) required comprehensive solutions to influence favourably the future pattern of urbanization and the form and quality of urban life;

• policies and programs of all levels of government required consultation, cooperation and coordination to successfully guide urban development and enhance the quality of life in existing and new urban centres.(Oberlander 1987, 20–21)

MSUA operated on the basis that urban concerns have an impact on all levels of government and vice versa and there existed a need for intergovernmental consultation and coordination of policies and programs affecting urban development in Canada.

While the Ministry served Canada well for seven years, it was abolished, primarily because of its inability to resolve the constitutional tension between the provinces and the federal government on municipal versus urban affairs.

The debate on the nature, scale and scope of urban problems in Canada has not abated; it has intensified. The fundamental source of "urban problems" is the process of urbanization itself.

For rational private and public economic reasons, people concentrate in Canadian cities in ever-increasing numbers and proportions as a matter of free choice. The consequences of these trends have generated problems *of* the city, as well as *in* the city. Both problems share one common characteristic; they are highly interdependent. Housing is related to transportation and land use, and vice versa. Land use and access to activities in all parts of the city affect the rich and the poor, they affect the revenues of the city as well as the natural environment and all of them loop back on themselves in a continuing cause-and-effect chain.

This sense and reality of interdependence is at the core of Canada's urban problems and deserves continuing and thorough attention by Ottawa as well as by the provincial capitals. The urban process is multi-dimensional, reaching back into the past and affecting the future.

MSUA was a creature and creation of its time. It was a strategic, significant and successful experiment in public administration in Canada. It was *strategic* because it was launched within the larger context of radical changes in governmental structure and administrative procedure during the first phase of the Trudeau years, 1968–72. It was *significant* because it challenged the conventional wisdom in public administration by advancing the concept of separating policies from programs and aggregating policy responsibilities in a single Ministry for strategic action while leaving the programs with appropriate delivery agencies. It was *successful* because it met its original mandate as envisaged in the Speech from the Throne of October 8, 1970:

> To foster coordination of the activities of all levels of government and contribute to sound urban growth and development. (Oberlander 1987, 21)

However, there were limits to federal initiatives in urban affairs in a federally structured country. Increasingly assertive provincial governments are involved in the tug of war between Ottawa and the provincial capitals. The municipalities became the innocent bystanders and were severely affected. While MSUA attempted to build an equitable structure and system through which to mediate and resolve urban issues that affected Canada as a whole, the provinces clearly refused to accept such a possibility. In their minds, urban affairs remained synonymous with municipal affairs and the municipalities ought to remain wards of their respective provinces. There was no constructive accommodation between the federal government, the provinces and their municipalities during the seventies or eighties and there is still no will for a Constitutional resolution.

The agendas of government have now changed; the primary issues are jobs, inflation, interest rates and other economic priorities. All these issues have a clear impact on the cities and towns of this country. MSUA pioneered the analysis of the interdependence of social, economic, environmental and political issues through its studies of urban settlements from coast to coast as a basis for a national urban policy.

MSUA was sacrificed on the altar of federal–provincial relations to satisfy the almost irrational preoccupation with Canada's nineteenth-century constitutional division and allocation of powers spearheaded by Ontario, Alberta, Québec and British Columbia. The issues that MSUA was established to deal with have not vanished. In fact, they have been exacerbated and have become more complex and more intractable as Canada increasingly becomes a dense urban industrial network.

Traditionally, it has been part of Canada's conventional wisdom that the federal government had no legitimate business in the provincially responsible and dominated cities. Conventional wisdom has also dictated that the infusion of program money was the appropriate solution to problems both *of* and *in* the city. MSUA's surprising success in raising public consciousness and political awareness, while fraught with ups and downs, threatened its own survival. The power to initiate a national urban policy and translate it into reality through federally available and effective means threatened the provinces, which challenged what they considered a major federal intrusion into provincial jurisdiction.

Herein lies the fundamental paradox of Canada's struggle to come to terms with its urban identity: the federal government has the power of the purse but little control over urban development; provincial governments have constitutional power but often lack sufficient resources to address urban issues systematically; and the municipalities have the problems, but neither the power nor the financial resources to address the problems systematically. The effects of conventional wisdom, coupled with constitutional paradox have militated against the creation of a lasting national urban policy together with relevant policy instruments.

What political structural conclusions can we draw from the federal initiative (MSUA 1970–78) to improve urban live within a prevailing constitutional strait-jacket?

1. The municipalities must be included in all urban policy/program/ project negotiations directly and by right.

2. Federal–provincial governance must encompass municipal needs on a continuing basis within a political and administrative structure balancing taxation powers with political accountability; responsiveness with responsibility.

3. Urban communities at the local and metropolitan level must be empowered to form and sustain local self-government as the foundation of Canada's democracy. More than 80 percent of all Canadians live *in* the city and all Canadians live *by* the city by choice. Constitutionally guaranteed local self-government must reflect this reality and thereby encourage federal/provincial/local administration to respond successfully to urban Canada's needs.

How Do We Move from Here to There?

1. Prevailing distribution of the power to govern and command the relevant resources to implement economic, social and environmental policies/programs/projects requires cooperation between existing political and administrative units. This *cooperation* must be based on early *consultation* and subsequent *coordination*. MSUA pioneered a process of tri-level consultation, nationally, provincially and locally.

1971–73	National:	Policy Alternatives
1971–75	Provincial:	Program Planning
1971–78	Local:	Project Negotiations

   Examples of tri-level consultations leading to cooperation and successful coordinated execution included:

National: Federal land management policies within municipalities and metropolitan areas

Provincial: Federal/provincial powers targeted for
    • urban railway relocation
    • urban housing

Local: Specific joint projects combining federal resources/land and program funds within municipal development proposals, for example
    • Waterfront Development, Halifax
    • Civic Centre and City Square, St. John's, Newfoundland
    • Vieux-Port, Montréal
    • Vieux-Port, Québec City
    • Harbourfront, Toronto
    • Rideau Canal Waterway, Ontario
    • Granville Island, Vancouver

2. Federal government's continuing presence in Canada's cities demands that its programs, initiatives and resources be coordinated within its own orbit and with the provinces and their municipalities. The best examples include: the changing federal presence in sea- and airports, in national transportation systems and its continuing substantial urban land ownership. Initially at the Cabinet level, a committee of Ministers ought to be charged with the initiative of consultation, cooperation and coordination over federal policies, programs and projects of explicit urban impact.

3. Ultimately, local government in its municipal and metropolitan form, charged with direct local governance, must be admitted to confederation as a legitimate partner in confederation. The current constitutional review ought to initiate the process by a declaration of principle: urban government, a constituent partner in federation, to be fully articulated and implemented through specific and detailed consultations throughout the decade, leading to full partnership status by the year 2000.

The year 1992 will be remembered as Canada's date with its constitutional destiny. The BNA Act of 1867, serving as Canada's constitutional surrogate framework, was patriated in 1982, resulting in the Constitution Act, 1982. The historical division of power remained unaltered, but a major addition was the Charter of Rights and Freedoms and a formula to amend the Constitution. The amending formula was based on the consent of 7 provinces encompassing within them 50 percent of the population. Nine of the 10 provinces agreed to this patriation process. Québec chose not to be included.

In 1984, the Progressive Conservative government of Brian Mulroney came to power and among its political objectives was "to include Québec in the constitutional process" by reforming the constitutional framework to meet Québec's unique social and political aspirations (Cairns 1988, 45).

While Canada's Constitution Act, 1982 legally and technically applied to all provinces and all Canadians, including Québec, Brian Mulroney chose to open up the century-old debate on Canada's governance. The result was the Meech Lake accord of 1987, cobbled together by the 10 provincial premiers at the Prime Minister's summer cottage north of Ottawa. While this accord appeared to represent full agreement among all provinces, including Québec, it needed ratification by all 10 legislatures and the federal Parliament. It failed to achieve unanimity when Manitoba and Newfoundland, for different reasons and with different methods, failed to ratify the Meech Lake accord.

Since then the federal government has struggled, by a variety of means, to maintain public debate and increase public participation in its drive to resolve the constitutional impasse established by the patriation of the British North America Act, without full political and institutional unanimity.

Québec decided to accelerate this public debate and the process of constitutional adjustments by passing Bill 50 in the Québec legislature, which provided for a provincial referendum on Québec's sovereignty by October 1992. Against this rapidly approaching deadline, feared by some, hailed by others, the federal government instigated a sequence of five regional conferences dealing with different aspects of Canada's constitution, from Halifax to Vancouver.

In Halifax "The Division of Powers" was considered; in Montréal, "Canada's Economic Union"; in Toronto "Canada's Identity, Rights and Values"; in Calgary "Institutional Reform." The Vancouver meeting provided the opportunity for bringing together the varied discussions and presentations into a consistent and integrated whole, dealing with eight issues, among them: Canada's distinct society, its linguistic duality, the need for Senate reform, the urgent requirement for an economic union coupled with a social charter and the framing of the "Canada Clause" as a preface to the new Constitution.

However, an unexpected and most startling discussion revealed an unscripted debate on the inherent right of Aboriginal peoples to self-government. Let the Report on the Vancouver Meeting speak for itself:

- Participants enthusiastically endorsed the idea that the inherent right of Aboriginal peoples to self-government should be entrenched in the Constitution. And like Québec's distinct society, it must be more than an "empty box." It must include not only jurisdictional powers, but also governance over land, resources, and protection of Aboriginal languages.

- The right of self-government should be exercised within the Canadian federation. Application of the Charter of Rights and Freedoms in Aboriginal governments, while generally endorsed, is a question for further study and debate.

- While the full dimension of the inherent right to Aboriginal self-government could not be well defined in a brief weekend, there was an overwhelming commitment to the principle and to developing a process by which it could be achieved expeditiously.

- It is vital to establish fair and effective processes to bring about Aboriginal self-government without delay. There was strong sympathy for the suggestion of one of the Aboriginal organizations—that the inherent right be given effect, with the approval of the national organizations, through treaty negotiations with each Aboriginal group. In this way, powers could be adapted to the particular circumstances of each community. Negotiations would proceed according to the Aboriginal peoples' own timetable. (Oberlander 1992, 2)

As Canada's Native community achieves its inherent right to self-government, can the general Canadian urban community be denied a constitutionally anchored right to local self-government within a united federal Canada?

There is some hope—perhaps this is the moment to act boldly and with some generosity within the constitutional spirit of innovation. The problems and issues that the 1970 federal initiative attempted to resolve, through creating MSUA's mandate to frame a national urban policy, have not gone away. Canada has become what was anticipated 20 years ago—a country of three mega-cities, supported by a network of smaller settlements stretching from Sidney, B.C., to Sydney, Nova Scotia, and beyond. Urbanization has proceeded with a vengeance and is currently confronting nearly all jurisdictions with nearly insurmountable problems at escalating public and private costs.

Canada is an urban society unable to establish an urbane system of administration. During the past 20 years the provinces have gradually abdicated their constitutional responsibilities, shifting more and more daily and seasonal urban tasks to the municipalities without also shifting to them appropriate financial resources. "Downloading" has become a way of life for Canada's 10 provinces.

The Constitutional debate turned and twisted its way through renewed public participation to its ultimate resolution, due to Québec's insistence on its October Referendum, and could lead to an urban national trauma without comparable policies or federal leadership. During the most recent turn of events in Constitutional politics, Canada's native population has wrung a promise from the federal government for the "inherent right" to self-government. Is it possible that Canada's native population will achieve self-government, including local self-government, while Canada's urban population, anchored in the 23 Census Metropolitan Areas, will continue to be denied a constitutionally enshrined right to local self-government?

So far Canada's struggle for a national urban policy with appropriate implementation instruments was indeed a short-lived hiccup in the continuing and evolving saga of Canada's political system, rooted in an escalating milieu of urbanization and industrialization. Does it have to remain an accidental blip in the continuity of Canada's evolving governance or could it serve as a reminder that urban Canada needs a national urban policy to meet its united destiny?

Postcript

The preceding article was presented to the May 1992 International Canadian Studies Conference in Jerusalem, based on the political joustings in Ottawa and the provincial capitals to that moment.

In the intervening two years Canada's political and economic circumstances have changed dramatically. Governmental priorities have been altered radically and, in particular, constitutional concerns have lost their place on the public policy agenda. Some of the following changes were in the making druing the late 1980s, others are new and some are still emerging.

1. The Charlottetown accord, based on the five regional conference consultations (*see* page 80) failed to achieve its required unanimity and has joined Meech Lake and the other previous ntional attempts in the archives of failure to update Canada's Constitution. The Québec referendum, in October of 1992, resulted in a constitutional and institutional draw (paralysis perhaps) denying everyone a mandate for radical change to the status quo.

2. Canada's economy is currently in the midst of adjusting to its globalization, encouraged and sustained by the Canada–US Free Trade Agreement and the North American Free Trade Agreement.

3. "Deficit Reduction," "Debt Elimination" and "Jobs" have become the slogans of the 1990s, leading to a dramatic changing of the guard in Ottawa after the 1993 national election. Provincial elections also resulted in new governments with changed views on the urgencies of constitutional change.

4. Urban issues, however, have not diminished; on the contrary, they are asserting themselves continuously and engender new public policy responses. The Liberal Party won its substantial electoral victory in October 1993 on its "Red Book" platform. The Liberals promised that, once elected, there would be no new expenditures and no new programs, with the exception of a federal government intrastructure initiative to kick-start local job creation. The Rt. Hon. Jean Chrétien, Canada's new Prime Minister, promised the "new money" to upgrade Canada's aging urban infrastructure with full provincial and municipal cost-sharing support—an extraordinary federal initiative considering historic constitutional hesitancy and fiscal stringency. Ottawa offered $2 billion of new budget funding to be matched in a variety of ways by the provinces and their muicipalities over the next two years. Currently [1994], the federal Treasury Board is negotiating ten federal–provincial agreements to allocate these funds, based on a formula reflecting differential prevailing provincial unemployment rates. The results will be ten different applications of this federal initiative without anticipating the explicit urban impact or consequences.

   While it clearly an urban program initiative, it is sectoral and segmental and independent, if not isolated, from other public policies. Explicitly, it is the only new federal cash contribution, leaving it to the provinces and the municipalities to establish urban priorities and procedures of regional distribution throughout the network of urban settlements regardless of size or location. It may once again reinforce the historic consequences of federal funds as an urban band-aid in lieu of a national urban policy reflecting continuing constitutional constraints and following traditional administrative procedures.

5. The most unexpected and surprising change in the federal government's atttitude towards the 1992 constitutional national consultation was contained in the stark policy announcement by the new Minister of Indian Affairs and Northern Development, Ronald Irwin, in the House of Commons and reported in the *Vancouver Sun* on February 15, 1994: "Aboriginal local government as proposed in the Charlottetown Accord can be achieved without opening up the 1982 Canada Constitutional

Act." The Minister assured everyone that the Chrétien government is committed to quick and expeditious negotiations between the federal government and the Native community, to achieve Native self-government. This is a radical and completely unexpected policy announcement and carries with it a new interpretation of "local self-government." At present, the Aboriginal leadership seems divided over this shift in federal policy: the urban Native community, living off reserve, is in support; other groups oppose it. It clearly presages yet another round of accommodating to political reality without radically changing Canada's constitution. This approach based on long historic precedent, will accommodate pressing needs of an urban/industrial society, and is characteristic of Canada's long history of adaptive federalism.

References

Cairns, Alan C. 1988. Federalism and Provinces. In *Meech Lake: From Centre to Periphery*. Vancouver: The University of British Columbia, Centre for Human Settlements.

Oberlander, H. Peter 1986. Submerged Third. In *Public Options* July.

———. 1987. Navigating Through Shoals: How to Create a Ministry while Operating It. In *The Ministry of State for Urban Affairs*. Vancouver: The University of British Columbia, Centre for Human Settlements.

———. 1992. Proceedings: Concluding Conference of the Policy Conferences on the Proposals for a Renewed Federation. Vancouver, September.

Rowat, Donald C. 1975. *Your Local Government: A Sketch of the Municipal System in Canada*. Toronto: Macmillan.

ROBERT SCHWARTZWALD

Pre-Referendum, Post-Meech Lake: Cultural Development Policy in Québec

As early as 1962, Québec novelist and essayist Hubert Aquin bemoaned the "cultural fatigue" of French Canada, expressing the hope that some day soon "our cultural existence could become something other than a permanent challenge and that this fatigue might cease" (Aquin 1977, 97). Yet, at least on the bureaucratic level, no such respite has occurred, and various Québec governments have produced no fewer than five major policy papers on culture and cultural development since those early years of the Quiet Revolution. This paper proposes to provide a comparative and critical analysis of the two most recent* of these documents: the first, *La Politique québécoise de développement culturel*—known informally as Livre bleu ("Blue Book")—was published in 1978 by a pro-independence Parti Québécois government that would hold an unsuccessful referendum on the issue two years later;** the second, *Une Politique de la culture et des arts* ("Arpin Report"), was submitted in 1991, one year after all ten provinces failed to ratify the Meech Lake constitutional accord and its recognition of Québec as a "distinct society" within Canadian Confederation. It was received by a provincial Liberal government caught between responding to the disillusion and restiveness of its supporters on the one hand and keeping the door open to further constitutional renewal with the rest of Canada on the other.

---

* Reference herein to "current" conditions should be taken to mean May 1992 when the paper was presented to the International Canadian Studies Conference in Jerusalem.

** On May 20, 1980 the citizens of Québec were consulted in a referendum on whether or not to give the Parti Québécois government a "mandate to negotiate sovereignty-association" with the federal government in Ottawa. By a 60 percent to 40 percent margin, the answer was NO.

Although we are here most concerned with drawing out the differences between the Livre bleu and the Arpin Report, it is important at the outset to be clear on what the two reports share, at least rhetorically: a commitment to culture as a democratic right; the notion that governments must be judged on their performance in improving the quality of life of their citizens, of which culture is a primary indicator; the conviction that sustained government intervention in the field of culture is appropriate, inevitable and necessary, particularly in the case of Québec; the idea that cultural producers have the right to a decent level of existence that requires governments to move beyond a grant-to-grant, subsistence-level approach; and finally the concept that the Canadian government's authority over certain key elements of the cultural sphere is incompatible with Québec's cultural development, and therefore that Québec must achieve exclusivity over cultural policy, regardless of future constitutional arrangements.

As products of two very different conjunctures and prepared for governments with distinct ideological orientations, the justifications provided for some of these areas of agreement, not to mention the scope and specifics of proposed policy, often diverge widely. Nevertheless, one can read these cultural documents as more than immediate reflections of the policy of the government of the day. They convey important information about discursive ruptures and continuities around notions of *culture*, cultural *development* and the role of the state in protecting and promoting these; they demonstrate to what extent culture is imagined as expressive or constitutive of a homogenous national identity.

Paradigms of Culture: Citizens, Producers, Consumers

A useful way to enter into a comparison of the two reports is to consider the import of their distinctly different provenances. The Parti Québécois document was published by the Minister of State for Cultural Development, Camille Laurin, one of the PQ's leading ideologues and strategists. Indeed, not only is his name listed as authoring the Report but an Introduction to it is also signed by him. Of course, the Report was drafted by high-level functionaries and academics aligned with the Parti Québécois, and particularly informed by the eminent sociologist Fernand Dumont, whose writings on culture and society are well-known and respected in Québec. (Dumont became the first Director of the Institut québécois de la recherche sur la culture, an independent research body proposed in the document and established shortly after its release.)

The tone of this Report, 472 pages in length and published in two volumes, is at once learned, philosophical and prescriptive. The entire first volume is a general enquiry into the question *"De quelle culture s'agit-il?"* ["What do we mean by culture?"] and it is required reading for understanding the policy dimensions addressed specifically in the second volume. Ambitious and confident in its objectives, this document is entirely elaborated in reference to two assumptions that appear in its concluding pages: *"En attendant que la province devienne un pays…"* ["While we wait for the province to become a country"] (Québec 1978, 472) and *"Il est des choses qu'une* province *peut faire"* ["There are things that a *province*, i.e. a mere province, can do."] (Ibid., 471). Here, we see at work the double discourse within which so much of the PQ's strategic and tactical planning was enmeshed: on the one hand, the assertion that nothing could fundamentally be ameliorated in *la condition québécoise* without the achievement of sovereignty; on the other, the need and desire to demonstrate that the PQ was capable *in the present* of implementing policies that would make a significantly positive difference to the quality of life in Québec.

To what extent would expanding the role of the state in cultural matters provide a foretaste of what could be achieved after independence, and to what extent would the successes of cultural policy implemented under the constitutional status quo obviate the need for independence? The Livre bleu attempts to resolve this double bind by defining culture in systemic terms, and confirming its elaboration and development as fundamental rights of modern nations. Consequently, the Report has a high stake in explicating Québec's status as a nation in order to demonstrate its inalienable right to promote its own cultural development. In this sense, it claims to be doing nothing less than what Canada itself had been doing ever since the publication of the Massey Report in 1947. But whereas Canada's cultural policy depended upon the "provincialization" of Québec and limiting its culture to performative and representational elements, a Québec policy would seek to restore the "globality" of the culture. One hears echoes of Hubert Aquin in this section of the Report; *"Seule l'abolition de la culture globale de la culture canadienne-française peut causer l'euphorie fonctionnelle au sein de la Confédération et permettre à celle-ci de développer 'normalement' comme un pouvoir central au-dessus de dix provinces administratives et non plus de deux cultures globalisantes"* (Aquin 1977, 87).

The scope of the Livre bleu is truly astounding when making its claim for what may legitimately be considered within the purview of a cultural development policy. It is precisely the kind of document that a *noveau-philosophe* such as Alain Finkielkraut condemns in his *La Défait de la pensée*

(Finkielkraut 1989), since in his view to designate such a vast range of human activity as "cultural" is to banalize the term and empty it of any notion of value. Finkielkraut's disparaging "boots to Bach" dismissal aside, though, it is clear that the Livre bleu is a very modern document, completely in harmony with the kinds of policy papers that have been developed in other advanced societies where governments legitimate their attempts to "develop" culture through maintaining a pluralist discourse. UNESCO documents at the ready to be quoted whenever required, the first volume discusses culture in terms of ethnicity, gender, age, class and urban and rural lifestyles; the second volume lists all the proposed areas of intervention: habitat, health, leisure, work, the media, scientific research, arts and letters, cultural industries, patrimony and the school system itself. Specifically, in the Livre bleu the reader is constantly interpolated as a *citizen* whom the government serves. Culture is not only a democratic right, but an inherently democratic field of intervention. It is repeated that it will be up to the citizen to realize and develop the culture, while the government responds to his or her aspirations by providing the necessary policy measures and support. Throughout, there is the strong assumption that the government is a faithful reflection of the people, springing from them and almost intuitively responsive to their desires. This is so because both government and the people are tied to the wellsprings of a common culture.

The most recent cultural policy paper is authored by Roland Arpin, a senior government functionary, in the name of "Le Group-consiel sur la politique culturelle du Québec," a commission of 11 men and women appointed by the government from a range of cultural sectors. In other words, this group was instructed to report *to* a government that in no way had the kind of investment in the eventual implementation of its Report that the PQ government had in its Livre bleu. Whereas the latter reads like an arm of government and party policy, the new report was written strategically to appeal *to* a government whose ideological leanings are anticipated and provided for in the rhetoric of the Report. Specifically, the Report must acknowledge, while hoping to moderate, the favourable bias the Liberal government has towards free market and private sector initiatives. This probably explains why the document is at such pains to argue that culture not be evaluated solely, or even primarily, in economic and productivist terms, and that provincial governments recognize unreservedly the major role the state will need to play in cultural development. Over and over again, the Report admonishes its (governmental) reader that what is required is a "Research and Development" approach to culture, but one that recognizes at the outset that short-term gains are unlikely and that, if you will, culture has its own rewards. There is a plea for government to understand that the economic interests of Québec are better served if there is a reservoir of cultural sympathy abroad that is resistant to the vicissi-tudes of economic cycles, not to mention changes in orientation and interest on the part of business and government alike. Hence, the need to support cultural organisms and promote their international visibility, albeit in accordance with the principles of sound business management. Accordingly, language about elevating younger or experimental artists and writers from subsistence status is countervailed by pronouncements on the need to stabilize major cultural organisms (symphonies, ballet companies) and prioritize support for what are called the "backbone" of Québec's cultural profile.

The Arpin Report interpolates its reader as either a *producer* or *consumer* of culture. On the "production" side, it stresses the state's responsibility to serve its "clients" by enabling them to be *competitive* in the cultural market: *"faire mieux, autrement, et plus tôt—c'est la triple et implaccable loi de la concurrence"* ["To do it better, in a different way, and before anyone else: that is the triple and implaccable law of competition"] (Québec 1991, 61). As for the "consumption" side, the emphasis is on access by non-profes-sionals to professional products that, by virtue of their "cultural" charac-ter, enhance the quality of life in the modern world. In other words, there are those who produce, and then there are those whose right to consume what others produce must not only be protected, but promoted through educational programs that enhance the appreciation of culture. The Report discusses at some length how this might be done in the family, in the school system and through the *mise en valeur* of Québec's patrimony.

The Arpin Report's definition of what constitutes legitimate culture is broad enough on its own terms, which involve taking conventional defini-tions of letters and the visual and performing arts and expanding the latter pair to accommodate forms that depend on new and sophisticated tech-nologies. More importantly, though, the Arpin Report eschews any rela-tional view of culture, focusing instead what is conventionally referred to as "high culture." Here, there is no recognition of what the Livre bleu refers to as authentic popular culture, which would consist of a series of knowledges, techniques and relations formed through interactions with geography, climate and familial structures in specific *regional* milieus. The Livre bleu speaks of rehabilitating these cultural forms, of providing them with material support and seeing in them rooted expressions of identity in opposition to the "mass culture" that is largely manufactured in faraway studios and imported to Québec where it "floods" the airwaves. The Arpin Report tends not to recognize the question of cultural forms, collapsing popular cultures with "recreation" or "crafts." For it, these are appropriate community activities, but ones that in a sense fall outside the scope of the Report. Instead, it seeks improved access to high culture for all, and it is assumed what most will desire is an "entertaining" middle-brow version of it.

At the risk of appearing somewhat schematic, then, we may sum up by observing that on the question of defining the key notions of culture and cultural development, the Livre bleu is synthesizing in spirit, painted in broad strokes and concerned with directly linking its notion of cultural development to Québec's viability as a modern national *state*. On the other hand, the Arpin Report is self-avowedly "empiricist" in orientation, and at once more reserved and more precise about what constitutes legitimate government support for culture. But as we will see in the following section, the Reports must ultimately be evaluated not only on the basis of their respective proposals, but by reading these proposals against, or as encoded by, the basic assumptions each has made about the nature of Québec society.

Paradigms of Culture: The Nation, The Homogenous, The Heterogenous

In the earlier part of this century, an individual who was not *de vielle souche** might have been forgiven for regarding Québec civil society as an extended family from which he or she was excluded. "State" and "citizenry" seem almost anachronistic terms when applied to this period, when economic hegemony was exercised mainly by an Anglo-Scots élite and upward mobility for immigrants and even the "French-Canadians" themselves occurred *outside* the national community defined in terms of a homogenous adherence to "*[notre] foi, langue et nos institutions*." In this context, Québec nationalism was decidedly more "ethnic" than "contractual," an important distinction to which we shall return. Yet, as Benedict Anderson reminds us in his *Imagined Communities*

---

* "Of old stock." In Québec, this would include the vast majority of the population. Their French ancestors came to North America primarily in the seventeenth century.

(1991), it is more productive to think of nationalism as a variegated "system" like kinship or religion than as a monolithic ideology. During the Quiet Revolution of the 1960s and 1970s, for example, francophone Québec seemed almost overnight to shed the ideological trappings of a quasi-corporatist, clerically driven society and to embrace both sides of the participatory/technocratic paradigm characteristic of modern democracies. In this instance, the nationalist impetus behind francophone Québec's self-affirmation helped turn the province's civil law into one of the most progressive in the democratic world on a whole range of questions, from women's rights and health care to laws concerning labour relations and electoral financing itself.

Since its emergence in the late 1950s, there has been a persistent tendency to decry modern Québec nationalism as a new form of tribalism. Perhaps the key text in this regard is Pierre Elliott Trudeau's "La Nouvelle trahison des clercs," which appeared in 1962 in the review he founded and directed, *Cité libre*.* This argument has been especially amplified in recent years by critics of the Parti Québécois and by perhaps its most controversial achievement, the Charter of the French Language, Bill 101. Bill 101 specifically prohibited the use of languages other than French on all commercial signs, with the exception of small, family-style businesses. The merit of such a policy is certainly a legitimate subject of debate, but most often the policy is either carelessly or deliberately misrepresented, especially outside Québec, as one of "banning English." Prohibitions have never been placed on signage for cultural, religious or social service establishments. [As of publication, the authority of this Bill has expired. Editor.] Far from viewing the Charter as a radical, albeit possibly Jacobinesque outgrowth of the Quiet Revolution, these critics see in Bill 101 the retrograde assertion of an archaic "nous" over a more modern civic pluralism. Whether it be based on blood, lineage, or some ineffable collective spirit, this "nous" would distinguish the authentic Québécois from "les autres," the others who either surround Québec or live within its borders. In recent years, this critique has been extended to the Québec Liberal Party itself, which many self-declared representatives of the anglophone community, including the newly-formed Equality Party, regard as virtually infiltrated by an *indépendantiste* "fifth column."

---

* In 1968, Trudeau became Prime Minister of Canada in a campaign marked by strong opposition to Québec nationalism. Since that time, he has been an unrelenting opponent of any "special status" for Québec, not to mention of the independence movement. Most recently, he spoke out against the Meech Lake accord [as well as the Charlottetown accord. Editor].

In the Livre bleu, culture is defined as *"Des ensembles plus ou moins vastes de façons de parler, de penser, de vivre, et en corollaire, des langages, des croyances, des institutions")* ["Larger or smaller ensembles with their ways of speaking, thinking, living and as a corollary, with their languages, beliefs and institutions"] (Québec 1978, 11). In the modern period, the document tells us, these are most often recognizable and legitimated as *national* cultures. Within this framework, the French language is recognized as a *"foyer de convergence"*; it is at once the language of the historical majority and the language through which all citizens should have an equal opportunity to manifest their own values. In fact, the Livre bleu's view of Québec as a nation is not centred around blood, but around an evolving commonality of experience derived from shared territory, history and language.

Indeed, the important changes to Québec's demographic landscape signalled by the unprecedented arrival of significant numbers of francophone immigrants of non-European origin, large new allophone communities from the developing world and the emergence of new forms of cultural self-representation for Québec anglophones have profound and ever intensifying cultural ramifications. In the "theoretical" first volume of the Livre bleu, the expressed desire is to encourage the participation of these "cultural communities." Their diversity is seen as a source of strength, provided they are able to communicate with the majority in its language. To the extent that the Livre bleu speaks of a "fraternity of culture" that will evolve around the French language, it adopts what may be termed an "integrationist" approach to the question of immigration.

Now, none of this should sound terribly strange to anyone following contemporary debates in Europe, for example. Particularly in France, it has become common to rehearse the various concepts of nationhood that developed from the French Revolution throughout the nineteenth century as a way of preparing a discussion on contemporary issues such as the assimilation or integration of immigrants, multiculturalism and democratic pluralism itself. Writers such as Alain Finkielkraut (1989) Julia Kristeva (1991) and Dominique Schnapper (1991) have reminded us of the division between the "universalist" view of the nation as *contract* bounded by common law and nation as defined in terms either of blood or specific "genius". (The latter view was not always so radically opposed to the former; in Herder, for example, the recognition of specifically national characteristics was in the name of the universal principle of self-determination; each people was to be free to "be itself," as it were, safe from the homogenizing, even assimilationist designs of greater powers.) Such a historical view also reminds us that language has often enjoyed a kind of linchpin status, alternately represented as the most profound expression of national genius, or as the most arbitrary yet palpable evidence of a common social pact to which an otherwise heteroclite population pledges allegiance. The Livre bleu presents French as the only viable *lingua franca* for Québec, but one that bears all the scars of the economic and political domination endured by that society. For historical reasons, it is the language most apt to convey the cultural specificity of Québec, and while its undermining leads directly to grave psychological trauma for the population, including loss of self-esteem and self-destructive forms of behaviour, its enhancement will have a correspondingly therapeutic and dynamizing impact on the nation.

How does the Arpin cultural policy paper measure up to its predecessor on these issues? This is not an unimportant question, since the policy it recommends and that is implemented will be of enduring significance, regardless of the precise redefinition of Québec's constitutional status that results from the current deliberations. In a comparative reading, it is hard not to be struck by how generally elliptical, if not downright evasive, the document is about what the specificity of Québec culture might be. Indeed, only 4 pages out of the total 325 are devoted to discussing this question! Instead, the Report seems to want to beg off, vaguely describing Québec as *"cette terre d'Amérique bien particulière"* (!) and its culture as somehow linked to *"un quelconque Amérique"* (Québec 1991, 40). In the absence of any substantive analysis, the document is content merely to affirm that French *is* the common language of public life and leaves it at that! This performative wilfully refuses to acknowledge the contentious nature of language debates in Québec, or indeed that there is, or has been, any debate. In particular, the relevance of these debates to the question of immigration is smoothed over.

Such silence is deafening when set alongside the very real tensions that exist in Montréal and their implications for its cultural ambience in the future. What will be done, for example, about the fact that immigrant children often attend French-language schools where fewer than half the students are in fact francophone? To date, impatient responses that range from proposing completely separate schools for those immigrants who are "culturally incompatible" to outlawing the use of English on school grounds have brought deserved discredit to many of the traditionalists within the Montréal Catholic School Commission. But even those who have opposed these "suggestions"—and there are many who have—often tend to subtly shift the burden of the failure of government resolve back onto immigrants themselves, confusing their use of English (for many of them, after all, this is a family matter, considering the network of relations they have through-out North America) with an unwillingness or refusal to use French. But what message do immigrants finally receive from witnessing the seem-ingly interminable and incoherent wrangling over language among fed-eral, provincial and municipal jurisdictions, not to mention the quarrels within the institutions of the francophone community itself?

Of course, the problem is that for the most part, issues of immigration and "cultural communities" are not considered cultural by the Arpin document, and are therefore situated safely beyond its scope. More pre-cisely, the document's bias towards well-established institutions implic-itly serves to relegate the initiatives of immigrants to mere local manifestations of a universal "Culture." The Arpin Report offers the immigrant cultural producer a "choice" between outright assimilation into a "universal" high cultural domain or remaining within the folkloric "recreational" world of the ethnic community. It rehearses the article of faith that universal culture is anchored in local specificities, but by refusing to acknowledge the *national*, it offers no unifying principle within which minorities may make their contributions. Ironically, it is the Livre bleu, precisely because it recognizes collectivities and has a strategic relation to them, that speaks much more explicitly, if not satisfactorily, about them.

Capital, Metropolis; Periphery, Centre

One area where the Arpin Report could represent a significant advance over the Livre bleu is in its proposed rehabilitation of Montréal as a cultural metropolis. I deliberately employ the term "rehabilitation," because the new document marks a departure from the horror and distrust with which functionaries and policy makers in Québec City, some 300 km downriver and with an overwhelmingly middle-class and francophone population, have tended to view the province's cosmopolitan centre. In this regard, the Livre bleu in particular resorts to language that portrays Montréal as an anomaly on an otherwise homogenous landscape.

In the Livre bleu, the city, where almost one half the population of Québec lives is refigured as an anomalous *region*, and indeed a region that has been relatively spoiled and pampered in comparison to others. This is never justified, merely asserted as an obvious truth with a gratuitous aside or two on Montréal's "uniqueness," defined in terms of its integration into the "Great Lakes megalopolis" (!) and the contacts it enjoys with the rest of Canada and the United States. The latter, however, are what make Montréal *"pas purement [Q]uébécois"* (Québec 1978, 96). Its cultural preeminence is grudgingly acknowledged—"*il peut se trouver des esprits pour le regretter [mais] qui saurait le contester?*" (Québec 1978, 97)—and presented almost as if necessitating redressment. The Report ominously refers to Montréal as a *"zone de péril"* and at times conjures up an almost exoticist fascination with the city: "*C'est là qu'au Québec la langue et la culture françaises vivent le plu* dangereusement!" (Québec 1978, 98).

Of course, it is true that Montréal is where the viability of French as well as its indispensability need to be firmly established, and in fact many of the provisions of Bill 101 were designed to facilitate this process. The requirement that immigrant children attend French schools and the measures that establish French as the *lingua franca* for commerce and services have demonstrably furthered this aim. The problem with the Livre bleu is not so much that it continues to present the linguistic situation in Montréal as one of "crisis"—after all, the document is contemporaneous with Bill 101 and not subsequent to any experience with its implementation—but that it can only imagine the resolution of this crisis through a homogenizing paradigm that tends to obliterate the real challenges presented by Montréal's diversity. The document's assertion that "You almost have to live in Montréal to be aware of the complexity of the language problem in Québec and the urgency for a solution…" (Québec 1978, 98) is in fact an understatement: it is no exaggeration to say that Montréal's linguistic situation *is* the "language problem" of Québec! Elsewhere, the francophone population is sufficiently hegemonic in all spheres to render the question of "choosing" to learn the national language completely academic for an immigrant. By definition, Montréal's position in Québec is unique, and policy cognizant of this reality should be expected to take this into account. Instead, the Livre bleu curiously refers to a range of programs and options to be applied in cities "like" Montréal! This rhetorical formulation serves only to deny Montréal's irrefutable difference, the better in fact to "regionalize" (i.e., provincialize) it. At this point the Report betrays a gap between pious wishes for reconciling integration and diversity and thinking concretely about the issues this involves. The process is imagined as occurring in relation to a largely homogenous indigenous population, an ideological construction based on the demographic reality of the entire province of Québec, but one which is clearly inadequate to the reality of Montréal. The result is a sudden recourse to authoritarian discourse that seems most interested in finger-wagging and stigmatizing the metropolitan population: "*Il incombe à l'Etat* d'empêcher la région montréalaise de se déraciner, *tout en* activant *et en* normalisant *les ferments d'innovation qui s'y développent*" (Québec 1978, 102).

And what would "normalizing" Montréal mean? This distrust of the metropolis is a throwback to theories of culture that bank on "authenticity," where urban inhabitants are at once written off as "impure" and subject to the operations of a state that wants to prevent the contagion from spreading. Ultimately, Montréal's exceptional status is acknowledged, but as "aberrant" or "marginal." Yet how could this really be so when the "language problem" there is the common experience of almost half the province's population, including many with the greatest education and contacts with the world at large? In the final analysis, the ideological imperative to see the question of language through the prism of homogeneity impedes the Livre bleu's ability to think coherently and imaginatively about Montréal's cultural development, which is to say about a crucial aspect of the presence a sovereign Québec would have in the community of nations.

The Arpin Report, on the other hand, explicitly breaks with the "regionalizing" orientation of the Livre bleu. It develops a tri-partite view of Québec in which Montréal's role as metropolis is *enthusiastically* embraced, to use the Report's own word. It speaks of the "necessity to use the only large city Québec possesses" for the common good: "Whatever happens to this city will determine the future of Québec" claims the document, which is why Montréal needs to be "fully recognized as the principal pole of cultural life in Québec" (Québec 1991, 126). Additionally, the Arpin Report proposes a range of programs designed to support training and production for younger professionals. Much of the Report is centred on programs and initiatives that would provide Québec cultural producers with the incentive to remain in Québec and the facilities that would enable them to produce "cutting edge" work while doing so.

Gone also is the Livre bleu's contradictory tendency to describe every sector of Québec culture as being mortally threatened by outside forces, usually American, while at the same time exhorting Québécois not to behave as if they were "besieged"! The Arpin Report notes confidently that despite the presence of many more American and English-Canadian television channels, for example, only 5 percent of the francophone population says it prefers to watch American sitcoms and dramas, while the vast majority actually prefer those "made in Québec" (Québec 1991, 115). As welcome as the Arpin Report's de-dramatization of these issues might be, however, it would be deceptive not to acknowledge therein a tendency to "wish away" the real tensions that exist in Montréal. For example, what access do francophone and allophone immigrants have to the media and other cultural institutions of the majority? What role do these play in encouraging the elaboration of a contemporary culture in Montréal, or alternately do they serve to reinforce boundaries between mainstream (self) representations and activities on the margins of society? The issues, as we suggested earlier, primarily involve ways of establishing Montréal's cosmopolitanism as a boon, rather than a threat, to Québec's cultural development.

In the view of the Arpin Report, Québec City should accept its role as capital, and develop the highest standards as the depositary of the national patrimony (archives, national museums, etc.). It should be no surprise that the development of the regions is largely equated with the construction of facilities able to receive and diffuse the culture that will mainly be produced...in Montréal! This brings us back to a problem identified earlier: local culture, such as it exists at all in the Arpin Report, is seen largely as recreational or centred around "self-improvement." Needless to say, there is no obvious reason why the recognition of Montréal as a metropolis should come at the expense of any serious attempt to deal with the cultural needs of the regions. Turning them into passive consumers of culture is as egregious as the Livre bleu's misguided desire to "regionalize" Montréal!

Some Current Implications...

Since the Livre bleu is in many ways not only the product of a previous government but of an earlier conjuncture, we will not ask of it a final question reserved for the Arpin Report: What may we expect from it over the coming period? It is clear that if implemented, cultural activity would be less subject to evaluation on the basis of an overarching political agenda that, under the Parti Québécois government, tended in practice to favour products that claimed to represent authentic expressions of national specificity. These were not so much distinguished by their explicit ideological orientation as they were by their localization at certain sites of cultural production. In other words, they were conceived of as being more "at home" in certain sectors, such as crafts, "popular" dance, folk-rock and historical novels. On the other hand, the entrepreneurial preoccupations of the Arpin Report, as much as they claim to encourage what might be called "cultural venture capital," will tend to direct resources to "proven values," and therefore to the cultural monuments of the status quo. In the hands of a government that has shown little ability to evaluate the importance of culture other than through box office receipts, there is every reason to expect an intensification of these tendencies, perhaps even to the point where some traditional pursuits are themselves sacrificed on the altar of "accessibility"!

Since the Second World War, Québec governments have regularly asserted their rights to jurisdiction over educational and cultural matters on the grounds that the British North America Act, 1867, reserves these portfolios for the provinces. Over the years, the Canadian and Québec governments have argued over grants to universities, television and telecommunications policy and representation at international meetings of cultural and educational associations, to name only a few areas of dispute. Hence, what of the necessity for Québec to achieve exclusivity over cultural affairs, a perspective the Arpin Report shares with its predecessor? Before closing, let us note two important recommendations in the Arpin Report that seek to prepare the terrain for this eventuality. First, that a Ministry of Culture be established that would blend the responsibilities of the current Ministry of Cultural Affairs and the Ministry of Communications. The Report characterizes the current MAC's profile as "discrete and self-effacing," and argues in favour of a powerful Ministry that is not constantly having to defend its legitimacy before those of more high-powered dossiers. Fusing with Communications, recognized as a *secteur de pointe*, would facilitate this. This proposed reorganization is more modest than the *dirigiste* experiment of the Parti Québécois government, which featured a "super-Minister" of State for Cultural Development (Camille Laurin) who lorded over a handful of Ministries, including Cultural Affairs, Communications, Youth, Leisure, Sports and Education! Nevertheless, it remains to be seen whether a Liberal government is willing to concede such weight to culture within the Cabinet, not to mention what relative weight "industrial" and "artisanal" sectors of culture would have within such a Ministry.

The Arpin Report also recommends the establishment of an Arts Council in Québec along the lines of the Canada Council. Specifically, such an agency would be created with an arm's-length relation to the government in order to ensure its autonomy in the awarding of grants and subsidies. The Livre bleu had explicitly rejected establishing a granting agency autonomous from the Ministry of Cultural Affairs, rationalizing that the peer review procedures in place were adequate and that it was illusory to believe such an agency could function viably if its general orientation was at odds with government cultural policy in any case! Such an attitude is largely responsible for the dearth of support the claim for exclusivity has until now elicited from the Québec cultural community, where widespread respect for the peer review and arm's-length work of the federal believe such an agency could function viably if its general orientation was at odds with government cultural policy in any case! Such an attitude is largely responsible for the dearth of support the claim for exclusivity has until now elicited from the Québec cultural community, where widespread respect for the peer review and arm's-length work of the federal granting agencies contrasts with the historical failure of Québec agencies to perform in the same manner. Whether or not the newly-announced policy will be sufficient to attain the explicit support of artists and writers remains to be seen; in any case, their hesitation is clearly not ascribable to some deeply held loyalty to the federal state—indeed, many Québec writers and artists are still firmly in favour of independence—but rather to the pragmatic ("opportunistic and unprincipled," their detractors have said!) reality that the current dual federal–provincial structure seems to allow for a greater margin of manoeuvre and the possibility of successfully funding an experimental or marginal project.

With a referendum on new constitutional arrangements imminent and the Québec government embroiled in other controversies, including the proposed further development of the James Bay hydroelectric grid over the objections of Native peoples, the attention the Arpin Report receives over the coming period is in any case likely to be limited. Some of its recommendations are being implemented, others have been rejected out of hand, and still others will be integrated, albeit in slightly modified form, into future cultural policy papers. Yet the Report, even if less obviously so than the *Livre bleu* that preceded it, is about more than policies themselves, however worthy any specific ones might be. It offers a further chronicling of Québec's (self) representation as a distinct society within the North American and international contexts, and an important insight into how a society prepares to deal with the changes that are imposed upon it by the world in which it evolves.

References

Anderson, Benedict. 1991. *Imagined Communities: Reflections on the Origin and Spread of Nationalism.* 2d ed. London and New York: Verso.

Aquin, Hubert. 1977. La Fatigue cultural du Canada français (1962). In *Blocs erratiques.* Montréal: Quinze.

Finkielkraut, Alain. 1989. *La Défaite de la pensée.* Paris: Gallimard.

————. 1991. Le Group-Conseil sur la politique culturelle du Québec. *Une Politique de la culture et des arts* ("Arpin Report"). 2ème éd. Québec: Gouvernement du Québec.

Kristeva, Julia. 1991. *Etrangers à nous-mêmes*. Paris: Gallimard.

Livre bleu. *See* Québec 1978.

Schnapper, Dominique. 1991. *La France de l'intégration : Sociologie de la nation en 1990*. Paris: Gallimard.

Trudeau, Pierre Elliott. 1962. La Nouvelle trahison des clercs. *Cité libre* 46(avril) 3–16.

ZACHARIAH KAY

Canada and Israel: Four Decades in Retrospect

Caution is a necessary ingredient of any state's foreign policy. That is self-evident regardless of the international system's nature. The extent of caution as a keystone in policy decision-making determines the degree of activity on the diplomatic front. Canada's relations with the Jewish state is a hallmark of caution mixed with a measure of conciliatory activism that became less active and more prudent in the decades subsequent to 1948.

Canada emerged from World War II as a major western ally and trusted middle power. Due to its antecedents and social structure, it was a firm component of the western bloc in the bi-polarized Cold War world. Still, the oldest Dominion was aware of its Commonwealth connections in conjunction with its nascent internationalism that found expression through the United Nations where its stature as international *persona grata* was acknowledged.

In retrospect, Canada's pre-1948 policy of non-commitment towards a Jewish state in Palestine was a mirror image of its British-policy-oriented Liberal Prime Minister, William Lyon Mackenzie King, a somewhat excessively cautious but nonetheless masterful politician. While there were vestiges of Christian support for Jewish restoration in the Holy Land coupled with the activities of the Zionist-led Canadian Jewish community, the Canadian leader remained supportive of Britain's Mandate policy in Palestine. That also accounted for the delay in recognizing Israel after its establishment on 14 May 1948.

King's retirement in November of that year and the installation of his successor, Louis St. Laurent, and, in particular, the new External Affairs Minister, Lester B. "Mike" Pearson was a harbinger of what was to follow. Pearson had already acquired a reputation as an internationalist, a United

Nations exponent for the solution of international disputes whose conciliatory, albeit cautious, approach had earned him kudos, particularly over
the Palestine partition plan. It was to emerge again towards the end of the
first decade and earned him a Nobel Prize.

Perhaps it is no less of a coincidence that Canada's grant of de facto
recognition of Israel on Christmas Eve 1948 occurred just over a month
after King's retirement. Canada then moved from a stance of non-commitment to one of diplomatic support for Israel's existence. However, Canada
was careful never to be too far in advance of its British and French allies and
within the bounds of American policy parameters.

Pearson's internationalism set the stage for the next two decades in
Canadian foreign policy, even during his period in opposition. Prime
Minister John Diefenbaker maintained the policy. The Progressive Conservative leader had been a supporter of the Jewish homeland and, subse-
quently, of Israel since his early days in politics.

The third and fourth decades bore witness to shifts in Canadian foreign
policy. While Pearson's conciliatory activism and well-timed ad hoc actions were examples of Canada's independence on the international scene,
External Affairs' caution was always in tow. With the arrival of the Pierre
Trudeau–led Liberal government and Canada's bi- and multi-cultural
soul-searching, the country turned away from international idealism towards greater concern for its international economic relations. The subsequent Joe Clark Progressive Conservative government, then Trudeau
again and finally Brian Mulroney's Progressive Conservative governments veered to what became known as "evenhandedness" or more
attention to Arab politics. Israel, which had become a regional power, lost
its Occidental underdog appearance and more pro-Arab voices—especially from commercial interests—gained Ottawa's ear.

While caution with less conciliatory activism was still the salient feature
of Canada's relations with Israel, the former remained committed to
Israel's existence and security but mindful of Arab viewpoint. Still, the
shifts in the latter part of the four decades did not dislodge the primacy of
caution in Canada's foreign policy approach.

The First Decade

Canada began its first term on the UN Security Council with the issue of
Israel's admittance to UN membership being tied to *de jure* recognition.
When Israel was voted into the UN on 11 May, 1949, Canada extended
recognition. Eight days later, Israel's first Consul General, Avraham
Harman, took up his post in Montréal. In September 1953, Israel's first

Minister Plenipotentiary, Michael Saul Comay, arrived in Ottawa and his status was raised to that of Ambassador the following September. T.W.L. "Terry" MacDermott was appointed Canada's first (albeit non-resident) Ambassador in Tel Aviv.

Although Canada had supported and worked for the passage of the 1947 partition plan, which included the internationalization of Jerusalem, the government accepted the subsequent recommendations of the Palestine Conciliation Commission concerning the reality of Jerusalem's division between Israel and the Hashemite Kingdom of Jordan. Canada opted for maximum local autonomy and protection of the holy places pending a final peace settlement. Yet it never recognized Israeli sovereignty over West Jerusalem, nor Jordanian sovereignty in the eastern part of the city nor over the West Bank of Judaea and Samaria. When Israel proclaimed Jerusalem its capital in December 1949, Canada had accepted the divided city as a fact but demurred from recognizing it as Israel's capital.

Canada's involvement with UN-sponsored activity led to General Howard Kennedy's appointment as the first director of the UN Relief and Works Agency (UNRWA) for the Arab Palestinian refugees, and Major-General E.L.M. Burns as head of the UN Truce Supervision Organization (UNTSO) in the Middle East.

While Canada had sold defensive weapons to Israel and Harvard aircraft trainers to Egypt, a serious imbalance occurred when the latter concluded a major arms deal with Czechoslovakia in 1955. In the House of Commons, the Liberal government faced stiff opposition from the Progressive Conservatives and the Cooperative Commonwealth Federation (CCF) as some of their members regarded the Harvards as offensive rather than defensive weapons. The opposition argued in support of Israel's position and requests. In the wake of the parliamentary debates, Israel formally applied for the purchase of 24 F-86 Sabre jet interceptor fighters. In September 1956, after long and arduous negotiations and consultations with the United States and other NATO allies, the Liberal government of Louis St. Laurent finally approved the sale to augment Israel's defence military capability in the light of Egypt's earlier acquisitions. When the Sinai was invaded on 29 October 1956, the sale was suspended and eventually cancelled.

The St. Laurent government's negative response to the Anglo-French action in the Sinai-Suez crisis of early November was opposed by the Progressive Conservatives, who felt that Canada should have stood by Britain and France and expressed sympathy for Israel's action; the CCF had also expressed sympathy for Israel. Later in November, Parliament was summoned into special session to debate government policy. This followed the first Emergency Special Session of the UN General Assembly, where External Affairs Minister Lester Pearson proposed the establishment of an international United Nations emergency force (UNEF) as an intermediary between the opposing forces in the Sinai-Suez region. His plan was adopted. It called for the Force's contingent, to which Canada contributed, to be composed of middle level powers. The success of UNEF earned Pearson the Nobel Peace Prize. Major-General Burns of UNTSO was appointed UNEF commander.

The election of June 1957 ended 22 consecutive years of Liberal rule when the government was defeated by the Diefenbaker-led Progressive Conservatives. The new Prime Minister was pro-British, but at the same time had been a long-time supporter of the Jewish homeland and a recent supporter of the Sabre jet sale to Israel.

The Second Decade

The Progressive Conservatives went to the polls again on 31 March, 1958 and won a landslide victory. Unlike St. Laurent, Diefenbaker had taken firm control of foreign policy, looking more towards Commonwealth relations while maintaining support for the UN. The government backed the United States invasion of Lebanon and the dispatch of British troops to Jordan in 1958. When the UN Observer Group in Lebanon (UNIGOL) was established in May of that year, Canada again contributed. It was also in the autumn of that year that Canada's first resident Ambassador to Israel, Margaret Meagher, was appointed.

In addition to furthering economic relations, Diefenbaker hosted an official visit by Israel's Prime Minister David Ben-Gurion in May 1961, when they also discussed development aid to the Third World.

From 1963 to 1968, Lester Pearson led a Liberal minority government. During this period, Canada was largely concerned with Francophone domestic issues as well as the French-speaking world, including the Third world and Arab countries.

The mid-east crisis of May 1967, which culminated in the Six Day War, placed Canada in opposition to Egypt's demand and UN Secretary U Thant's consent to remove UNEF. On 8 June, Pearson outlined a peace plan in the House of Commons calling for UN presence, freedom of passage, demilitarized zones and a concerted effort to solve the Arab refugee problem. Opposition leader Diefenbaker was more demanding, emphasizing the need to support Israel's right to exist and its right to Jerusalem, which Israel's forces had just reunited. At the UN, External Affairs Minister Paul Martin reiterated Pearson's plan, adding the need for a Secretary General's representative. This eventually led to the Security Council's passage of Resolution 242 on 22 November 1967, with Canada's full support.

Prior to the Six Day War crisis, Israel's third President, Zalman Shazar, made the first state visit to Canada during the country's centennial celebrations.

The Third Decade

In the 1968 election, a majority Liberal government led by Pierre Trudeau was brought to power. With External Affairs Minister Mitchell Sharp, the government inaugurated a series of studies dealing with the country's international relations. Veering moderately from the internationalism of the previous two decades and having become more cognizant of the Arab states, the government sought what it considered to be a more "even-handed" policy vis-a-vis the Middle East. The decade bore witness to increased trade with Middle Eastern states, economic interests exerting more influence on policy. In the 25-year period ending in 1974, Canada had also contributed $32 million in aid towards the Arab refugees.

One of the major repercussions of the 1973 Yom Kippur War was the Arab oil embargo. Despite Canada's wealth of fossil fuels, it still depended on Arab oil for its east coast domestic market. As well, the Arab boycott of Israel affected the Canadian business community. Although the federal government promised to enact anti-boycott legislation, that promise never came to fruition. Ontario, however, the largest and most industrialized province, did pass such a law.

Canada's movement in favour of Arab Palestinian rights caused a number of public controversies. Contending that Palestinian rights must be taken into account, Canada favoured Palestine Liberation Organization (PLO) representation at international UN–sponsored conferences. There was a stir over Canada's hosting of the UN Congress on the Prevention of Crime in September 1975. The Canadian government demurred and the Congress was then shifted to Geneva. However, the government did allow the 1976 Habitat conference to proceed in Canada with PLO representation.

The "Zionism is Racism" resolution adopted by the General Assembly in 1975, was opposed by the government. On 12 November, former Progressive Conservative leader Diefenbaker presented a resolution that was unanimously adopted by the House of Commons condemning the UN resolution. A cabinet decision of February 1976 stated Canada's desire to trade with *all* nations in the Middle East.

The Fourth Decade

In 1978, Canada joined the UN Interim Force in Lebanon (UNIFIL). Israel's Prime Minister Menachem Begin visited in November of that year and urged Trudeau to move the Canadian Embassy to Jerusalem. In the following year's election, the Progressive Conservatives led by Joe Clark won power as a minority government. During the campaign Clark had promised to move the Embassy to Jerusalem if he were elected. The ensuing controversy, however, stirred by Arab and Canadian commercial interests, compelled him to backtrack in spite of counter-pressure by the Canada-Israel Committee (CIC), the pro-Israel lobby. A commission headed by former national Progressive Conservative leader Robert Stanfield recommended against the Embassy move and the Clark government accepted Stanfield's recommendation. The issue was not revived even after the election of the Trudeau-led Liberals the following year. The Liberal government continued to expand its trade interests with North Africa as well as with other Arab states.

Canada supported the Camp David accords and the subsequent Israel-Egypt peace treaty of 1979, and continued to back efforts to foster an overall Arab-Israel peace process. In the election of 1984, the Progressive Conservative party, led by Brian Mulroney, won an unprecedented majority. A more critical attitude towards Israel followed in the wake of the 1982 Lebanon War. This was noted in a report on *Canada's Relations with the Countries of the Middle East and North Africa* submitted by the Standing Committee on Foreign Affairs of the Canadian Senate in June, 1985. While supporting Canada's contributions to UN forces in the Middle East including the Multinational Force and Observers in Sinai (MFO), the report also called for the curbing of terrorism and violence; ensurance of Israel's security; the halting of Israeli settlements in the Administered Areas; and Palestinian representation in the peace process.

Towards the Fifth Decade

External Affairs Minister Joe Clark continued to shift his policy, moving it closer to the pro-Arab European Community's position, although it was less pronounced than their's, and did not diverge significantly from U.S. President George Bush and Secretary of State James Baker's policy in the Middle East. A clear break with Canadian government traditional attitudes towards the Arab-Israeli conflict occurred when Joe Clark delivered a speech at the annual CIC dinner on 10 March, 1988, in Ottawa, that was highly critical of Israel. Somewhat taken aback, he tried to assuage the critical impact in a subsequent speech. Nevertheless, Canada's largest newspaper, *The Toronto Star*, agreed with Clark's criticisms, as did a number of other anglophone newspapers and a sizable number of those in the electronic media. The francophone media had been moving in that direction long before the separatist Parti Québécois with its pro-Arab sentiments had gained power in Québec. Canada had now become more forthright in its policy of supporting Palestinian rights and PLO participation. When Clark was replaced by Barbara McDougall in 1991, Canada was in the midst of constitutional soul-searching but was also an established member of the Group of Seven (G-7) major industrial powers. Eventually, it found itself as the initial refugee moderator in the multinational Middle East peace process.

One might ask whether Canada has bowed to the political mathematics that 22 Arab sovereigns are bigger than one Jewish state. Has Canada, in the definition of its late foreign policy savant John Holmes, shed its traditional "Middlepowermanship" that, in the eyes of this observer, portrayed greater elements of "evenhandedness" than has occurred in recent decades? Whatever transpires in the latter part of the fifth and subsequent decades, the cautionary premise undoubtedly will remain a hallmark in Canadian-Israeli and Middle East relations.

This paper is based upon an article to appear in the forthcoming *Encyclopaedia of Zionism*, to be published by the Associated University Presses, New Jersey, summer 1994.

Bibliography

Primary Sources

Ben-Gurion Diaries. Ben-Gurion Archives. Sdeh Boker, Israel.

Canada, Department of External Affairs, publications: monthly, annual, Statements and Speeches; 1970. *Foreign Policy for Canadians* Ottawa: Queen's Printer.

———, House of Commons Debates, Proceedings of the Standing Committee on External Affairs, Senate Debates. The Standing Senate Committee on Foreign Affairs. 1985. *Report on Canada's Relations with the Countries of the Middle East and North Africa*. Ottawa: Ministry of Supply and Services, Canada, 1985.

Israel State Archives, Documents on the Foreign Policy of Israel, Volumes 1–7 and Companion Volumes 1948–52. Jerusalem: Israel State Archives, 1981–92. Foreign Office files, from 1948.

National Archives of Canada, Files of the Department of External Affairs from 1947, Privy Council Office files, Papers: E.L.M. Burns, John G. Diefenbaker, L.B. "Mike" Pearson, Louis S. St. Laurent.

Submissions by the Canada Palestine Committee, Canada–Israel Committee, the Canadian Jewish Congress–United Zionist Council of Canada.

Secondary Sources

Books

Bercuson, David J. 1985. *Canada and the Birth of Israel: A Study in Canadian Foreign Policy*. Toronto: University of Toronto Press.

Canadian Institute of International Affairs, *Canada in World Affairs*, series since the 1946–49 volume.

Canada–Israel Committee. 1979. *Canada–Israel Friendship, The First Thirty Years*. Toronto.

Dewitt, David B., and John J. Kirton. 1983. *Canada As a Principal Power*. Toronto: John Wiley and Sons.

Holmes, John W. 1979, 1982. *The Shaping of Peace: Canada and the Search for World Order, 1943–57*. 2 vols. Toronto: University of Toronto Press.

Kay, Zachariah. 1978. *Canada and Palestine: The Politics of Non-Commitment*. Jerusalem: Israel Universities Press.

———. Forthcoming. *The Diplomacy of Prudence: Canada and Israel. The First Decade, 1948–58*.

Pearson, Lester B., 1973, 1975. *Mike: The Memoirs of the Right Honourable Lester B. Pearson*. 3 vols, edited by John A. Monro and Alex I. Inglis. Toronto: University of Toronto Press.

Stein, Janice. 1989. Canadian Policy in the Middle East. In *From Mackenzie King to Pierre Trudeau: Forty Years of Canadian Diplomacy*, edited by Paul Painchaud. Québec: Les Presses de l'Université Laval.

Taras, David, and David H. Goldberg, eds. 1989. *The Domestic Battleground: Canada and the Arab–Israeli Conflict*. Montréal: McGill–Queen's University Press.

Thompson, Dale C. 1967. *Louis St. Laurent: Canadian*. Toronto: Macmillan of Canada.

Journals and Quarterlies

Behind the Headlines series of the Canadian Institute of International Affairs

Canadian Journal of Political Science–Revue canadienne de science politique

International Canada

International Journal

International Perspectives

Middle East Focus

Selected Canadian newspapers since 1948

PART II
ESSAYS IN CANADIAN
POLITICAL ECONOMY

SALLY F. ZERKER

Introduction

Before economics, before political science, there was political economy. Those sagacious philosophers of the late eighteenth and early nineteenth centuries, who authored the classics in political economy, laid the foundation for both economics and political science, which ultimately became separate and distinct areas of scholarship, analysis and policy formulation. Our predecessors, unlike many modern disciplinarians, emphasized the functional interdependence of wealth and power. Three of the four essays in this section of the book are indisputably in the tradition of that earlier era. The binding feature among them is neither theme nor focus, but rather an interdisciplinary approach to their specific topic, such that all three papers treat the issues of wealth and power as logically interactive. The fourth essay, by ten Raa and Mohnen, will be seen as the work of specialist economists, but their subject matter, that of potential gains for Canada from free trade, has had and will continue to have enormous political implications, as evident in the election debate of 1988 and, later, in the discussions about the North American Free Trade Agreement.

This section begins with an essay by Sally Zerker, and it is a most appropriate beginning for this segment of the book because her paper re-examines the work of the pre-eminent Canadian political economist, Harold Innis. It may be stretching a point a little, but only a little, to claim that Innis was to Canadian political economy what Adam Smith was to fundamental principles of political economy. Both were founders, although admittedly Smith's legacy is broader and more familiar. But it is precisely the lack of familiarity with Innis' body of work that Zerker is undertaking to correct in this essay. Zerker's argument here is that Innis has been dichotomized into two supposedly unrelated fields of scholarship, the first dealing with Canadian economic development and the staple approach; the second analyzing society through the prism of his concept of the bias of communication. The former is perceived as the work of the "early Innis" and the latter that of the "later Innis."

The irony, according to Zerker, is that Innis was a thinker who decried sharp disciplinary divisions as contributing to the weakening of understanding, and thus would have been disappointed that the unity in his thought has been largely ignored. Zerker's essay addresses this problem by demonstrating how the thought of the earlier work is consistent with and embedded in the later work. The common and underlying factor throughout Innis' thought is the centrality of communication, taken in its broadest sense. Zerker's objective is evident throughout the paper, but in effecting this task she thereby also improves our understanding of the concept of staples in the context of Canadian political economy, and we have a clearer view of the significance of the bias of communication in the context of social theory.

Peter Clancy's paper, "The Political Significance of Maritime Economic Union," is undoubtedly a study in political economy. Clancy has attempted to avoid over-generalization and simplistic argument by exploring the impact maritime economic union (MEU) would have on a concrete business sector. He has chosen the forest industry, one of the most important business sectors of the region, for his case study. But Clancy also notes the significance of the provincial and federal politics that are the precondition of any economic transformation. Hence, this paper serves a number of functions.

First, it provides an historical survey of the politics behind prospective maritime economic integration. Clancy shows how and why the Canada–United States free trade agreement of 1989 (FTA), the failure of the Meech Lake accord, and the constraint on federal government transfers to the provinces acted as inducements to the premiers of the maritime provinces to consider (or more correctly reconsider) economic integration. Second, one finds here an interesting and thoughtful discussion of options that might be useful for implementing economic union, not a simple task by any means. It would involve financial, political and economic provincial harmonization. Third, Clancy examines the effects that MEU would have on the forestry industry. It is the secondary pulp and paper processing sector rather than primary logging activity where the impact would be felt most significantly, and here Clancy projects major changes should MEU become a reality. By focusing on the forestry industry, Clancy achieves what he sets out to do, that is, penetrate the "thick layer of generalities that seem to surround the union initiative."

Allan Warrack writes about the Alberta Heritage Fund, but his essay is not merely about the Fund itself, but about the political economy of the province of Alberta. Hence, the rationale underlying the Fund, that of putting aside incomes from non-renewable resources for future uses and thereby transforming this capital into a form of renewable resource, is set in the context of Alberta's specific economic and social problems. Warrack emphasizes the policy objectives of such a project in the light of economic vulnerability associated with resource-based economics in general, and that of Alberta in particular. In addition, Warrack provides important information about the history of the Fund, its composition, its stated goals, as well as data on its investment record.

The most significant contribution of this essay, however, is Warrack's analysis of the Alberta Heritage Fund's overall failure to meet the policy objectives set by provincial legislation. The developmental goals that were at the heart of the Fund's purpose have not been achieved, and the prospect for the Fund taking an important role in solving emerging debt problems are extremely doubtful, according to the evidence shown here. Warrack's data and analysis make that negative assessment difficult to refute. For most Canadians, who were aware of the existence of the Fund, Alberta seemed to have secured itself from downturns in the business cycle, and it has come as a surprise, if not a shock, that this presumably rich province has run into severe deficit and debt problems, much like other regions and provinces in Canada in 1993. Warrack demonstrates why faith in the Alberta Heritage Fund to manage cyclical effects was unwarranted in the first place, and he shows how mismanagement or misdirection of the Fund has reduced its anticipated effectiveness. The mystery that most Canadians associate with the Alberta Heritage Fund is here exposed.

The last essay in this section of the collection is by Pierre Mohnen and Thijs ten Raa. These two economists have used the techniques of modern economics, specifically linear programming, to test out a very controversial issue in Canada, the benefits (or losses?) of trading freely. They use the single year, 1980, as the test period for evaluating the gains Canada would have from free trade. The reader will see that the authors divide up the Canadian economy in that year into 29 sectors and 92 commodities, and that they utilize input-output tables to attend to interindustry flows of goods and services. Clearly, this is an abstract and somewhat static study, but given that one is aware of that condition, it fulfils a very useful appraisal of a problematic issue.

The specialist economist will undoubtedly be interested in the methodology that Mohnen and ten Raa use here to arrive at their conclusions, but the conclusions themselves will be easily accessible to specialist and non-specialist alike. Their study defines what kind of specialization would occur in a world of perfect competition, where the demand for intermediate inputs and the existence of secondary products are taken into account. Under these assumptions, the authors find that the gains from free trade are bigger than is generally reported in the literature. Although one cannot therefore conclude that the magnitude of gains realized in this exercise can translate directly to a world in which competitive imperfections exist, nevertheless such experimentation gives us the ground upon which further adjustments can be calculated and analysis undertaken.

SALLY F. ZERKER

Transportation and Communication in Innis' Thought

Oneness in Innisian Duality

Harold Adams Innis has come to be known as one of Canada's outstanding
social scientists, with both national and international recognition, primarily as a result of two important and unique conceptual contributions. First
he gave Canadians the staple approach, an analytical tool that revamped
their perception of political economy as it related to their own country, and
by which he offered them an indigenous, independent outlook in this
regard. Then he presented the whole world with a brilliant, fascinating
theory of society that focused on technologies of communication and
appraised these in terms of their relative emphasis (bias) on time or space,
and from which he drew implications about the values that emerged in the
cultures where the different kinds of communication systems were embedded. Unfortunately, all too often people familiar with one part of Innis'
writings and ideas have only a superficial acquaintance with his other area
of creativity. Canadianists from a variety of disciplinary fields are usually
thoroughly grounded in the "early Innis," while the "later Innis," the
communication theorist, is set aside for the specialist of mass communication. This separation of his thought is an ironical legacy from a man who
decried sharp disciplinary divisions, who foresaw in this partitioning a
weakening of understanding and who therefore would have been disappointed (although not surprised) that the unity in his thought by and large
has been overlooked.

That unity derives from the centrality of communication, taken in its
broadest sense, to his life's work. This feature is of course obvious in the
focus and the results of his later interests but, though less glaringly

conspicuous in his staple analysis, it is there nonetheless. In the early phase of his work it takes the form of assigning to transportation technology the single most important influence on Canadian economic and political change. It is not an exaggeration to argue that, in the final analysis, Innis' staple approach is more than anything else a study of the role of transport in shaping the Canadian fabric and landscape. It is worth remembering too that Innis' first important research effort produced the volume, *A History of the Canadian Pacific Railway*, and that from that interest in Canada's transcontinental transport facility he went on to elaborate on the significance of resource exploitation to this nation's development. Furthermore, the continuity of this central theme is noticeable in another facet of his early work, his treatment of the price system as a vast communication network.

But to appreciate this constancy in his thought one should begin by explaining the staple approach. Innis saw the origins of Canada as an appendage to western civilization, living on its periphery. As such, immigrants from the metropolitan heartland were immediately dependent on the export of raw materials for the satisfaction of their cultural attachments. That situation was due to a characteristic condition of "new" or "empty" lands, wherein shortages of both labour and capital prevailed. Therefore, Europeans expecting to duplicate the essentials of their accustomed way of life in the new land—which inevitably required imports of familiar artifacts and manufactured goods—were obliged to exchange an export product in demand at home, which they could produce efficiently despite these two acute limitations.

It was just such commodities that attracted migrants to Canada's shores in the first instance—the substances of nature's abundance that could be separated from their respective settings with relative ease and low cost. More specifically, only such commodities that could command a price high enough to cover long-distance transport costs could fulfil the immigrants' export aims. Two broad categories of raw materials met these various constraints; either luxury goods for a small but high-income market, or necessities not available in sufficient quantity to satisfy European demand from indigenous sources. In naming these products "staples," Innis indicated his appraisal of their weighty role in the economic activity of the colony, and this reality provided him with the serviceable tool he had sought in order to address the unique problems of a new country. For, as he wrote, a "new country presents certain definite problems which appear to be more or less insoluble from the standpoint of the application of economic theory as worked out in the older highly industrialized countries" (Innis 1956, 3). It was foolhardy for Canadians "to attempt to fit their analysis of new economic facts into an old background." Therefore, the "only escape can come from an intensive study of Canadian economic problems and from the development of a philosophy of economic history or an economic theory suited to Canadian needs." Thus the staple approach answered his search for a philosophy of economic history for Canada.

It must be stressed, however, that Innis' staple approach was not circumscribed by the narrow limits of economics. Some followers of Innis, by their adaptation of his analysis to a theory of economic growth, may have publicized falsely—and probably unintentionally—the impression that the original work was also confined to economic considerations alone (Watkins 1967; Marr and Paterson 1980, 11). By contrast, his own method emphasized the political and social consequences of economic activities generally and those arising specifically from difficulties encountered in a young society dependent upon staple exports. Hence, his study of the by-now famous series of staples that dominated Canadian development—cod, furs, lumber, wheat and minerals—that took their place more or less sequentially in Canada's export record, was pursued with a broad sweep of vision.

The image of Canada that emerged from this approach was that of a country overwhelmingly reliant on staple exports; a reliance which had unfortunate consequences. It was a condition that evoked an exceptional dependence on foreign markets and foreign policy-makers and thereby determined a high degree of vulnerability to forces over which Canadians had no control. But at the heart of that vulnerability was the role of transportation. This was due to the obvious particularity of transport techniques for the efficient delivery of each staple. The mode of transporting cod was clearly inadequate for the fur trade, and fur trading transportation technique had little to offer the sawn lumber trade, and so on. Those methods suitable to submerged drainage basins were inappropriate for drainage basins, and those within the continental area useful for water transport could not serve the needs of overland shipping. This interlocking of each staple with its complimentary transport technique meant that as the Canadian economy experienced a loss or depreciation of the value of one of the export commodities and was forced to switch to another staple, the nation automatically was faced with an adjustment in transport facilities. However, such a procedure necessarily involved major outlays of capital for infrastructure construction, and that expenditure—indeed, series of expenditures—imposed political institutional revisions to underwrite the heavy charges.

Staples and Transport

Innis began his essay, "Transportation as a Factor in Canadian Economic History," with a self-evident truth; that the "early development of North America was dependent on the evolution of ships adopted to crossing the Atlantic" (Innis 1956, 62). Where Canada was concerned, this advancement brought fishing ships from four different European nations—Spain, Portugal, France and England—to adjacent North Atlantic fishing grounds, in search of a rich protein food that could satisfy Catholics' demand for their numerous meatless days. Cod's abundance in Canada's coastal waters appeased that quest. The cod fishery's transport facility was at one and the same time the processing plant, that is to say, the fishing ship was a self-contained unit of production. Capital requirements were therefore limited and, given the common practice of share financing, entry was relatively easy. This economic dictate in combination with the geographical environment of this industry, which operated on an open sea and was organized over numerous "scattered harbours and bays formed by the drowned system of rivers and their tributaries" gave the fishing industry its highly decentralized structure (Innis 1940).

Innis also familiarized us with the conduct of two different forms of fishing technique—wet and dry fishing—and he explained the significance for Canada of the alternative methods. Only dry fishing actually brought Europeans onto the lands of North America, because only that process required land-based stages and beaches for drying purposes. Where dry fishing produced an ideal foreign trading good, wet fishing was mainly a domestic activity in response to an internal domestic demand. Hence, the former was a stimulant to settlement while the latter by-passed the New World. For Protestant England, with its limited access to plentiful and cheap supplies of salt and its weak domestic demand for fish, the dry technique that depended mainly on sun and air rather than on salt for preservation and that finished a product that could be stored and carried to distant markets, the choice was obvious. English fishermen relied on drying methods and as a result they became early settlers in Canada, on the Avalon Peninsula. The French also eventually came around to adopting dry fishing techniques, but in their case it led them to penetrate the continent by the St. Lawrence River to shores along the Gaspé coast suitable for drying (Innis 1940, 486).

Once a start was made on land, settlement was also stimulated as a consequence of unused capacity in the transport of fish. During the outgoing leg of the voyage the holds were empty, or rather they were filled with huge boulders for ballast that were dumped offshore Newfoundland on arrival at this side of the Atlantic. But that carriage, while providing weight and balance for safety, added no income to cover overhead costs. The general rule for efficient use of transport equipment requires income-earning cargo on both ends of the journey. Fishing ships turned to carrying labourers for payment on the outgoing leg of the trip, men who hired out to bye-boat-keepers or who offered their services to operators of dry fishing. Some were seasonal employees, but others stayed behind and remained permanent residents. Hence, the transport dictates of Canada's first staple was an instrument of settlement.

The legacy of this decentralized industry with its emphasis on individualism, initiative and entrepreneurial skill was an intense spirit of autonomy. "The competition between small units, together with flexibility of organization, weakened government control," wrote Innis. Accordingly, "France was driven in turn from Nova Scotia, Cape Breton, the Gulf of St. Lawrence, and the French Shore; New England was driven from Nova Scotia, the Gulf of St. Lawrence and Newfoundland; and Nova Scotia was driven from Newfoundland" (Innis 1940, 506–7). Thus, the fishing industry, which was both economically and geographically diffuse, also spawned political diffusion. It was an industry peopled with spirited, competitive and adaptable human beings, typical of aggressive commercialism, such that their economic liberty led to demands for political liberty. It was no accident, thought Innis, that Nova Scotia was the first province in Canada to achieve responsible government, or that the Maritime region proved to be an unsuccessful base for empires. However, one should bear in mind that the original ingredient determining that claim on freedom was the self-contained, independent fishing ship, floating freely on the unbound sphere of submerged drainage basins.

Transportation in the fishing industry had nothing to offer the fur trade. This continental activity was in fact in sharp contrast to the fishing industry in almost every respect. Where fishing was decentralized, the fur trade flourished best with a centralized industrial structure. Where fishing clung to the coastal regions and set its sights eastward, the fur trade penetrated deeper and deeper across the continent in a continuously westward thrust. Moreover, it did so in advance of European settlement, integrating the whole northern half of the North American continent into a transcontinental economy, linking Europe to lands from the Arctic and across the Rockies to the Pacific. The territory of the fur trade established the geographic boundaries, more or less, of Canada, while the North-West Company can be said to have been the forerunner of this nation.

This achievement was clearly only possible as a result of a remarkable system of transportation and communication. In adapting the transport technology of the Native peoples to European demand for furs and the profit-seeking motives of the newcomers to this continent, the fur traders were able to surmount the barriers and hazards of forest and plain, of mountain and bog, in the absence of either European settlers or their infrastructural support systems. And the benevolence of geography was theirs too, in the form of expansive, accommodating river systems draining primarily in an east-west flow. River and canoe, Amerindians and Europeans, bound together in pursuit of a raw material to satisfy a frivolous item of fashion in the export market, this was the origin of the foundation of the Dominion of Canada.

But one cannot deny that the fur trade left behind a very strange bequest. In a microcosmic way it demonstrated Innis' dictum that the "economic history of Canada has been dominated by the discrepancy between the centre and margin of western civilization" (Innis 1962, 385). Here Innis was pointing to an imbalance in development between the industrialized, advanced centre of the economic empire, and the weak, vulnerable, staple producing marginal economy, leaving a wide gap between the two ends of the interdependent exchange in its wake. In a similar way Canada itself inherited an internal regional imbalance from the fur trade. The discrepancy between the decision-making, financially strong, politically influential centre and the periphery's feeble, dependent position was first introduced through the agency of the fur trade's centralizing character, the discrepancy that continues to this day.

In the end, centralizing pressures reduced the fur trade to two giant corporations—the Hudson's Bay Company and the North-West Company—each of which aimed aggressively at dominating the same northwestern territorial fields of operation. The rampant, fierce, even murderous competition that resulted had to be repressed, as it was in 1821 when the two companies merged under one corporate board of directors. The majority control was held by Nor-westers, but they took the name and the base of the Hudson's Bay Co. By one stroke the fur trade was eliminated from the St. Lawrence economy. A staple that had led and distorted a society in its own image was gone, and gone for good. Canadians, particularly the merchant class, were forced to look elsewhere to satisfy their zealous trading interests. But to replace the fur trade on the transportation base it had established would not merely be difficult, it would be impossible.

As luck would have it, a new staple was emerging just as the old one fled. No doubt those European participants engaged in the long, deadly and costly war known as the Napoleonic Wars would not appreciate its characterization as fortuitous, but for the colonists of the St. Lawrence it proved to be an unmixed blessing. When Napoleon tried to hem in the military might of the British navy by blockading its supply of masts from the Baltic—which in its own time was the military equivalent of modern jet fuel—the British turned to North America for this strategic commodity. For the mother country, its British colonies represented a reliable controllable region, rich in woods of all sizes and shapes. But because, until then, Canadian timber could not overcome the burden of long-distance transport costs to effectively compete with the Baltic, the British now provided Canada with the protection of steep tariff walls aimed against all foreign timber, while colonial timber passed through free of duty.

At first, the most primitive, wasteful form of timber making—squared timber—was produced in the Maritimes and the two Canadian provinces. As long as that was the situation, the untamed rivers were adequate to handle the huge timber rafts that were floated to the ports of disembarkation. But once Canadians refined their output into one or another type of sawn lumber, whether deals, planks or boards, no longer could extensive immersion in water be tolerated—it would spoil the goods—and it was therefore necessary to carry the lumber on barges. Now Canada's wonderful, accommodating river system required very expensive "repairs" to circumvent rapids and barriers in order for it once again to resume its role as the main thoroughfare of the colony. Canals for the St. Lawrence were unavoidable.

This necessity imposed a major revision of the political structure of the colony and represents one of two major transformative effects of lumber's transport technology on Canada's development. The other was the unused capacity in this industry's transport and its impact on settlement. Efficient use of the equipment used for shipping those heavy, bulky wood products eastward across the Atlantic demanded an equivalent cargo in weight and volume paying its way westward. The balancing cargo found to pack the timber ships' bottoms were the victims of the industrial revolution. They came by the thousands in rat- and disease-infested lumber ships, where conditions were so inhuman and death so common that they came to be known by the ghoulish term "coffin ships." Nevertheless, the lumber industry helped to people Canada, and in turn this immigrant flow stimulated the expansion of the industry by providing it with the required labour force.

The second implication—the political dimension—of lumber's transport technique derived from the demand for restructuring the river system by means of canals. But undertaking a common goal involving very heavy capital expenditures while Upper and Lower Canada were politically separated presented grave difficulties. The Act of Union was therefore a political response to transport problems that arose with the transition from fur to lumber, and a solution that would meet the needs of the latter would also accommodate growing exports of agricultural products, especially from Upper Canada.

However, the size of capital outlays on canal construction could not be seen to be warranted on the basis of Canadian traffic alone. Nor were private investors prepared to risk their wealth without assurances that government "rescues" would be forthcoming. Thus, Canadian government involvement and eventual ownership of transport facilities was an inherent feature of staples dependency. Also, because capital expenditures on canals were laid out in advance of their economic justification in relation to colonial traffic, these risky ventures were undertaken with an eye to a new economic strategy.

The old strategy was one of linking the mother country and Canada directly, reflected in colonial protection, in which the peripheral society produced the raw materials to feed the machines of the industrial heartland. "Industrialism has been poured into the moulds of wood," wrote Innis (Innis 1956, 250). In turn, the colony was expected to purchase finished industrial products from the metropole. However, this strategy was workable only as long as the cost of the transportation infrastructure was modest and manageable in relation to the colony's own needs.

The new strategy aimed at a scheme to help defray the costly new burdens that accompanied canal construction. The idea was to make a completed efficient St. Lawrence system so attractive to American shippers that a substantial share of the large and growing volume of mid-western business would be diverted in that direction. But as Robert Burns might have reminded the Canadian planners, "the best laid schemes o' mice and men gang aft a-gley." No sooner was a start made on the Canadian system when a wonderfully serviceable American link between Lake Ontario and a year-round open port on the Atlantic was completed. The Erie Canal was opened for business in 1825, four years ahead of only the first phase of the St. Lawrence's reconstruction. However, the new strategy was still counting on imperial preferences, which might well counter the Erie's attractiveness, since U.S. goods going to Britain by way of the St. Lawrence would be received on Canadian terms. But Canada's completion of its canal system in 1848 had the untimely misfortune of coinciding with the free trade movement in the mother country and hence the abolition of preferential treatment. Worse still (as if that were not enough), the Canadian water throughway, on completion, found itself faced with an expanding American land-based railway system, which altered the whole nature of transport competition.

Here was a situation that was to repeat itself again and again in the Canadian experience. The powerful, aggressive, adjacent neighbour to the south forced Canada's technological pace, not by the substance of Canadian needs and ability to pay, but by the imposition of rapid obsolescence on Canada's equipment in comparison to the more advanced U.S. technology. The case of canals was prescient of the future. The Canadian canal era had only just begun when the provinces were prodded into the railway age, taking upon themselves burdens far heavier than that affordable by a population of not quite 2.5 million at mid-century. Necessarily, private funds were sought and were granted security by governments, thereby concocting the worst of all possible combination, that of private rights underwritten by the largesse of the public purse.

Some means was required to pay for this extravagant transport infrastructure. Neither the first nor the second strategy was working out. Thus yet a third policy was formulated, one that looked to U.S. markets—as distinct from U.S. traffic—to open borders in the exchange of primary goods. For more than a decade Canada and the United States enjoyed a period of reciprocal free trade, between 1854 and 1866. But the traditional protectionism of the U.S. asserted itself and brought an end to the Reciprocity Treaty by their abrogation of it. The third economic strategy was over.

Finally, Canadians in the central province, the region that had been generated by the fur trade as the focus of authority and power, looked westward to the old fur trading boundaries as the one reliable, indigenous potential source of trade and economic growth. It was a land admirably suited to agricultural production at a moment in the history of western civilization when the industrialized nations turned to the periphery, not only for raw materials to feed the machine, but also for food products to nourish the human adjuncts of those machines. But no major carriage operation, either of settlers in or of wheat out, could be harnessed without a transcontinental rail hook-up to bind the extremities of this vast continent both physically and politically. Confederation and transportation were an intricate unity in more ways than one, but it was undoubtedly a political solution to an economic and technological problem. The transition from one transport technology to another imposed the political adjustments that led to Confederation.

Canadians were then asked to foot the bill for the transcontinental railway by following the lead of their protectionist southern neighbour. The National Policy was to be the fourth economic strategy. It introduced a high tariff wall that was meant to stimulate manufacturing mainly in the central provinces, and these would serve the tariff-enclosed whole of the Dominion of Canada. Meanwhile, the traffic of exports from western Canada outbound to Europe would help assure a profitable return to private investors in the Canadian Pacific Railway. But Innis also indicated the communication significance of the CPR when he wrote, "The history of the Canadian Pacific Railway is primarily the history of the spread of western civilization over the northern half of the North American continent" (Innis 1971, 287). Reducing the cost of long distance transportation is not only a factor in the transmission of goods; it also brings people in touch with each other over longer distances by means of an advanced technological network.

Innis and Continuity

Confederation and the National Policy is obviously not the end of the story of staples, transport and Canadian development. But it is sufficiently explanatory to illuminate the shape of Canadian political evolution on the one hand, and the incidence of Canadian economic vulnerability on the other. Innis' staple approach is thus not about numbers, size and growth, but about the social and political fabric of the society; about the origin of regional distribution of power; about Canada's economic storms that were generated by small external economic winds; about political upheaval as a consequence of economic problems; and about the place of Canada in the wider spectrum of western civilization.

From an intellectual standpoint one cannot then justify an artificial separation of Innis' being into two discrete scholarly types; an early Innis whose view of the world was through a very narrow, provincial lens emphasizing national interests, and a later Innis who broadened out into grand, universal, philosophical issues. Unquestionably, the one led neatly into the other in a smooth, progressive, consistent line. This continuity is apparent from a correct reading of his staple approach and from his early interest in communications. By 1938, some years before he began his research into communication systems, he had already considered and written about the dissemination of information and values by means of the messages of the market (Innis 1956).

Innis described the integration of the entire world through the tentacles of the price system. The Old World sought out the New World in response to the rise in prices and the profitability of trade. It was the price system that stimulated the dried cod industry by its attraction to the treasure-rich Spanish market. Products from Virginia and the Far East, from Africa and the West Indies, from Canada and Europe—all were part of an inter-global network of exchange brought with remarkable precision to those spots on the map where effectual demand was manifest.

But market forces were not only agents of material communication, they were also instruments of social revolution. The price system "swept aside the feudal system" (Innis 1956, 252–72) and wiped out "the inequities of the Colonial system itself." So powerful was the pull of the price system that even Aboriginal peoples, in North America and elsewhere, were unable to escape its gripping reach. No system was inviolate from the force of the price system; as it "destroyed feudalism so it destroyed the defenses of commercialism." Industrialization and capital deepening followed on the heels of earlier competitive structures. "The emergence of free trade by the middle of the century reflected and enhanced the efficiency of the price system and the growth of industrialism. The ebb of commercialism was the flow of industrialism." All of this, and more, Innis attributed to the increasing effectiveness of the price system. Hence Canada, its staples, and its transportation facilities were one small but important segment in the world-wide transformation that saw the integration of industry, techniques and values.

Innis' interest in Canada was therefore in the context of his wider attention to global considerations. It was also a logical forerunner to his fears for the survival of the civilization of which it was a part. He had seen how Canada's development was by and large a function of imperial will and needs, and he had noted that as communications improved they enhanced the potential for centralized direction and authority. The large-scale political organization now and in the past that ultimately affected all aspects of life was the "empire," and the history of the west could well be told as a story of the growth and decay of empires that had preceded the current one. Therefore, to appraise the potential for his own civilization's success or failure he determined to examine the records of past imperial experiences.

But how to do that with a measure of objectivity? How does one get outside one's own cultural bias and conceit?

> We must all be aware of the extraordinary, perhaps insuperable difficulty of assessing the quality of a culture of which we are a part

or of assessing the quality of a culture of which we are not a part. In using other cultures as mirrors in which we may see our own cultures we are affected by the astigma of our own eyesight and the defects of the mirror, with the result that we are apt to see nothing in other cultures but the virtues of our own. (Innis 1951a, 132)

To escape from one's own bias one first had to appreciate that each civilization believes in its own uniqueness and its own superiority to other cultures. The very notion of progress starts from the premise of others' inferiority. Moreover, such an escape is infinitely more difficult for generations disciplined in the written tradition and the printed word, for they scarcely can perceive the nature and values of societies based on the oral tradition. But Innis proposed a way out of this intellectual snare. He asserted that societal values were very largely defined by the communication media by which they were transmitted. Therefore, were one to study past and present empires through concentrating on the different communication technologies each depended upon, one could examine them from within, so to speak.

Of course Innis was thoroughly practised in such an approach to societal analysis. Communication media would take the place of staples as the cutting edge of research and insight, only this latest technology would be employed on the world stage, using empires for his unit of analysis. Moreover, he had already worked out the significance of centralizing and decentralizing characteristics in the staple approach as these worked their impact on social and political phenomena. Centralizing and decentralizing factors were also prevalent in communication media as he was to tell us in his usual terse way:

> The concept of time and space reflect the significance of media to civilization. Media which emphasize time are those which are durable in character such as parchment, clay, and stone....Media which emphasize space are apt to be less durable and light in character such as papyrus and paper. The latter are suited to wide areas of administration and trade....Materials which emphasize time favour decentralization and hierarchical types of institutions, while those which emphasize space favour centralization and systems of government less hierarchical in character. Large-scale political organizations such as empires must be considered from the standpoint of two dimensions, those of space and time, and persist by overcoming the bias of media which over-emphasize either dimension. (Innis 1950, 7)

Thus Innis set out to uncover the inner truth about his world, for which he devised a tool of analysis that was a direct descendent of Canadian staples, and that followed faithfully from his earlier lines of inquiry.

The Bias of Communication

When Innis shifted his scholarly interests away from the subject of Canadian economic history to a searching enquiry into the nature and significance of cultural bias in the 1940s, both the subject and his method of analysis raised eyebrows among his colleagues in the field. How was the study of media and societies connected to the discipline of economic history or even to the broader area of political economy? But though it may have seemed far-fetched to some, actually it was not. While recognizing that Innis was never one to be constrained by the limits of convention—the staple approach was itself an unorthodox tool for the study of Canadian economic and political questions (see Pomfret 1981)—in this instance one is persuaded that consistency and links are evident between his earlier and later interests. This is because, on the one hand, a main concern of economic history has always been the growth and decline of particular societal structures, a concern that was also specifically emphasized in Innis' study of communications and society. On the other hand, since the study of technology and its implications was then and remains today a focal point of much scholarly exploration in the field of economic history, there is no logical reason why the technology of communication media should be viewed as an odd, inappropriate digression. Thus, for Innis, the progression to media and bias, while highly inventive, was a "natural" step taken by a thinker who had already followed his own creative path to his and the intellectual world's great benefit.

Innis undertook his deep probe of modern western society by delving far into its distant past, to the beginnings of recorded history. But "unrecorded" history, or a civilization based on the oral tradition, though more difficult to make intellectual contact with, was as essential to scrutinize as those with written traditions. Perhaps more so! For Innis believed that part of the inherent bias of writing-bound cultures is that they block out awareness of possible alternatives. To alert his students to the narrowness of their perceptions, Innis opened his course, Empire and Communications, with this warning; "the oral tradition has been pushed so far into the background that we do not realize that a culture can exist on the oral tradition" (Innis 1951b,1). Although he was somewhat less than optimistic regarding the ability of "students steeped in the written tradition" (Innis

1950, 55) to grasp the nature and importance of an oral culture, nevertheless he thought it compelling to take up the challenge. What was at stake was nothing less than relearning a lost sense of the power of the spoken word, while at the same time sensitizing the modern western world to the danger of an inflated self-image. For, according to Innis, a culture obsessed with its own uniqueness "is the ultimate basis of its decline" (Innis 1951a, 133). Innis thus laid the groundwork for studying our own civilization by turning first to the ancient world where there were memories of both written and oral media of communications.

He began by analyzing empires in antiquity that were dominated by media that possessed fully antithetical effects from those evident in his own society. Ancient Egypt's use of stone and Babylon's reliance on clay offered him two case studies of societies monopolized by media of communication that were overwhelmingly attuned to an interest in time. Both media were durable in character, but also cumbersome to use for transmission of information rapidly and over long distances. As a result, these time-biased empires manifested an enormous concern with eternity, which in that era was inevitably associated with religion. On the other hand, for these civilizations, problems of space—such as the administration of territory—received relatively little sympathetic attention. That is precisely why, according to Innis, societies obsessed with time were seen to favour decentralized political structures where the hierarchical institutions formed the mechanism of authority and where state power was not the major organizational force. By contrast, media "that emphasize space favour centralization and systems of government less hierarchical in character" (Innis 1950, 7).

Innis' demonstration of the incidence and meaning of time-bias, drawn from antiquity, did not mean that such conditions of communication were confined to the cradle of writing. Similar characteristics would again surface in medieval Europe, when Christendom's monopolization of thought and learning would dominate through the control of parchment. Furthermore, one should not think of space and time as two factors that are inherently counterposed to each other. On the contrary, the thrust of Innis' analysis was to emphasize the hazards of excesses in the direction of either space or time, and to make a case for the need for balance between the two. Civilizations "have tended to flourish," he wrote, when they "reflect[s] the influence of more than one medium and in which the bias of one medium toward decentralization is offset by the bias of another medium towards centralization"(Innis 1950, 7).

He believed that either end of the time-space continuum distorted human existence. Societies dominated by intrinsically time-biased media were bent on defending against change of any kind—economic, political, social—using tradition and custom as the agents of rigidity, where the ultimate objective was to realize undiluted sameness, generation after generation. Such rigid, static cultures were enormously detrimental to the flowering of human genius. But at the other extremity of the time-space continuum one could expect only a different kind of deformity, not the absence of it. Where space bias dominates, human development is diminished by creating a societal myopia, in which only the present counts because there is no vision and no perspective.

Achieving balance was an extremely rare phenomenon in the history of western civilization. It happened infrequently, usually as a result of a medium invasion into an area already in the monopolized grip of an entrenched alternative medium. But on those rare occasions, such as during England's Elizabethan era, a heady creativity breaks loose that touches all aspects of society; the arts, law, government and economic activity. One very special specimen of a society in graceful balance was that of ancient Greece, which blossomed and shone on a foundation built on the oral tradition, a medium of communication that was both flexible and powerfully resistant to encroachment.

Innis outlined the power and adaptability of the oral tradition in such important areas of social development as the arts, science, philosophy, politics and religion; in each case the height of accomplishment was achieved just prior to the spread of writing. Although the existence of writing was known as early as the eighth century B.C., it infiltrated very slowly into Greek society. Additionally, when the transition to writing finally took hold (post-Socrates) (*see* Innis 1950, 68), it embodied a unique characteristic. The Phoenician alphabet was adapted to the Greek language in such a way that for the first time symbols depicting vowel sounds were integrated into the alphabet. That is to say, writing was bent to the requirements of the spoken word, and in turn the Greek language was freed from the bond of writing and the emphasis of only the eye and the hand. As the ear took its place in the new writing form, it became possible to transpose some of the best achievements of the oral Greek culture to the written word. In the end, Greece was able to fulfil the Delphic maxim, "nothing overmuch," or "nothing in excess" through this unique balance between the oral and written traditions with the following outcome:

The powerful oral tradition of the Greeks and the flexibility of the alphabet enabled them to resist the tendencies of empire in the East towards absolute monarchism and theocracy. They drove a wedge between the political empire concept with its emphasis on space and the ecclesiastical empire concept with its emphasis on time and reduced them to the rational proportions of the city-state. The monopoly of complex systems of writing, which had been the basis of large-scale organizations of the East was destroyed. The adaptability of the alphabet to language weakened the possibilities of uniformity and enhanced the problems of government with fatal results to large-scale political organization. But the destruction of concepts of absolutism assumed a new approach of rationalism which was to change the concept of history in the West. (Innis 1950, 100)

It is a long, long step from ancient Greece to our western civilization of the twentieth century, a cultural chasm, so to speak, but one that Innis managed to cross with his examination of papyrus, parchment, paper and the printing press, to the point that it became evident that the modern West was overwhelmingly dominated by the space-bias extremity of the time-space continuum. In many respects, the printing press was a turning point, although its initial impact, like that of earlier novel media in the process of breaking down a pre-existing monopoly of knowledge, was that of political, religious and economic liberation. However, when the print-paper medium ultimately overpowered its competitors, its technological dictates steadfastly pushed on towards the spatial obsession. "The printing press and the inventions associated with it...[were] concerned with the destruction of time and continuity" (Innis 1951a, 187–88).

The technological criterion that influenced that evolutionary process most directly was the fact of mechanization. Machine industry applied to communication imposed the same kind of dictates that other capital intensive industries experience. To pay for the heavy outlay for overhead or fixed costs on a continuing basis, investors must seek wider and wider markets. This condition spawns intense competition between independent units, resulting in consolidation, mergers and takeovers. Capital-intensity in the communication industry has its centralizing implications, not unlike that of the fur trade. But while it was always clear that the fur trade was in the business of selling furs, it was not always obvious what the communication industry was selling, until Innis pointed out that the product of newspapers, radio and television is advertising. (Innis obviously did not write about television per se because he died in 1952, just as television was making its entry into the communications industry. Nevertheless, what he had to say about mechanized commercial communications applies equally well to television, only with greater intensity.) The unique attribute of this product is that its price is determined by the volume of its sale, hence, the larger the audience the higher the price per unit. Again, there are inherent centralizing tendencies as a result of this condition. Moreover, the drive for a larger market inevitably requires that newspapers, radio or television appeal to the lowest common denominator in the reading and viewing public.

Therefore, the cultural decay of the modern era was anticipated by Harold Innis, in accordance with his analysis of the new media and their impact. It was a vision that haunted him towards the end of his life, and he tried to warn us all to alert us to the danger. In "A Critical Review," delivered at the University of Oxford in 1948, he had this to say:

> Mechanization has emphasized complexity and confusion; it has been responsible for monopolies in the field of knowledge; and it becomes extremely important to any civilization, if it is not to succumb to the influence of this monopoly of knowledge, to make some critical survey and report. The conditions of freedom of thought are in danger of being destroyed by science, technology, and the mechanization of knowledge, and with them, Western civilization.
>
> My bias is with the oral tradition, particularly as reflected in Greek civilization, and with the necessity of recapturing something of its spirit. For that purpose we should try to understand something of the importance of life and of the living tradition, which is peculiar to the oral as against the mechanized tradition, and of the contributions of Greek civilization. (Innis 1951a, 190)

There was a time when Innis placed his hopes for nourishing the spirit of the oral tradition on that institution to which he had devoted his life, the university. But he was forced to admit that the university's cloisters were not impregnable, and that this cherished community was no more immune to decay than the world around it. It too exhibited the symptoms associated with a bias in the interest of space; in particular, an obsession with the material and the immediate. The bitterness he must have felt on this account is evident when he wrote: "The blight of lying and subterfuge in the interests of budgets has fallen over universities, and pleas are made on the grounds that the universities are valuable because they keep the country safe from socialism, they help the farmers and industry, they help in measures of defence. But of course they do no such thing and when such topics are mentioned you and I are able to detect the odour of dead fish" (Innis 1951a, 85.)

The new mass media were as illusory as a magician's trick. One was led to believe that their ability to assemble vast stores of information automatically translated into cultural growth. But Innis knew that culture was not about stores of information; it was about the "capacity of the individual to appraise problems in terms of space and time and with enabling him to take the proper steps at the right time." (Innis 1951a, 85) He saw around him a tragedy in the making, for Canada and for the civilization of which it was part, as modern mechanized media with their cultural consequences continued on the path of the destruction of a sense of time. But beware, said Innis, "Without vision the people perish." (91)

References

Innis, Harold A. 1940. *The Cod Fisheries*. Toronto: University of Toronto Press.

———. 1950. *Empire and Communications*. Oxford: Clarendon Press.

———. 1951a. *The Bias of Communication*. Toronto: University of Toronto Press.

———. 1951b. Lecture notes, p. 1. This author has a set of notes taken down almost verbatim directly from Innis' lectures in 1951 to the fourth year class in Economics and Political Science. The course was entitled Empire and Communications and was credited as the requirement in economic history.

———. 1956. *Essays in Canadian Economic History*. Toronto: University of Toronto Press.

———. 1962. *The Fur Trade in Canada*. Toronto: University of Toronto Press.

———. 1971. *A History of the Canadian Pacific Railway*. Toronto: University of Toronto Press.

Marr, William, and Donald Paterson. 1980. *Canada: An Economic History*. Toronto: Macmillan of Canada.

Pomfret, Richard. 1981. *The Economic Development of Canada*. Toronto: Methuen.

Watkins, M.H. 1967. A Staple Theory of Economic Growth. In *Approaches to Canadian Economic History*, edited by W.T. Easterbrook and M.H. Watkins. Toronto: McClelland & Stewart.

PETER CLANCY

The Political Significance of Maritime Economic Union: A Case Study from the Forest Industry

Perhaps the most intriguing "post-Meech" policy initiative in Maritime Canada is the campaign for a regional economic union. One telling political dimension of this issue has been the battle over terminology. "Maritime Union" has been abandoned by most parties to avoid the connotations of political union. The Council of Maritime Premiers favours "maritime economic integration,"while the technocrats associated with the issue prefer to describe it as the "co-operation initiative." The phrases "maritime economic co-operation" or "union" both figure prominently in press accounts. In this paper I will employ the term "economic union" in order to capture both the aim of achieving a single market and the process of joining three provincial economies which are in some respects distinct.

Yet despite the mounting visibility of the issue, it remains poorly articulated and, one suspects, poorly understood, within the region. This paper offers a critical appraisal of its political significance. I argue that the cornerstone concepts such as "international competitiveness" and "policy harmonization" are not adequately specified. As presently formulated, they constitute an ideological outlook rather than an analytic-strategic one. Indeed, once these concepts are examined closely, they reveal a limited understanding of the problem, one more compatible with the small business proprietorship than the complex fabricator of traded goods and services.

These arguments emerge by considering the Maritime Economic Union (MEU) project against a single but significant case study. To avoid over-generalized and, therefore, simplistic, argument, it is necessary to explore the impact of economic liberalization on concrete industrial sectors. For this purpose, the strongest cases are likely to be today's leading business sectors. I have chosen to focus on the forest industry, with particular attention to the pulp and paper sector. I find that a number of significant policy impacts would follow from the MEU initiative, primarily by way of "removing barriers" to the flow of factors of production. As this proceeds, the effect will be either to harmonize provincial policies at the lowest common denominator, or to eliminate state interventions altogether.

However useful this may be to particular business entities in the short run, it is of questionable relevance to the goals of regional economic development. The competitive prospects of the forest sector hinge on much more than the dismantling of state regulations to facilitate increased economies of scale. Like most advanced industries, the maritime forest sector consists of several discrete markets, of varying importance and potential. The place of maritime firms in the international forest industry will depend on the pursuit of business strategies of a more complex sort. In this, the elimination of interprovincial barriers may not be a sufficient or even necessary condition for long term viability.

The following section will briefly review the rise of the MEU project over the past 18 months. The next section considers the "strategic" aims of this program, and the logical links between goals and instruments. The third part will survey some changing patterns in the maritime pulp and paper industry and their "fit" with the MEU project. This is followed by a brief review of regional forest policies as prospective barriers to trade, with particular attention to measures affecting wood fibre supply.

The Rise of Maritime Economic Union as an Issue

For the past two years, broad and persistent efforts have been made to elevate "maritime economic integration" to the centre of the region's policy agenda. This campaign began in October 1990, with the release of Charles McMillan's report, *Standing Up to the Future*. Commissioned by the Council of Maritime Premiers (CMP), McMillan called for the systematic elimination of interprovincial trade barriers as a necessary step towards a market-driven business expansion in the region. Already the CMP had taken one step in this direction in December 1989, by negotiating a Memorandum of Understanding on Government Procurement. This required that all goods contracts worth more than $25 million, all service contracts exceeding $50 million and all construction contracts over $100 million be tendered regionally, without discrimination based on province of origin (CMP 1989, 2–3).

However the full extent of the Premiers' support for the McMillan strategy was not clear until the spring of 1991, with the release of the discussion paper *Challenge and Opportunity*. Echoing enthusiasm for a consolidated market of 1.7 million people, the document sets out 15 areas for prospective policy "harmonization," to be jointly studied over the next several years. To underline the priority attached to the matter, a joint meeting of the three provincial Cabinets spent several days exploring these questions in June, before they were referred to administrative working groups in the respective bureaucracies. Complementary to these governmental initiatives were a series of private sector conferences, at which the Atlantic Provinces Economic Council and the Atlantic Provinces Chamber of Commerce offered unqualified endorsements of the basic thrust and effusive predictions of a plethora of gains, as reported in the *Chronicle-Herald* 26 March and 11 June 1991 in articles entitled "Maritime Union Backed" and "Regional Co-operation Urged." Indeed, with the exception of the regional trade union leadership, who fear an assault upon the organized industrial work force and on the provincial state, few public figures have voiced criticism, as noted in the *Chronicle-Herald* 27 March 1991 in an article entitled "NSFL Chief Wary of Economic Union." It should be noted that the smaller rival union central, the Canadian Federation of Labour, has offered "conditional support" to the union initiative. However it does call for a Maritime Social Charter to guarantee social and environmental programs. (See the *Chronicle-Herald* article "Labour Group Offers Maritime Union Conditional Support" 28 November 1991. For the comprehensive APEC assessment, see *Atlantic Economic Co-operation* [APEC 1991]). The APCC position is expressed by its Chairman Rick LeBlanc, in An Atlantic Economic Initiative (LeBlanc 1991). The editorial support of the daily press reported, in the *Chronicle-Herald* of 10 and 11 June 1991 ("Economic Transition Necessary—Mazankowski and "Maritime Union Studied"), has been virtually unqualified, and senior federal ministers such as Mazankowski (Finance), Wilson (Trade) and Crosbie (Fisheries and ACOA) have bestowed their blessings. By any normal standard, this appears to be an issue whose time has come.

For high political purposes, this is undoubtedly true. Maritime economic integration is on that privileged agenda where a few broad thematic issues can win the endorsement of Ministers. It is true that the three provinces sometimes display differing levels of enthusiasm for the project. But in general, the issue is well-suited as a paradigmatic policy. It is comprehensive in the grand goal of constituting new economic domains. Yet it is also incremental, since the goal can be approached in small, successive steps. Within the governmental system, its issue appeal is partly crass: interprovincial "accords" will sprout freely to commemorate Ministerial achievements over the next electoral cycle. For their part, entrepreneurial bureaucrats will exploit this significant new opportunity for program and career aggrandizement, while it lasts.

Yet to dismiss the economic-union issue as a shallow expression of partisan and bureaucratic politics would be a major error. In reality, it is a complex product of multiple forces, both structural and conjunctural. Their convergence over the past 18 months explains both the rapid rise and the over-generalized rationale for economic integration. In its present amorphous state, the issue meets a number of quite separate needs. Only as this initiative generates concrete outcomes over time will its full political significance become clear. At present, the outcome remains significantly underdetermined. A brief survey of the animating forces should explain the contradictory possibilities. (*See also* Savoie 1991, 161–82.)

Broadly speaking, maritime integration is a reaction to both the program achievements and failures of the Mulroney government in Ottawa. In increasing order of importance, these are the implementation of the Canada–United States Free Trade Agreement (FTA), the mounting federal fiscal constraint applied to welfare state and intergovernmental transfers and the collapse of the Meech Lake constitutional initiative.

Although it will take years for the full extent of the FTA to register, the sheer breadth of the new policy harmonization has triggered a parallel review of trade practices within Canada. At the federal–provincial level, progress to date has been slow. As the *Globe and Mail* reported on 2 November 1990, efforts to conclude a federal-provincial agreement on internal trade were delayed in 1990, when Nova Scotia failed to sign by the 31 October deadline. The *Chronicle-Herald* reported on 21 November 1991 that a more limited protocol on government procurement was signed one year later. However, the *Globe and Mail* noted on 22 November 1991 that a comprehensive agreement on eliminating internal trade barriers remains several years away. But the demonstration effect of both processes has been salient to the maritime regional initiative, particularly when aggravated by the other political pressure points. More specifically, the advent of the FTA has sharpened political concern about the economic dislocations faced by the maritime region. Each province has canvassed its exposure and addressed the need for adjustment policies.* Indeed the prospect (and in certain quarters fear) of a renewed wave of locally targeted adjustment measures may have accelerated the campaign for regional harmonization.**

The Mulroney government's fiscal strategy has been clear since Michael Wilson's Economic Statement of November 1984 (Canada 1984). Ottawa's ostensible war against the deficit implied the systematic constraint of welfare state transfers to individuals and provinces. Since the enactment of new restrictions on Established Programs Financing (health and education) and the Canada Assistance Plan (welfare) in 1990, Ottawa has imposed formula cuts in each successive budget cycle. While this has aggravated the fiscal imbalances faced by maritime treasurers, it is the prospect of inexorable future cuts that has set off sharp political alarms. Indeed one of McMillan's most forceful arguments was the need for a regional regrouping in the face of federal fiscal disengagement. Tied to this was the proposition that an "over-governed" region could either consolidate or abandon many traditional fields of high-cost, state intervention.

Neither of the preceding factors can fully explain the abrupt plunge of the maritime Premiers into the integration issue. Since 1987, Mr. Frank McKenna (Liberal) has served as Premier of New Brunswick. Mr Joe Ghiz (Liberal) held office in Prince Edward Island from 1986 to 1992, when he was succeeded by Ms. Catherine Callbeck (Liberal). In Nova Scotia Mr. John Buchanan (Conservative) served as Premier from 1978 to 1991. After a six month (interim) tenure by Mr. Roger Bacon, Mr. Donald Cameron assumed the Conservative leadership in 1992. As a result of the May 1993 election, Mr. John Savage (Liberal) became Premier.

Indeed the traditional patterns of executive federalism, not to mention the performance of the Council of Maritime Premiers, might have predicted that the chance for rapid movement was remote. Only in the aftermath of the Meech collapse were most "normal" expectations shattered. Regional political anxieties were perhaps most sharply captured in the prospect of geographical partition, with the Atlantic periphery cut off by an emergent sovereign Québec. (Perhaps the most hysterical reaction came from Nova Scotia's premier John Buchannan, who expressed fear for the region's inevitable annexation by the United States should Québec

---

*For example, see the 1989 Report of the Nova Scotia Adjustment Advisory Council, *Adjusting to the Challenge*. At the outset this discussion was strongly influenced by the framework policies proposed by the federal de Grandpré Report (Canada 1989a). Provincial measures could expand the focus, or fill the gaps, by dealing with special local problems.

**For a detailed discussion, see Ottawa's 1991 constitutional proposals, with their extensive focus on protecting the Canadian "economic union." (Canada 1991). *Canadian Federalism and Economic Union: Partnership for Prosperity*. Ottawa: Supply and Services Canada.

attain sovereignty.) More immediately, with Québec again isolated on the intergovernmental scene, old expectations were of questionable relevance. As Premier Ghiz explained in July 1990, "in the new reality of bilateral negotiations our bargaining power has been reduced. We are on our own. Each of the provinces is now on its own in a new era of intergovernmental relations where *conquest*, not consensus, is the order of the day" (Ghiz 1990). In this light, joint regional positions could enhance maritime leverage. In addition, joint regional endorsement of preferred federal themes could work to advantage if the maritime experiment emerged as a prototype for broader pan-Canadian initiatives.

To this must be added situational factors that removed previous roadblocks. Prime among these was the political leadership transition in Nova Scotia. After a six month interregnum following John Buchanan's resignation, Donald Cameron adopted, in part by choice and in part by necessity, the strategy of distancing his government as far as possible from the patronage-driven politics of his predecessor. In contrast to Buchanan's caution and reluctance in the face of expanded regional initiatives, Cameron had every reason to embrace the project as part of his "new politics." Where in the past Nova Scotia was reluctant to surrender the sovereign powers of petty influence, Cameron could bend the new competitive procurement procedures, the review of administrative rules and the commitment to economic renewal, to his own cause.

For Frank McKenna, the regional economic initiative offered an intriguing economic prospect. For some years New Brunswick has led the region in balanced growth prospects. Moreover its proximity to New England suggests a locational advantage at the centre of the maritime bloc. Of the three leaders, PEI's Joe Ghiz is no doubt the most circumspect. However, while he must harbour reservations about the prospective union, it can clearly be shaped more effectively from the inside than the outside. As the next section suggests, the structural forms of union remain to be determined.

Modes of Constituting a Regional Economic Union

The future institutional form of the maritime economic union remains somewhat of an open question. At least two competing approaches can be identified. One seeks the progressive down-sizing of the public sector economy as administrative bureaus are merged, regulatory regimes are dismantled and maritime entrepreneurial energies are released with vast new pools of capital and suitably trained labour. The end point is an "internationally competitive industrial base in Atlantic Canada" (CMP1990, 16), and the preliminary goal is a 50 percent increase in the value of exported products. This is the future sketched by McMillan of the CMP, driving the agenda with the support of an elite business-oriented Advisory Board. By this account there is virtually no room for political discretion, since "international forces and influences must guide domestic initiatives" in the 1990s (17). In fact, politics seems to draw a string of pejorative connotations. It is narrowly identified with partisan political concerns, those electorally driven eccentricities of parochial societies.

Against this neo-liberal agenda stands a second possibility, less clearly articulated to date, but capable of emerging from the same starting point. This might be called a "neo-institutional" approach. It is similarly concerned with the future of fiscal transfers, and public sector diseconomies as they presently exist. However it assumes that public authority has a necessary and potentially positive role in any successful transformation of the maritime economy. Rather than seeing the problem rooted in state regulation per se, it points to the differential regulations that may obstruct and distort continuous operations. In this second version, interprovincial barriers can be eliminated through policy *harmonization* instead of through *de-regulation*. Rather than simply viewing provincial interventions as a source of higher business costs and choked off competition, regional strategic interventions can be seen as an integral part of the new economic agenda. Without it, no successful economic transformation is likely to occur in a peripheral economy. While McMillan may be correct in concluding that the status quo is not viable in the long run, this approach asserts that an alternative to competitive restructuring is absolute industrial decline, which an unmediated market strategy might well exacerbate.

At stake in this debate is the scope of policy intervention available in the regional economic union. If the market rules absolutely, then the pattern of policy harmonization is clear. It will converge around the lowest common denominator presented by the three provinces. Particular policy interventions will be washed out as regional authorities seek to enlarge market space. If however, the legitimacy of state intervention is accepted, then interprovincial harmonization may move "up" as well as "down" the regulatory scale, as the strategic calculus dictates. Grahl and Teague have pointed out that the European Community confronted these same options over the past decade (Grahl and Teague 1989). The harmonized regional policies could entail significant "market-shaping" measures, pursued in concert by the three provincial authorities.* This could permit a more ambitious transformative agenda, looking well beyond the creation of more companies "such as the Irving's" (25). Of necessity, it would include the interests of sometimes numerous primary producers located earlier on the production chain. To be sure, the neo-institutional approach harbours its own dysfunctional extreme, particularly if additional layers of intergovernmental machinery get wrapped in administrative isolation. But generally this approach more accurately concedes the inherently *political*, though not necessarily *partisan*, dimensions of an agenda of transformation.

Versions of both the neo-liberal and the neo-institutional options can be seen in the contemporary debate. The former is reflected in the discussion papers developed by Nova Scotia's Voluntary Planning organization. As far back as 1988, this private sector advisory body called for a new provincial economic development strategy. Invited by Premier Buchanan to initiate the process, Voluntary Planning drew on its own members, together with provincial civil servants and hired consultants, in the design of the March 1991 draft statement. In language echoing the CMP, it calls for enhanced skills training, a focus on "traded goods and services," technology diffusion, enlarged interprovincial markets, enhanced entrepreneurship and expanded capital pools. However the most telling comments concern the new role of government, in balancing budgets, ensuring business input, shifting to tax-based policy incentives and privatizing assets (Voluntary Planning 1991a, 28–31). This strategy has now been accepted as formal policy by the Government of Nova Scotia. Clearly the Voluntary Planning perspective is more explicit in its market co-ordinates than is *Challenge and Opportunity*. However the proximity of the two proposals illustrates the potential, and indeed the mechanisms, for economic union to be bent decisively in a neo-liberal direction. In May 1992, Voluntary Planning reviewed the CMP initiative in order to report to the provincial cabinet. Undoubtedly there is an affinity between the two initiatives. The Executive Director of the CMP described them as "two parts of a single whole," sharing core values that are "either identical, compatible or complementary" (Fanjoy 1992).

On the other hand, a number of academic commentaries have focused critical attention on the policy mechanisms, the scale of benefits, and their distributional impact. Michael Bradfield argues that with estimates of gains ranging from one-half to one percent of gross regional

---

* Although McMillan occasionally invokes the language of a concerted planning system, it is never seriously projected beyond the business advisory channels.

product, the real impact of the economic union package is relatively slight. By comparison, he suggests that "reducing unemployment by one percent would increase output on the order of 2.5 percent, hence to bring unemployment down by 4 percentage points (close to the Canadian average) would increase output by 10 percent" (Bradfield 1991, 15. *See also* Bazowski 1991). However, as Bradfield concedes, this is the realm of federal rather than provincial policy. If this suggests that provincial or even regional capacity for macroeconomic management is slight, its capacity for micro- or sectoral-level management remains considerable. Here the distributional impact of integration must be addressed, and Bradfield cautions that "economic integration must not be an excuse for giving still more power to vested interests through ill-considered de-regulations or for the dilution of standards in areas such as environment or worker safety" (Bradfield 1991, 1).

There are still interests that look hopefully towards economic union as a means for harmonizing policy "upwards." By this account, the more progressive policy initiatives, which have been achieved by popular political movements in single provinces, may in this way be generalized across the region. For instance, the President of the Maritime Fishermen's Union noted that:

New Brunswick is the only one of the three Maritime provinces that has passed legislation allowing [the] MFU to take part in collective bargaining with the companies to set the price of fish. Both Nova Scotia and PRI have promised such legislation on many occasions, but it has never materialized.... Provincial protectionism tends to work against fishermen. (Fraser 1991, 16)

Yet for the present, several factors suggest that the neo-liberal option is more likely to prevail. While maritime business organizations are far from hegemonic, their political influence easily outweighs that of labour and small producer groups. Furthermore, regional political values will play a significant role. The CMP paper takes pains to excise the spectre of *political* union, which has remained highly contentious since it was last raised in 1970. The advent of prominent new *regional* authorities can only serve to resurrect this spectre. Accordingly, the more eligible form of policy harmonization may be policy disengagement, which will suggest a common move towards less government. The alternative strategy of forming super-authorities to guide the regional economy remains much more distant. In this, recent maritime experience will offer little guidance. The Maritime Provinces Higher Education Authority likely has reached the limits of its effectiveness, as its task has shifted from managing university expansion to managing rationalization and decline. The Maritime Land Registration System is presently being phased out and privatized, a foreshadowing, perhaps, of the emerging policy agenda.

Furthermore there is scant tradition of economic planning on which to build. It is true that the proposals arising from the Joint Maritime Cabinet meeting included a consolidated Maritime Securities Commission. However this exception is better understood as necessary infrastructure for capital mobilization than as a prototype for future joint regulatory regimes. To be sure, there are appropriate fields for joint regulation. For example, each province is committed to ongoing consultation on environmental regulation and sustainable development. This has spawned the new institution of the Environmental Roundtable or Sustainable Development Commission, to mediate relations between business and environmental advocates (Howlett 1990, 580–601). Since the fields of primary resource harvesting, management and conservation offer such a voluminous source of interprovincial barriers, there may well come a point when *regional* roundtables and management regimes play a critical role in advancing the MEU project (*see* Nova Scotia Roundtable 1991). In fact, the Atlantic Accord on Environmental Cooperation, concluded by the four provinces late in 1991, allows issues of mutual concern to be addressed on a joint or, failing that, a bilateral, basis.

The Maritime Forest Industry

As we have seen, the case for maritime economic union is grounded in the increased efficiencies and competitive advantage that are expected to follow from the consolidated market. For the public sector, this accrues largely from reduced administrative costs of operation. In private markets, it appears in more profitable business in intermediate or end-use products that are "tradeable" beyond the province of origin. So in the case of the forest industry, attention centres less on the primary logging sector than on the secondary pulp-and-paper processing sector. It is important to note the general neglect of the logging sector, since this dismisses the interests and conditions of primary producers, relegating them to the margin of strategic policy. As we will see in the following section, primary wood supply fits the economic union paradigm only as an input factor cost for the pulp and paper mills.

However the case for economic union is equally tenuous when its generalized prescriptions are examined against the conditions and trends in the secondary pulp and paper industry. Here it is necessary to briefly survey the maritime industry. Descriptive data on the mill complexes is offered in Table 1 and their locations are shown on Map 1.

Of the three provinces, the New Brunswick industry is by far the most important, traditionally ranking fourth and currently standing fifth in provincial size of forest industry production in Canada. Nova Scotia ranks a more distant sixth in the national ranking, with an aggregate output less than half that of New Brunswick. This ranking is based on total forest product exports per province (Canada 1989b, 72). There are no processing facilities on Prince Edward Island, and its pulp exports to the mainland are insignificant.

In 1990, New Brunswick's ten mills displayed a wide range of production technologies and end products. Pulp was manufactured by the sulphite process at three locations, by the kraft or sulphate process at three others, by the thermo-mechanical process at two, and by the groundwood process at one. (For a useful description of pulping technologies see Sinclair 1990.) These mills produce varieties of northern softwood pulp, for market sale and for integrated fabrication of paper products. Significantly, pulp production was directly linked to paper product manufacture at seven of the ten mills. This segment reveals considerable variety, ranging from newsprint (three sites) to corrugated paper (two sites) to tissue products and coated papers (one site each). A majority of these firms are Canadian-controlled, though most headquarters lie outside of the province. Only two mill complexes are American-owned, while a third is a Canadian-Japanese joint venture.

In Nova Scotia, the three largest mills produce pulp by the sulphite, sulphate/kraft and chemi-thermal mechanical techniques. One of the three ships pulp only, while the other two combine market pulp sales and newsprint production. All three form part of multinational operations, headquartered in Sweden, the United States and the United Kingdom respectively.

In an important strategic review of the Canadian forest products industry, the consulting group Woodbridge Reed identifies the strengths and weaknesses that domestic producers will face in the 1990s. Traditionally, the export strength of the industry has been based in three sectors: construction grade lumber, softwood bleached kraft market pulp, and standard grade newsprint. While the first remains market-competitive, Woodbridge argues that both kraft pulp and newsprint are undergoing structural change. For the former, fast growing fibre stocks, particularly in the form of tropical hardwoods, are shifting the locational matrix away

Table 1
A Survey of the Maritime Forestry Industry

Products Company	Location	Ownership	Production Complex		Market
			Pulp	Paper	Pulp/Paper
Fraser Inc.	Edmundston, NB	Noranda Forest (Toronto)	Bleached Sulphite Unbleached Sulphite Groundwood	410 t/d 592 t/d 360 t/d	Link to Madawaska Maine paper mill
Atholville Pulp Co.	Atholville, NB	Fraser Inc. (Noranda)	Bleached Sulphite	360 t/d	
St. Anne-Nackawic. Pulp Co., Ltd	Nackawic, NB	Landegger (NY)	Bleached Hardwood Kraft	675 t/d	Bleached HW Kraft 233,000 t/yr
Stone Consolidated Ltd. (Bathurst Div.)	Bathurst, NB	Stone Consol. (Chicago)	Chemi-TMP		CTMP 168,000 t/yr Corrugated Medium Paper 150,000t/yr
NBIP Forest Products Ltd.	Dalhousie, NB	Canadian Pacific Oji Paper/Mitsui & Co.	Groundwood SCMP	600 t/d 400 t/d	Newsprint 1100 t/d
Mirimichi Pulp and Paper Inc.	Newcastle (1) Nelson-Mirimichi (2)	Repap Enterprises	Kraft Groundwood	575 t/d 125 t/d	Coated Paper 1300 t/d
Irving Pulp and Paper	Saint John, NB Dieppe, N.B	J.D. Irving Ltd.	Semi & Bleached Kraft	900 t/d	Semi/Bleached kraft 285,000 t/yr Tissue 209 t/d Tissue/Towel/ Napkins
Rothsay Paper Ltd.	Saint John, NB	J.D. Irving Ltd.	TMP Groundwood	300 t/d ——	Newsprint 340,000 t/yr

Table 1 cont'd

Products Company	Location	Ownership	Production Complex		Market
			Pulp	Paper	Pulp/Paper
Lake Utopia Paper Ltd.	St. George, NB	J.D. Irving Ltd.	NSSC Sulphite	—	NSSC Medium Corrugating Paper 120,000 t/yr
Scott Maritimes Ltd.	Abercrombie, N.S.	Scott Paper (US)	Bleached Kraft	232,000 t/yr	Market Pulp Scott 80/20
Stora Forest Industries Ltd.	Point Tupper, N.S.	Stora Kopparberg (Sweden)	Bleached Sulphite	120,000 t/yr	Market Pulp Storafite Newsprint 180,000 t/yr
Bowater Mersey Paper Co. Ltd.	Liverpool, N.S.	Bowater Washington Post	CTMP		Newsprint 230,000 t/yr
Minas Basin Pulp & Paper Ltd.	Hantsport, N.S.	CKF Ltd.			Packaging Products
Canexel	Chester, N.S.	Canadian Pacific Forest Products Ltd.			Hardboard

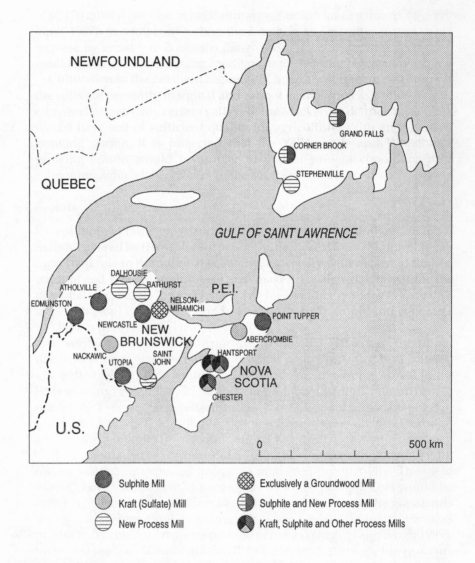

Location of direct discharge pulp and paper mills in the Atlantic provinces according to process category—1987

Source: Reproduced from Environment Canada. 1990. *Controlling Pollution from Canadian Pulp and Paper Manufacturers: A Federal Perspective*, 73–4. Reprinted with permission of the Minister of Supply and Services.

from the northern forest zones, while the new mechanical pulping proc-esses threaten to displace high-cost, small-capacity kraft mills. Those that survive will restructure in one of three directions: increase the plant efficiencies and scale of kraft operations, integrate with some paper or paperboard products or substitute a more favourable pulping process. The alternative will be to close the existing mills in favour of new sites.

In the newsprint sector, standard grades are being superseded by a differentiated range of mechanical printing papers for flexible uses. Given the extensive new capacity added during the last investment wave, kraft newsprint prices will remain soft and unprofitable to all but the largest scale mills. Meanwhile, demand will grow in uncoated mechanical papers, lightweight coated (catalogue and advertising) paper and other coated grades. Of particular potential is the U.S. printing and writing paper market. Summing up the re-structuring challenges faced by the pulp and paper sector, Woodbridge observes that:

> Canada already has many state-of-the-art, cost and quality com-petitive supermills. Others fall into an average category: some facilities are marginal except under very favourable product price conditions. (Woodbridge Reed 1988, 27)

The implication for the sub-optimal categories is clear. Parts of the industry that are dedicated to producing low-value commodities in small-scale mills must adapt decisively to newly emerging conditions. Woodbridge argues that the Canadian industry has focused in the past on *process* research, while largely ignoring *product* research and innovations in marketing. However, the key business challenge has now changed from the low-cost, high-volume supply of standard commodities to the supply of high-grade, differentiated products that are not marketed on the basis of price alone.

This analysis frames the maritime industry in a far different light from the MEU paradigm. Certainly New Brunswick reveals quite a diversified field of products, from newsprint to tissue, corrugated papers and light coated papers. This suggests greater aggregate stability over time and the possibility of a variety of growth strategies over the next decade. By contrast, Nova Scotia seems to be locked into precisely the mill and product mixes that Woodbridge identifies as most problematical.

In both cases, however, the scale of plants gives cause for concern. If the profitable future in standard grade commodities lies in supermill facilities, none of the regional pulp plants would appear to qualify at present, and only a few of the larger New Brunswick mills appear to offer a prospective platform for such expansion. Since there is only a very modest surplus of wood fibre within the maritimes to fuel expansion, it seems clear that the only viable route to supermill capacity lies in the closure of existing plants. This would be followed by the reassignment of crown leases and sale of private corporate forest holdings to the survivors. As will be seen below, the rationalization of the New Brunswick industry is now well underway. As this unfolds, the question of industrial linkages will loom large. Woodbridge points out that a crucial advantage of integrated facilities is to capture upstream profits from the sale of higher value-added commodities. If this factor is combined with the scale variable, it is possible to anticipate a triangular cluster of regional manufacturing complexes: the Fraser newsprint operations in the northwest; the Repap coated paper operations in the northeast; and the Irving newsprint, board and tissue operations in the south.

However strategic this may appear from the perspective of *industry* organization, any re-structuring will be mediated and controlled in the last instance by considerations of *company* strategy. This invokes a separate set of factors, including the differential efficiencies of facilities in multi-plant operations such as Noranda (Fraser), Repap, Stone or NBIP. Another constraint involves the financial position of both forest companies and their diversified parent firms. It is quite possible for fundamentally sound operating assets to be shuttered or sold by over-leveraged owners who are unwilling or unable to ride out the present slump in the pulp and paper sector. This was the case the *Globe and Mail* reported on 27 September 1991 regarding Donahue/Rexfor's greenfield pulp mill at Matane, Québec.

This point applies even more forcefully in Nova Scotia, where each of the three leading mills is an "orphan" branch plant of a foreign-based parent firm. As a subsidiary of Scott Paper (U.S.), Scott Maritimes is a moderate scale mill that ships pulp to Scott's tissue mills on the eastern seaboard. Stora combines a pulp and newsprint mill that is larger in total size, but remains dwarfed by the facilities in Stora Kopparberg's mainly European empire. Bowater Mersey is now the only remaining Canadian mill for the British Bowater Corporation, which owns it jointly with the *Washington Post*. Bowater's North American operations are overwhelmingly centred in the pine forest regions of the southern United States. Only six months ago, Bowater acquired the much larger Great Northern Paper complex at Millinocket, Maine, raising questions about the future role of the Mersey mill.

It is clear that the strategic adjustment of the maritime forest industry to the market conditions of the 1990s involves a variety of complex forces. Many of these are unique to the forest sector and the region's position within it, while others are company-specific and subject to a decision-making calculus stretching well beyond the region and even beyond the industry. When such factors are taken into account, the relatively simplistic assumptions of economic integration are seen to be sharply limited. As a growth and investment-generating initiative, the MEU attacks only one set of competitive variables. These are what Woodbridge labels "fundamental cost factors" or the cost of factor inputs. Here the advantage is unleashed by lowering the cost of raw wood fibre, of labour, of purchased energy and of delivery or transportation. Important as these may be, they may not in the end be determinants. Of perhaps greater importance are "product quality or service factors," which include reliability of supply and consistency of quality. These come into play because "few purchasers of higher value products buy on price alone" (Woodbridge Reed 1988).

This carries a further implication for the rationalization process which the industry presently faces. Any major reductions in fundamental cost factors may serve to postpone (and in effect, prevent) the necessary restructuring of marginal operations. In other words, if the logic of the integrated market unfolds as specified above, triggering major reviews of public policy aimed at lowering business costs at the processing plant level could well extend the status quo past the point at which structural change can succeed. More concretely, a policy adjustment to reduce the delivered price of pulpwood by 10–20 percent may prompt the owners of kraft pulp and newsprint mills to continue "normal" operations in the maritimes for an added few years, while affecting the long-term plant and product adjustments elsewhere in the company's domain.

Forest Policy and Economic Union

While the primary resource industries are no longer the backbone of the maritime economy (as they were before the Second World War), they remain substantial and strategic sectors today. The fields of agriculture, fishing and forestry continue to account for a significant share of the region's traded products and exports. Furthermore, they are critical employment and income-generating activities in the rural parts of the region, which have been under continual stress for the past generation. Finally it should be noted that all three fields remain firmly based in petty-bourgeois enterprise, though tensions with large-scale capital shape the politics of all three.

It was not surprising, then, that *Challenge and Opportunity* dealt in considerable detail with the resource sectors. Perhaps the most striking words were aimed at farming, where the Premiers called for a strategic plan "to improve the competitive position of maritime agriculture." To this end they struck a joint policy committee "to co-ordinate and harmonize maritime agricultural policies." In the fisheries field, the proposals took a similar theme, as the Premiers announced their intention to "reduce barriers in the fishing industry caused by restrictive provincial regulations." In particular, boat building loans would be portable throughout the region. More generally, the three provinces would "harmonize fees, schedules and conditions for buyer and processing licences" (CMP 1991, 4).

Given the scope and energy of these provisions, it is surprising that forestry did not figure in the broad inventory of action plans. Clearly the logic of policy harmonization, barrier reduction and easing regulations will not stop where field and sea meet the tree line. This is acknowledged in *Challenge and Opportunity*, which defers explicit action on forestry until a second round of economic union initiatives, when it will constitute one of five priority areas (Howlett 1990). In the meantime, many decisions with direct salience for forestry will be taken. Consider, for example, the proposed regional environmental accord. This will promote "complementary environmental policies and legislation" and at the same time "harmonize environmental standards and develop joint strategies to address regional environmental issues." In the maritimes a plethora of forest management practices, including pesticide and herbicide spraying, clearcut and selection logging practices and alternative regeneration techniques, rank high on the environmental agenda.

In sum, both the logic of the integration program, and the specific list of action proposals, signal that new forest policies will be integral to the new restructuring program. The list opposite sets out a range of measures that could reasonably come under review. However, the balance of this section will focus on the question of wood fibre marketing in New Brunswick and Nova Scotia. This is a particularly revealing policy study. Not only is it an important factor in the economics of pulp production, it is also a field in which the two provinces have pursued strikingly different strategies. Furthermore, since the marketing question links primary producers, industrial buyers and state authorities, it poses sharp political questions about distributive impacts. In effect, any movement towards harmonizing the pulpwood marketing regimes would trigger a fundamental conflict of interests and a re-ordering of power relations.

Labour Force/Employment
Workers compensation rates
Training programs
  woods
  mill
Labour mobility
Bush camp standards
Professional certification
  foresters
  technicians
  silviculture contractors

Transportation
Highway trucking rules
  load limits
  seasonal limits
  licence fees
Gasoline taxation

Land Ownership
Crown land policy
  licences
Private land ownership
Private land taxation
Silviculture practices

Wood Fibre Supply/Marketing
Crown stumpage
Private wood marketing
Pulpwood export

Secondary Mill/Processing
Power supply
Procurement
Effluent

The land tenure patterns in both provinces ensure that privately produced pulpwood will play a major role in industrial supply. Three-quarters of the forest land in Nova Scotia and just under half that in New Brunswick are privately owned. Prior to the 1960s, woodlot owners or wood producers were forced to deal directly with pulp buyers, generally faced with a price set by the companies. In the subsequent period, each province has established procedures for small producers to organize supply groups, and to bargain with the buyers over volumes and prices (Parenteau 1992; Clancy 1992). The results, however, offer a study in contrasts. New Brunswick presently supports six regional supply groups and a central federation that together cover the majority of private woodlot owners in the province. Nova Scotia supports only two regional supply groups, several additional (and quite rivalrous) small, woodlot-based organizations and no central, federated body. All of this occurs on a far narrower representative base. Over the past two decades, the roadside price for privately marketed New Brunswick pulpwood has consistently led Nova Scotia by $10 to $20 per cord.

While many factors shape this contrast in market conditions, perhaps the most significant policy element involves a single clause in the New Brunswick Crown forest act. This requires each pulp or paper company to sign a delivery contract with its registered private supply groups each year *before* the company can commence logging on its Crown lease forest lands. No similar provision exists in Nova Scotia. In New Brunswick it serves as a powerful inducement to concluding prompt agreements, rather than resisting and boycotting supply group talks as is common in Nova Scotia. Throughout this period, the New Brunswick regime has provided a model to which Nova Scotia woodlot groups have aspired. Yet all efforts to date have foundered on the resistance from the organized industrial forest lobby, the provincial Forest Products Association.

The economic union initiative threatens to pose the choice most sharply, for if a regional policy on this critical sector issue is to be achieved through harmonization, both pulpwood marketing regimes must converge on one level. Moreover the outcome carries profound distributional implications. Companies in the regional pulp and paper industry are virtually unanimous in favouring the Nova Scotia option (if not outright deregulation), while independent woodlot owners and small operators support the New Brunswick version. Consequently, the exemption of forest policies from the current round of union initiatives is highly significant, given that it postpones consideration for several years. Evidently the Premiers could not agree even to study the forest field at present.

It is quite possible that the deferred consideration of forest policy stems from the remarkable flux in that industry today. The restructuring patterns associated with the product cycle have already been discussed. The state policy domain has been no less active. In the marketing field alone, marketing authorities in Nova Scotia spent the past five years preparing a marketing regime modelled on New Brunswick (for an account of this struggle, *see* Clancy 1990). This initiative ultimately ended in deadlock and therefore political defeat. Alternately, the province of New Brunswick has, over the past 18 months, taken major steps in dismantling its marketing regime. This is tending towards a less rigorous, lower fibre-price regime that looks increasingly similar to the Nova Scotia model, as noted in the *Telegraph-Journal*, 10 January 1992. This occurs in the midst of the present forest sector slump, with the McKenna government offering wood- and labour-cost concessions in a desperate attempt to prevent mill closures. It has proceeded despite an unprecedented mobilization of the provincial woodlot owner movement to condemn and resist the "forest survival policy."

Conclusion

There are obvious limits to assessing a fundamental shift of policy paradigms by the impact of a single measure in a single industry sector. However this analysis was prompted by the dearth of concrete referents in the economic union debate, and I hope it has demonstrated the need for more empirical analyses. By penetrating the thick layer of generalities that seem to surround the union initiative, it can be better understood in realistic political terms. Each exercise in harmonization, rationalization or deregulation will be contested and resolved to the advantage and disadvantage of identifiable interests. It will be in the hundreds or even thousands of narrow, technical and possibly obscure policy adjustments that industrial politics will be determined in the future.

The particular case examined above suggests that a combination of business cycle pressures, varying organizational capacity among industry segments and ideological proclivities of state authorities, point to the downward harmonization of private, wood-marketing regimes. Should this follow the normal course, it will shift the terms of exchange, either marginally or decisively, in favour of industrial processors at the expense of small primary producers. Particular features of the maritime forest sector have dictated that a form of "pre-harmonization" occur *before* the formal process of co-ordination can be triggered. In less politically volatile settings, it is to be expected that the process will assume a more bureaucratic form, far more masked by the machinery of this incipient regional state. It will be no less political for this fact, though it may well go unrecognized as such.

I gratefully acknowledge the financial support of the Social Sciences and Humanities Research Council under Research Grant No. 410-91-0460.

References

Atlantic Provinces Economic Council. 1991. *Atlantic Economic Co-operation: An Exploration of the Concept, Its Benefits and Costs*. Halifax.

Bazowski, Raymond. 1991. Maritime Economic Integration: Neo-Classical Growth Strategies for Regional Development. Presented at the Annual Meeting of the Atlantic Provinces Political Science Association, St. John.

Bradfield, Michael. 1991. *Maritime Economic Union: Sounding Brass and Tinkling Symbolism*. Ottawa: Canadian Centre for Policy Alternatives.

Canada. 1984. House of Commons. *Debates*. Economic and Fiscal Statement. 8 November.

———. 1989a. Advisory Council on Adjustment. *Adjusting to Win* ("Grandpré Report"). Ottawa: Supply and Services Canada.

———. 1989b. Ministry of Natural Resources, Forestry Canada. *Selected Forestry Statistics, Canada 1988*. Ottawa: Forestry Canada.

———. 1991. *Canadian Federalism and Economic Union: Partnership for Prosperity*. Ottawa: Supply and Services Canada.

Clancy, Peter. 1990. Renegotiating a Regulatory Bargain: Probing the Limits of a Progressive Bureaucracy. Presented at the Annual Meeting of the Atlantic Provinces Political Science Association, St. John's.

———. 1992. The Politics of Pulpwood Marketing in Nova Scotia, 1960–1985. In *Trouble in the Woods: Forest Policy and Social Conflict in Nova Scotia and New Brunswick*, edited by L. Anders Sandberg. Fredericton: Acadiensis Press.

Council of Maritime Premiers (CMP). 1989. Press Communiqué. 76th Session, Halifax, 10 December.

———. 1990. *Standing Up to the Future: The Maritimes in the 1990s*, by Charles J. McMillan. Halifax: Council of Maritime Premiers.

———. 1991. *Challenge and Opportunity*. Halifax.

Fanjoy, Emery. 1992. Address to the Maritime Economic Co-operation Workshop. Halifax, 11 May.

Forestry Survival Plan in Works: Graham. 1992. The *Telegraph Journal*, 10 January.

Fraser, Sharon. 1991. Co-operation Yes, Superbureaucracy, No. *The Atlantic Co-operator*, May.

Ghiz, Joseph. 1990. Transcript of speech to the Charlottetown Rotary Club, 23 July. Government of Prince Edward Island press release.

Grahl, John, and Paul Teague. 1989. The Cost of Neo-Liberal Europe. *New Left Review* 174(March–April):33–50.

Howlett, Michael. 1990. The Round Table Experience: Representation and Legitimacy in Canadian Environmental Policy-Making. *Queen's Quarterly*, 97(4)(Winter):580–601.

LeBlanc, Rick. 1991. An Atlantic Economic Initiative: A New Vision for Atlantic Canada. Presented at the Annual Meeting of the Atlantic Provinces Political Science Association, St. John.

Nova Scotia Roundtable on Environment and Economy. 1991. *Sustainable Development Strategy for Nova Scotia: A Draft*. Halifax.

Parenteau, Bill. 1992. In Good Faith: the Development of Pulpwood Marketing for Independent Producers in New Brunswick, 1960–1985. In *Trouble in the Woods: Forest Policy and Social Conflict in Nova Scotia and New Brunswick*, edited by L. Anders Sandberg. Fredericton: Acadiensis Press.

Savoie, Donald J. 1991. The Search for the Holy Grail: Maritime Co-operation. In *Canada: The State of the Federation, 1991*, edited by Douglas M. Brown. Kingston: Institute of Intergovernmental Affairs.

Sinclair, William F. 1990. *Controlling Pollution from Canadian Pulp and Paper Manufacturers: A Federal Perspective*. Ottawa: Supply and Services Canada.

Voluntary Planning. 1991a. *Our Province, Our Future, Our Choice*: A Consultation paper for a Nova Scotia Economic Strategy. Halifax.

———. 1991b. *Report of the Public Consultation Process: Will to Win*. Halifax.

Woodbridge Reed and Associates. 1988. *Canada's Forest Industry, The Next Twenty Years: Prospects and Priorities*. Vol. 1, *Strategic Analysis*. Vol. 6, *Cost Projections*. Ottawa: Canadian Forestry Service, Industry, Trade and Technology Directorate, Economics Branch.

ALLAN A. WARRACK

Alberta Heritage Fund: Opportunity to Restructure Towards Sustainable Economic Development

Interest in the Alberta Heritage Savings Trust Fund (hereafter the Heritage Fund) is widespread. Most of that interest is on a financial basis. Perceptions of the Heritage Fund are wide-ranging; from positive to negative, from accurate to far-out misconceptions. Through it all, the primary perception of the Fund is as a financial "pot."

The Alberta Heritage Fund primarily is a policy instrument for resources management. As such, the Heritage Fund concept and experience is relevant to any jurisdiction where an economy is substantially based on resources. As any experienced policy-maker knows, there is far more to public management than wise policy choices. Strategic plans for effective implementation are imperative. Like any new idea, the Heritage Fund idea posed a major challenge to public understanding and acceptability. The basic concept of the Heritage Fund is a simple one, yet it is not fully understood. The concept is a reflection of Alberta's history, geography and economic structure. Historic and current perspectives will help explain the Alberta Heritage Fund. Hence, a short history of the Fund will provide a necessary context for later discussion.

Historical Perspectives

Economic Geography
Alberta is young, large and sparsely populated (2.5 million). It is the fourth largest Canadian province in both area and population. Although differing from Saskatchewan and Manitoba in many ways, much reporting of (Alberta) statistical aggregates is provided on a "prairie" region basis. Like Saskatchewan, Alberta is land-locked. Even more than Saskatchewan,

Alberta settlement patterns and resources potential require north-south transportation systems. The national context for such systems is primarily east-west in perspective.

Alberta has an unusual array of geographic features. There is shortgrass prairie, black-loam parkland, northern boreal forest, foothills, mountains and an extensive Lakeland zone. Resources have always comprised the primary economic base. Until about 1950, that base was predominantly agriculture—farming and ranching. Agriculture remains a basic industry; Alberta is a major cereal crop producer and is Canada's largest producer of red meat. A future geographic constraint on economic development may be watershed distribution. Most of Alberta's watershed flows "down" north; most of the watershed is away from population density. Moreover, downstream regions have water rights to be respected.

Another feature, harsh climate, hardly requires comment. Such a climate imposes higher energy costs and greater infrastructure requirements.

About two-thirds of Alberta's land surface is Crown-owned. Public land tends to be intensively used (e.g., provincial parks), extensively used (e.g., livestock grazing), specialized in use (e.g., transportation corridors or military reserves) and land with special features (e.g., national parks). Nearly all agriculture production is from privately held land. Commercial forest production is wholly from public land. While about 80 percent of Alberta conventional oil and gas is from public subsurface (mineral) lands, the ownership of surface and subsurface lands is not systematically contiguous. There is limited private ownership of coal reserves—mostly thermal (as distinct from metallurgical) coal. The massive tar sands area is a publicly owned resource.

The changing demographic character of Alberta's sparse population must be noted. Until the 1950s, the population was largely rural. During the 1950s and 1960s, economic and population growth was far greater in Calgary and Edmonton than elsewhere in the province; rural areas were deeply concerned about stagnation and decline. During the 1970s, population percentage in rural areas continued to fall absolutely, at the same time that city growth was exceedingly rapid. Today over 60 percent of Albertans live in Calgary and Edmonton.

Alberta's economic history is tied to resources. Prosperity levels have been relatively low and subject to severe economic cycles. As of early 1982, Albertans had just experienced an unprecedented decade of high prosperity. This was followed by a lengthy economic recession.

Energy Resource Development in Alberta

Early this century Alberta's first oil discoveries were made in the "Black Gold" area southwest of Calgary. These discoveries thrust Calgary into its historic and present position as Canada's centre of conventional oil and gas exploitation. While the Black Gold discovery was important at the time and continues to produce today, it is now minor in relation to subsequent energy events and contemporary requirements.

In February 1947 a huge discovery was made in central Alberta at Leduc (near Edmonton). A frantic pace of exploration, discovery and production ensued. Soon there were thousands of producing oil wells with grasshopper pumps dotting the rural landscape. Alberta had entered the big league of oil.

Originally, natural gas was handled as an inconvenient by-product and "flared-off." Natural gas pools now are recognized as highly significant. An important dimension of Canadian energy policy has been the fuel substitution of natural gas for oil. As of 1991, Alberta has nearly completed a unique rural gas distribution system.

The dominating event of Alberta's energy resource development was the Natural Resources Transfer Act of 1930. It is important to note that both renewable (e.g., forestry) and non-renewable resources were included in the scope of that legislation. The transfer of ownership of public* resources from the federal to provincial sphere had been included in the terms of Alberta and Saskatchewan becoming provinces in 1905. It was a quarter century later before the transfer was implemented. Ownership of resources is the basis for lessor-share royalty (for oil and gas) and stumpage (for forestry) regimes. Resource economic rent is the pivotal concept underlying the Alberta Heritage Fund.

The economic structure of energy industry development has been that of many small and geographically dispersed operations. A web of pipelines traversed the province as Alberta became a world leader in pipeline technology. The hydrocarbon resources found were high quality, abundant and reasonably accessible. While oil and gas operations were large in provincial aggregate, individual operations were relatively small and thus reasonably compatible with host rural communities. These circumstances held into the early 1970s.

By the late 1970s a surge of enthusiasm had developed for energy megaprojects. Aside from coal-fired power plants, the Great Canadian Oil

---

* Only Crown resources were transferred; privately owned (freehold) resources were not directly affected.

Sands plant (now Suncor) was built in the mid-1960s and Syncrude was completed in 1978. Alsands, Cold Lake Heavy Oil and Northern Gas Pipeline megaprojects were soon proposed. It appeared that the economic structure of the energy industry was transforming from many small operations to a few large ones. However, by mid-1982 most Canadian energy megaprojects had collapsed or were put on hold.

There are four summary characteristics of energy resource development in Alberta:

1. The bulk of energy production is from provincial public resources.
2. Energy industry activity is primarily in the private sector.
3. The economic structure primarily is numerous smaller operations with a few large operations.
4. The pace of development historically has been limited by markets rather than by production capacity.

Policy Background to the Fund

The Heritage Fund concept was proposed by the Alberta Government in late 1974. The concept was widely debated in the 1975 Alberta election. Draft legislation was developed in the fall of 1975; modified legislation was brought forward and given assent in the spring 1976 Alberta legislative sitting. The initial money flow into the Fund ($1.5 billion) was provided by late summer of 1976.

The content of the new government's policy focused sharply on re-sources. Compared to the past, resources policy was given much higher priority in relation to competing areas of policy. In the new government's perception, managing the province's natural resources was central to economic development strategy and to financial management by the provincial government. In the early 1970s the Alberta Government was deficit-financing its budgets. Several dimensions of resources policy directions were specified. These were:

- the public's ownership share* should be markedly higher;
- the non-renewable resources of oil and gas were priced below value and must be revised;
- resource upgrading and thus employment opportunity in Alberta must be increased dramatically; and

---

* This royalty share had been limited to a 1/6 maximum in oil and gas leases; this could only be changed by legislation that forced changes in the public/private lease contracts

- Albertans should have greater investment opportunity as their publicly owned resources are developed (the eventual vehicle for implementing this policy direction became the Alberta Energy Company).

During 1974, OPEC actions sparked a price revolution, quadrupling oil prices. As a result, Alberta had begun to receive a much higher oil and gas royalty share on far-higher-priced commodities (oil and natural gas). Despite federal government and consuming region efforts to suppress price increases, the fundamental fact was that resource revenue funds began flowing to Alberta (and, to a much lesser extent, to Saskatchewan and British Columbia) in amounts that greatly exceeded expectations.

The ready availability of large resource revenues was a prime condition leading up to the Heritage Fund idea. It was also a source of concern that current revenues could induce government expenditures that would be unsustainable over the long term.

Resources Economics and Management

The Alberta Heritage Fund can be viewed in many ways. Most public attention, certainly that of the media, has focused on the Fund from a financial viewpoint. However, that should be secondary. While the Heritage Fund is a pool of capital, the primary questions are why and how the pool of capital evolved. The core of the Alberta Heritage Fund idea lies within the concepts of resources economic management.

The Heritage Fund is a financial instrument for resources management over time. Capital management principles are applicable. The Fund can convert non-renewable resource assets into renewable resource assets and human capital assets. The Fund in general, and the Capital Projects Division in particular (detailed explanation on page 172), is founded on economic rents and time preference as they pertain to public resources management policy.

Basic Issues

Natural resources constitute an essential input into all goods produced in a modern economy. Resource sectors are industries that supply basic commodities. Canada's Macdonald Commission (1985) was attentive to natural resources development and identified five such major categories: agriculture, forestry, fisheries, minerals and oil and gas. Many analysts would broaden the scope by referring to land, air, water, wildlife and so on. A useful distinction is between renewable and non-renewable resources. The resources assets can be "drawn down" or utilized. Renewable resources stock can be built up as well as drawn down. Non-renewable resources are finite but the magnitude of the finite asset is unknown.

The Alberta Heritage Fund monies stem from non-renewable resources. Hence these resources will receive more attention in this paper. However, the principles could be adapted to apply to renewable resources. Only revenues from publicly owned (Crown) resources flow to the Heritage Fund, therefore royalties (owners' share) monies rather than taxes pertain to the Fund. Yet the concept of the Heritage Fund need not be confined to economic rents in the form of royalties (hydrocarbons or minerals) and stumpage (forestry). Resource endowments are assets, regardless of ownership, and can be made subject to property taxation or other tax provisions. In some western American states (e.g., Montana), severance taxes are levied on coal sales.

Resource conservation is the attempt to establish the socially most desirable levels of resource development and consumption over time. Having proper regard for future generations, to what extent of finite non-renewable resources can a particular generation feel entitled? In this judgement, resource high-grading (using the cheapest/highest quality first) must be taken into account. At a given point in time the renewable resource stock is finite. But this stock can be utilized and replenished concurrently. Human capital stock can be accumulated in the forms of education, training and experiential skills. A more complex notion of resource conservation would allow interchange between non-renewable, renewable, and human resource assets. Viewed in this way, drawdowns of non-renewable resource stocks can meet the issue of resource conservation by flowing to renewable resource/human capital stock build-up.

In earlier and simpler economic eras, there was little to resources policy beyond continuity of supply considerations. With sparse populations surrounded by vast resource stocks, virtually all resources could be perceived as infinite. Moreover, in those harsh and often desperate times, primacy was given to survival. With the world population explosion and dramatically higher standards of living, pressure mounts on our resource endowment. A serious issue is sustainability of aggregate production and a livable environment over the long-term.

Resource Economies

There is little disagreement that natural resources have played a seminal role in Canada's economic development. This is particularly true for the early economic history of each Canadian region. It is especially so for newer regions today; e.g., the western provinces, Newfoundland and Canada's North. What of the future to and beyond the year 2000? Perspectives differ by region—so then do policy prescriptions for natural resources in Canada's economic future.

The economics of resources is notoriously cyclical. Economies substantially dependent on natural resources, whether regional or national, tend to be cyclical. The cycles can be large in magnitude and occur in rapid surges (booms) and slides (busts). Constant adaptation and adjustment is needed to exact prosperity from the cyclical reality that characterizes resources economic development. Moreover, the timing of cycles is virtually impossible to predict. Resource sectors in Canada total about a third of gross national product (GNP) and half of the merchandise export revenues. These proportions are higher in Alberta and in the rest of the West.

There are three basic types of cycles: weather, markets and policy cycles. Weather uncertainties are particularly vexing to agriculture. Variable supply riding up and down in elastic demand results in both price and farm income instability. Another repeated observation is dependence of the resources sector on international markets. The markets are inherently volatile; so too are the employment opportunities and income streams associated with natural resources development. The instability is magnified when the developments are megaprojects (Warrack 1992). Resource economies also are vulnerable to public policy cycles; the policy risk can emanate from either domestic or foreign decisions. Two recent examples are forestry resources (U.S. import legislation) and energy resources (the National Energy Program). Sparsely populated regions have little political clout and thus are more likely to be public policy victims.

Economically viable resource development in Canada is highly dependent on international trade and foreign capital flows. A large project requires commensurately large capital investment and size of market. Canada's markets and capital pools are relatively small.

The environmental context of natural resource development is exceedingly important. There need be no long-term conflict between economic growth and environmental concerns. We must leave a healthy environment and sustainable resource base for future generations. Mitigating environmental damage is appropriate for resource development cost accounting. In meeting enlightened environmental consciousness, it is important to recognize the special costs in remedial upgrading of aging resource projects. Often, improvements are best done in conjunction with major project expansion. However, the central policy issue ought to be "how" rather than "whether" adverse environmental impacts will be remedied.

Alberta has been and continues to be primarily a resources economy. Each of the above contexts is pertinent to any evaluation of the Alberta Heritage Savings Trust Fund. Meanwhile the Alberta Government aspires to economic diversification (Alberta 1984). For some time to come the nature of the Alberta economy will be accurately characterized as a resources economy. Thus it is appropriate that a resources policy and management perspective be applicable to the Alberta Heritage Fund.

Economic Rents and Time Preference

Society's supply of things worthwhile emanate from our physical resource environment. In sloppy moments, economists, bureaucrats and politicians may assume supplies—wishing rather than producing. Mother earth, however, is niggardly. Supply is contingent upon technology, information and effort. Management involves combining these factors to result in supply availability. Costs are incurred in releasing needed supplies.

The concept of economic rent is pivotal to revenue flows into the Alberta Heritage Fund. Economic rent is defined as the amount by which the price of a natural resource exceeds its cost of supply. In the usual quadrant graph of the supply curve (marginal cost function), the appropriating of economic rents (royalties or stumpage) shifts the supply curve upward on the vertical axis. Production will cease if royalties exceed economic rent. There must be "room" in the cost structure for royalties to be paid and production to proceed. Costs may be highly variable in response to a variety of cost-inducing production and transportation factors, etc. Less difficult and higher-quality finds have lower costs, the economic rents are thus large in magnitude. Royalty regimes frequently reflect these cost variation realities. For example, in Alberta "old oil" royalties differ (higher) from those applicable to "new oil." Scarcity of the resource induces the value of economic rent. Unlimited supply of a resource, relative to demand, will result in little or no economic rent. Clean air and water have only recently become somewhat scarce. OPEC's actions after 1973 dramatically enhanced the scarcity-induced value of crude oil through its successful monopoly pricing techniques.

Up to the early 1970s, Alberta royalties on oil and natural gas were legislatively limited to a one-sixth (16.67 percent) share. Resource policy changed, resulting in dramatically increased royalties and established variable royalty regimes congruent with cost differences for new finds, lower-production wells, and enhanced recovery systems. Royalty shares of resource economic rents had become a substantial share of Alberta government revenues. These revenues increased dramatically in 1974 and 1975 as oil and natural gas prices escalated.

Until 1976, Alberta resource economic rents (100 percent) were used for year-by-year general revenues of the provincial government. Commencing in 1976 in Alberta, 30 percent of Crown resource economic rents was set aside into a separate trusteeship—the Alberta Heritage Savings Trust Fund. The other 70 percent continued to flow into general revenues of the province. In 1982, the portion set aside was changed to 15 percent; the residual 85 percent went to general revenues. The principle is that a share of resource economic rent revenues is withheld from current use and can be deployed instead for future benefits. Since 1987, no non-renewable resource income has been deposited into the Alberta Heritage Fund.

There are implementation difficulties in a policy of deferring benefits into the future. Many individuals have trouble saving for their own or their family's future. It is far more difficult on a societal (government) basis. The future "gain" is distant, diffuse and uncertain: the current "pain" is immediate, specific and certain. Although the economic principle may be sound, the politics may be exactly contradictory.

The notion of time preference underlies interest rates; "good things are better sooner" and "bad things are better deferred." So a price (interest rate) must be paid for the use of someone else's money. In economic terms, present consumption must be deferred to provide a loan to someone else. Nominal interest rates must add risk and inflation components to time preference. Risk is never zero; the prime interest rate includes a limited risk provision of 1.5 to 2 percent. Most borrowers face a "prime plus" market interest rate.

The foregoing refers to private capital markets and interest rates. The Heritage Fund belongs to Alberta as a society. Hence, the social discount rate is relevant. What is the difference? By convention social discount rates are conceived in real terms where nominal-less-inflation results in real rates. Most public policy analysts agree that the social discount rate is properly lower than the private capital market interest rate. A public investment can include intangible as well as financial benefits. The social discount rate is defined as the minimum real rate of return that a public investment must yield if it is to be worth undertaking. In economic terms the social discount is the real rate of return foregone in the private sector when resources are shifted (e.g., taxation) to the public sector. Society is better off if the public investment yields benefits (i.e., return) in excess of the social opportunity cost of withdrawals from the private sector. There are at least three reasons why social discount rates are appropriately lower than real market interest rates:

1. Intergenerational equity—society has a special trusteeship responsibility for the young and unborn.

2. Intragenerational equity—provision of needed public services and capital investments.

3. Risk pooling—risks are, like the principle of insurance underwriting, more predictable and manageable in a large pool than a small pool.

Like so many things in economics, the social discount rate magnitude is debatable. It should be viewed as a range rather than scalar number; more severe social needs would apply to the low end of the range. I submit the range of 4–7 percent. This range is relatively low to guard against the danger of capital-starving public institutions and services.

Context of Heritage Fund Policy

Why establish a Heritage Fund? The royalty share of oil and gas revenues had been increased with legislative changes in the early 1970s. Shortly thereafter came the OPEC oil price shock. The resource revenue flow could be stemmed by curbing production levels—an unthinkable alternative in the mid-1970s. While this alternative has some economic rationale, it would have had severe divisive implications within Canada (Warrack 1985). Oil supply for Canada was already overly dependent on vulnerable overseas sources of high-priced oil. Projections of non-renewable resource revenues showed large budgetary surpluses for a period of years. Yet Alberta already had among the highest levels of public services and the lowest taxation level in the country.

"Why a Heritage Fund?" was a central question in the 1975 Alberta election. A consensus was forged favouring the Heritage Fund idea. Four basic reasons emerged supporting the concept: 1. to be fair to future generations—recognizing that the non-renewable resources are depleting; 2. substantial capital investment would be instrumental in an economic structuring; 3. to provide quality of life improvements that Alberta otherwise could not afford; and 4. to provide an alternative revenue base for the future if required.

There were many complex factors involved in policy and design of the Alberta Heritage Savings Trust Fund. These are economic, financial, social and public perception factors. Some considerations were more decisive than others.

Economic

Alberta is comparatively prosperous. But the level of prosperity is precarious. Alberta employment and incomes are highly dependent on primary resource development activity. For some years over half of the provincial government budget revenue came from the non-renewable resource revenues; now that amount is about one quarter (Alberta 1992). The economic basis for Alberta's prosperity is narrow; such an economy is not strong.

The economic development requirements in Alberta are consistent with macroeconomic goals for Canada. The Alberta problem is vulnerability; economic activity that reduces this vulnerability contributes to its economic development. An economic issue for Alberta is greater economic stability for the future.

Economic growth must be harnessed to restructure Alberta's economy. Alberta has a declared six-element economic strategy:

- agriculture processing,

- resources upgrading,

- gateway to northern development,

- technology and skills centre,

- financial and allied services and

- tourism.

Underlying this strategy is the reality that comparative advantage determines the chances of success. As a technology and skills centre, Alberta might expect to achieve a comparative advantage in oil and gas expertise, certain areas of medical research (a major thrust of the Fund's Capital Projects Division), livestock production and processing and telecommunications technology. Resource upgrading can occur in petrochemicals based on resource (especially natural gas) feedstock availability. Shifting to a provincial corporate income tax system is intended to open a wider array of incentives for enhanced economic activity. The acquisition of Pacific Western Airlines (now privatized) helped position Alberta to compete effectively in servicing northern development.

Alberta government's policy position since 1971 was that diversification is vital to strengthen its regional economy; this approach was reaffirmed in 1984 with the Alberta White Paper. Here it was argued that strengthened regional economies are consistent with a stronger national economy.

Changing the structure of an economy is a capital-demanding process. Economic growth of a given amount is less capital-demanding when little restructuring is involved. More capital is required when a higher proportion of the investment is for totally new facilities as distinct from replacement and/or expansion capital. Moreover, greater infrastructure investment is required so facilitative services are available. Much of the infrastructure must be provided by the public sector.

The investment factor is enormously important in Alberta's economic strategy for development; thus capital availability is vital. As a pool of capital, the Heritage Fund was meant to help meet capital requirements. Loans to Alberta Crown agencies and other Canadian governments (and some of their agencies) total large amounts (*see* table 2b). Several infrastructure installations have been funded directly by the Fund (Heritage Fund Reports, annual and quarterly). The Fund is a potential policy instrument for an economic policy role involving conversion, through the Heritage Fund mechanism, of non-renewable resources assets into physical and human capital for future economic development.

Financial

It is an axiom of practical politics that the highest level of public service provided becomes the minimum expectation of the public. Thus the provider of public service (government, utility company, and so on) will be wise to have a strategic financial plan that assures the capacity to pay indefinitely for public service improvements it implements. Normally government spending is constrained, with reasonable public understanding, by affordability limits in the short term. When more is affordable in the short term but not in the long term, there is a grave risk that public expectations will mount unconstrained. If so, the political pressures for massive spending increases would be fierce and ultimately must be heeded. For Alberta in the second half of the 1970s, large budgetary surpluses over a series of years resulted in very, very large provincial budget increases in spending. What happens when (not if) non-renewable resource revenues wither away? If the foregoing axiom is correct, the only choices would be a dramatic and permanent pattern of tax increases and mounting public debts. As of 1992, Alberta has had some tax increases (but no sales tax, yet) but has a recent series of whopping deficits ($2.3 billion for 1992–3) (Alberta 1992).

The preceding section notes that economic restructuring is a capital-demanding process. Hence Alberta's economic strategy for development would be well-served by a concurrent capital-supplying process. Moreover, the revenue source under examination materializes from non-renewable resource utilization that represents a drawdown on resource stock (a form of capital). Finally, more capital investment is possible with more limited levels of current expenditures.

A related matter was that Alberta initiated a challenge to the fiscal equalization system in Canada. Revenues from non-renewable Crown resources had been treated like any other revenues. Alberta took the position that these revenues, which were capital and non-recurring in nature, should be viewed differently from current and recurring revenues sources; only a "current portion" ought be counted in the equalization calculations. The federal government countered with the valid point that Alberta's financial management handled non-renewable resource revenues no differently from other revenues. One result of the Heritage Fund was a change in this regard.

Social
Social progress is the objective of economic progress. Greater economic capacity makes meeting more needs affordable. Should affordability be gauged in shorter or longer-term perspectives? If the needs fulfilled are perceived by recipients as permanent, then long-term affordability is essential. If an expenditure is interruptible a more myopic view is appropriate.

Quality of life improvements (social dividends) are a reason for favouring the Heritage Fund idea. This factor underlies the Capital Projects Division of the Fund. Social and environmental improvements, which Alberta could otherwise not afford, are made possible. Many of these yield immediate and continuing benefits. Other projects are in the nature of economic infrastructure; these are meant to enhance future economic productivity. Thus such infrastructure investments should make further future social and environmental improvements more affordable.

In addition to absolute capital costs, the operating-to-capital cost ratio characteristics are exceedingly important in project evaluation. How much future operating costs are compelled by a given capital investment? As examples, compare hospitals, reforestation and parks. Hospitals: each capital dollar forces an operating cost dollar expenditure within about two years—a high ratio. Reforestation: incremental operating costs are negligible—a low ratio. Parks: significant but moderate operating costs are implied—a medium ratio. The affordability question must include operating cost projections. If these are small or moderate in magnitude, conventional budgeting may be satisfactory. If large, a specific financial strategy is warranted; a Medical Heritage Endowment has been established to support the Medical Research facilities of the Alberta Heritage Fund. The purpose was to assure continuity of the established social benefits.

Heritage Fund decision-making should face the social issues of fairness to future generations of Alberta citizens. Is it fair for a current generation to spend all the non-renewable resource revenue on themselves? The legacy would be a very high (and probably irreversible) level of government expenditures combined with resource depletion. The issue is more serious than quantitative resource depletion. The best and cheapest resources are utilized first. There is a danger of leaving future generations with a higher level of expenditure and a poorer resource base to support it.

Alberta Heritage Fund (AHF) Financial Status

The original 1976 Legislation provided for three divisions of the Fund: Canada Investment Division (CID), Alberta Investment Division (AID) and Capital Projects Division (CPD). A final residual category (not division) of the Fund handles cash management and money-market (not equity) securities.

In 1980, legislative amendment provided for two additional divisions: Commercial Investment Division (CMID) and Energy Investment Division (EID). CMID and EID implementation was very slow (until 1982), and by that time the Federal Government's National Energy Program had started to impose severe economic limitations on Alberta and its hydrocarbon sector.

Detailed information is available from annual and quarterly AHF reports. The Fund grew rapidly until 1983; since then its growth has barely matched inflation's erosion of purchasing power. Table 1 highlights AHF data from inception to 1992, with division-by-division for every year.

From a financial perspective only about $200 million of CPD is marketable, leaving the AHF size at just over $12 billion. In addition, financial assets are carried at book value and some have dubious market value due to the sustained economic recession. A recent study calculated that the actual AHF value had dropped to $9.6 billion (Mumey 1992).

The Alberta Government has begun to incur large deficits, $1.5 billion for 1991–92 with 1992–93 forecast of $2.3 billion (Alberta 1992) The provincial government's accumulated debt has overtaken the magnitude of the Alberta Heritage Fund.

Table 1
Size and Composition of the Alberta Heritage Savings Trust Fund
Fiscal years 1976/77–90/91, as of 31 March of each year
(dollars)

Category	1977	1978	1979	1980	1981	1982	1983	1984	1985	1986	1987	1988	1989	1990	1991
Canada Investment Division	50 m	96 m	270 m	929 m	1.5 b	1.9 b	1.9 b	1.9 b	1.9 b	1.9 b	1.9 b	1.5 b	1.4 b	1.3 b	1.2 b
Alberta Investment Division	704 m	1.1 b	2.8 b[3]	3.1 b	4.5 b	6.3 b	8.2 b	8.1 b	8.1 b	8.2 b	7.8 b	7.5 b	7.4 b	6.9 b	5.9 b
Capital Projects Division	36 m	123 m	255 m	733 m	960 m	1.3 b	1.6 b	2.1 b	2.4 b	2.6 b	2.8 b	2.8 b	3.1 b	3.3 b	3.4 b
- Financial Assets	-	-	-	-	-	-	-	200 m	200 m	200 m	200 m	200 m	200 m	200 m	200 m
- Deemed Assets	all	all	all	all	all	all	all	1.9 b	2.2 b	2.4 b	2.6 b	2.8 b	2.9 b	3.1 b	3.2 b
Commercial Investment Division	n/a	n/a	n/a	n/a	nil	189 m	199 m	199 m	201 m	217 m	233 m	263 m	287 m	316 m	340 m
Energy Investment Division	n/a	n/a	n/a	n/a	25 m	25 m	25 m	25 m	24 m	16 m	8 m	1 m	nil	nil	nil
Cash and Marketable Securities	1.2 b	1.8 b	1.2 b[3]	1.4 b	1.3 b	849 m	576 m	808 m	1.4 b	1.8 b	2.3 b	2.8 b	2.8 b	3.2 b	3.9 b
CCITF[2] Deposit, Accrued Interest, and Accounts Receivable	262 m	266 m	152 m	190 m	287 m	392 m	491 m	532 m	447 m	467 m	347 m	310 m	299 m	332 m	592 m
TOTALS	$2.2 b[1]	3.4 b	4.7 b	6.4 b	8.6 b	11.0 b	13.0 b	13.7 b	14.5 b	15.2 b	15.3 b	15.3 b	15.3 b	15.3 b	15.3 b

[1] The Alberta Heritage Fund began with a special capital allocation on August 30, 1976.
[2] Consolidated Cash Investment Trust Fund of the Province of Alberta.
[3] Reflects Alberta Government Telephones and Alberta Municipal Financial Corp. debenture transfers to the Alberta Investment Division.

Canada Investment Division (CID)
The Alberta government wanted the Heritage Fund to have a Canadian
dimension. Loans were to be available to other Canadian governments and
their agencies. Starting in early 1977, there have been 33 loans totalling $1.9
billion. The scope includes six provincial governments and/or agencies;
the exceptions are Ontario, British Columbia and Saskatchewan. Three
loans have been made to Hydro-Québec though not to the province itself.
The federal government has not borrowed from the Heritage Fund.

The first loan, to Newfoundland in February 1977, warrants special
attention. It was the first province-to-province loan in Canada's history.
Another historic context of that first loan is that a separatist government
was elected in Québec only three months before; U.S. financial markets had
viewed the Québec event with some anxiety and were reassessing the risk
of Canadian loans. While Canada Investment Division loans are on commercial terms, these terms were decided with a credit rating as if loans were
to the best non-Alberta government-related borrower (e.g., Ontario Hydro); hence the interest rates contain less risk premium than would foreign
capital markets. Moreover nearly all of these Heritage Fund loans, especially the earlier ones, have resulted in a substantial exchange rate bonus.
The Canadian dollar began to plummet in 1977. Repayment of foreign
borrowing would have been more expensive than present principal and
interest repayments to the Alberta Heritage Fund.

No CID loans have been made since 1982. Existing loans are being
liquidated as they mature. From a high of $1.9 billion, CID is now $1.2 billion
and will continue to fall.

Alberta Investment Division (AID)
This is by far the largest component—nearly half of the total Fund. The
division is made up of loans to Alberta Crown corporations and shares of
some provincial government investments. Detailed breakdowns are available from sources cited earlier. Both Canada and Alberta Investment
Division undertakings are directed toward financial return—principal,
interest, and dividends.

Three sets of loans dominate: Alberta Mortgage and Housing Corporation is the largest borrower ($2.1 billion), followed by Alberta Agricultural
Development Corporation ($1.1 billion), Alberta Municipal Financing
Corporation ($710 million) and Alberta Opportunity Company ($150
million). Due to privatization, Telus (formerly Alberta Government Telephones) Corporations loans ($700 million) are about half of former levels
and are to be liquidated fully.

Private placement of the above debentures saved considerable monies in fees and commissions. However, the process insulated the AHF and recipients from market forces and disciplines. Alberta Heritage Fund difficulties are partly the result of market detachment.

There was one major economic development use of AID in the 1970s: about $500 million participation in the successful Syncrude Oil Sands megaproject. Over the 15 years of AHF, only a handful of other AID economic development investments have been made. Overall the AID economic development investment effort has been about $1.6 billion— only a modest effort in view of the "need to strengthen and diversify the provincial economy" (Alberta, Heritage Fund Reports, preamble).

Capital Projects Division (CPD)
A fundamental CPD premise is that CPD investments are for improved social and economic well-being in the longer-term future. Financial yield, on an ongoing basis, is a minor consideration. For the other divisions, commercial financial return is a declared primary objective.

One area of confusion is the calculation of the Heritage Fund's overall financial return. Because CPD (as a matter of policy) does not normally involve such return, the percent financial return should be calculated on a base that excludes the Capital Projects Division. As well the regular budget process must still include the normal capital components. All CPD developments are to be capital in nature but not all capital deployments should come from CPD. Projects undertaken in this division have been for improvements Alberta could otherwise not afford in the normal budgetary circumstances.

Many and varied projects comprise the Capital Projects Division. The top priority to date has been medical research facilities and an accompanying endowment. The medical projects focus has been on cancer, cardiac and children's disease research facilities. Because the capital expended to build these facilities necessitates high future operating expenditures, an Endowment ($300 million) was established—the financial yield funds on-going research programs.

Other CPD projects include agriculture (irrigation works and grazing reserves), transportation (airstrips and terminals, grain hopper cars), renewable resources (land reclamation, flood control, forest nursery and forestation), parks and hydrocarbon technology research (especially oil sands). Education projects have included special library development funds and an array of substantial Heritage Fund Scholarships.

Table 2a, Schedule 5, and Table 2b, Schedule 6, are excerpts from the AHF quarterly report dated 31 March 91 along with the most recent AHF annual report. The 1991–92 annual report will become available later, but it will not differ significantly from that of 1990–91.

The thrust of this paper is to evaluate the economic development use of AHF. Some CPD efforts are economic development in nature, others are not and still others are debatable. In an enumeration of economic development Schedule 6 investments, the parks and health and substance abuse items would be excluded. If all else is included, the economic investments are $2.1 billion; adding $200 of Vencap Equities from Schedule 5 results in a total of $2.3 billion of CPD economic development effort. Thus about two-thirds of CPD monies of $3.4 billion have been designated towards economic development purposes.

Commercial (CMID) Energy (EID) Investment Divisions

Neither division is consequential. CMID is the vehicle for holding a portfolio of equity securities protecting AHF purchasing power during inflationary times. If AHF were to be managed as a endowment, CMID would be a crucial division. Lack of CMID initiative is a subject of AHF criticism.

Similarly EID is inconsequential; there was a corporate debenture investment made in 1981. That debenture was paid off in late 1989 and now EID is empty.

Economic Sustainability

A recent study assessed Alberta's problems of economic instability (Mansell and Percy 1990). By any measure, particularly through the 1980s, the

Table 2a
Capital Projects Division Investments—Assets—31 March 1991
(unaudited)
Schedule 5

	Legislative Appropriation 1990–91	Investments Made During Three Months Ended 31 March 1991 (thousands of dollars)	Investments at 31 March 1991 at cost
Department/Project			
Economic Development and Trade			
Venture Capital Financing -			
Vencap Equities Alberta Ltd	$ –	$ –	$ 199,993

Alberta economy ranks among the most unstable in Canada.

Alberta's prosperity and stability was impaired severely by the Federal Government's early 1980s National Energy Program. In addition, hydro-carbon and agricultural prices collapsed mid-decade. Energy royalties and tax revenues to the Alberta Government fell precipitously. Moreover, economic recession greatly dampened individual and corporate income tax revenues.

From a public finance perspective, a crunch is inevitable when "hard" expenditures are supported by "soft" revenues. The Alberta Government faces an economic circumstance of revenue instability concurrent with expenditure level permanence. Greater revenue stability is needed. The Heritage Fund could "bridge finance" the gap for a time, but the Fund is much too small to solve the public finance problem. The entire Heritage Fund is barely a year of the Alberta provincial budget. For the first time, serious debate has begun in Alberta regarding the sales tax revenue option.

The protracted constitution crisis in Canada holds adverse economic repercussions for the country and for the province of Alberta (Boothe 1992). Several economic topics, for three alternative constitutional scen-arios, are analyzed. Magnified instability and risk would worsen a structural problem of the Alberta economy, yet there is grave danger of just such a future reality. The result would "overmatch" the Alberta Heritage Fund to an even greater extent.

Alberta economic development policy has emphasized sustainability through diversification, including the Alberta Heritage Fund statement of objectives. Many surveys confirm that the Alberta public supports this approach to lessen economic instability. Despite broad political support, the diversification policy focus does not stand up well to economic analy-sis. Mansell and Percy (1990, 139) conclude that Alberta economic sustainability will be enhanced with diversification as one of four concur-rent policy strategies. Moreover, they urge a broadened definition of diversification in Alberta's economic strategy. Instead of a focus on specific industries with low variance (that may have little or negative comparative advantage), Alberta should diversify primarily by building on strengths (e.g., expand product lines, vertically integrate and diversify markets of existing industries). The study concludes that Alberta economic sustainability will be enhanced more by a broadened and expanded policy rather than by seeking to change the economic base.

A purpose of this paper is to evaluate the Alberta Heritage Fund's impact on economic sustainability in Alberta. As Alberta Heritage Fund legisla-tion and policy was framed, the mechanism for that impact was to be

Table 2b
Capital Projects Division (CPD), 31 March 1991
Schedule 6

Capital Projects Division Investments — Deemed Assets — 31 March 1991
(unaudited, thousands of dollars)

| | Investments made during | | | Investments |
Department/Project	Legislative Appropriation 1990–91	Three Mo. Ended 21 Mar. 1991	Twelve Mo. Ended 21 Mar. 1991	at 31 Mar. 1991 at cost
Advanced Education				
Alberta Heritage Scholarship Fund	$ –	$ –	$ –	$100,000
Clinical Research Building	–	–	–	17,632
Library Development	–	–	–	9,000
Agriculture				
Farming For The Future	5,000	1,209	4,839	58,054
Food Processing Development Centre	–	–	–	9,013
Irrigation Rehabilitation and Expansion	25,000	155	24,990	311,942
Private Irrigation Water Supply	3,068	86	254	446
Economic Development and Trade				
Rail Hopper Cars	–	–	–	53,661
Education				
Alberta Heritage Learning Resources	–	–	–	9,222
Energy				
Alberta Oil Sands Technology and Research Authority	–	–	–	418,700
Renewable Energy Research	1,000	227	422	499
Environment				
Irrigation Headworks and Main Irrigation Systems Improvement	40,400	21,255	38,934	472,657
Land Reclamation	2,500	981	2,298	37,665
Lesser Slave Lake Outlet	–	–	–	2,889
Paddle River Basin Development	–	–	–	41,781
Executive Council				
Occupational Health and Safety Research and Education	1,218	371	1,142	9,816
Forestry, Lands and Wildlife				
Alberta Reforestation Nursery	–	–	–	14,739
Grazing Reserves Dev. & Enhancemt	1,392	365	1,385	40,479
Maintaining Our Forests	–	–	–	24,960
Pine Ridge Reforestation Nursery Enhancement	3,100	828	1,373	1,373
Health				
Alberta Children's Provincial General Hospital	–	–	–	40,477
Applied Cancer Research	2,800	–	2,800	43,983
Applied Heart Disease Research	–	–	–	29,341

	Legislative Appropriation 1990–91	Investments made during		Investments at 31 Mar. 1991 at cost
		Three Mo. Ended 21 Mar. 1991	Twelve Mo. Ended 21 Mar. 1991	
Department/Project				
Tom Baker Cancer Centre and Special Services Facility	–	–	–	93,204
Public Works, Supply and Services				
Capital City Recreation Park	800	385	485	44,008
Fish Creek Provincial Park (Land)	–	–	–	27,107
Walter C. Mackenzie Health Sciences Centre	–	–	–	391,073
Recreation and Parks				
Fish Creek Provincial Park (Development)	–	–	–	16,859
Kananaskis Country Recreation (Development)	–	–	–	224,728
Municipal Recreation Tourism Areas	2,825	750	2,370	13,185
Urban Parks Development	3,150	2,231	3,143	90,718
Technology, Research & Telecommunications				
Alberta Heritage Foundation for Medical Research Endowment Fund	–	–	–	300,000
Electronic Test Centre	–	–	–	6,175
Individual Line Service	66,725	91	66,454	217,842
Microchip Design & Fabrication Facilities	–	–	–	7,750
Transportation and Utilities				
Airport Terminal Buildings	–	–	–	16,359
	$158,978	28,934	150,889	$3,197,338

economic diversification. An interpretation of the Mansell and Percy study is that Alberta relied too heavily on the diversification economic strategy. Thus expectations of the impact of the Alberta Heritage Fund may have been unrealistically high. Nonetheless, it is important to evaluate how effectively the Alberta Heritage Fund has contributed to economic sustainability in the province.

Division-by-Division Evaluations
The Canada Investment Division (CID) was established because the Alberta Government wanted its Alberta Heritage Fund to have a Canadian dimension. Most loans were to poorer provinces and at concessionary interest rates. From a high of $1.9 billion, the loans are being liquidated as they mature. It is unlikely that any new CID loans will be made, so CID will become empty. CID was not based on any *Alberta* economic purpose, so

should be evaluated accordingly. However, the concessionary interest rates "shadow" is that Alberta Heritage Fund revenues were lower than market values. Presumably the revenue gap could have been used for other purposes, including economic diversification.

The Alberta Investment Division (AID) should have been a primary policy instrument for economic development. From this perspective, AID management has resulted in *poor* performance. As noted earlier, only a handful of the AID investments were of an economic development character; the $1.6 billion of such investment represents only 20–25 percent of the Division over the last decade. AID monies have predominantly gone to finance Crown corporations, with no opportunity to reap capital gains. Thus AID has had "downside" risk exposure but no "upside" gains potential. These transactions have been insulated from market forces, with dubious results for recipient entities as well as for the Alberta Heritage Fund itself. Private placement fees and commissions savings should have translated into case savings for microeconomic uses by individuals and companies in Alberta. A portion of the savings may have gone into economic development investments.

The Capital Projects Division (CPD) is a major instrument for economic development. Apart from the venture capital item (Vencap), no financial return is appropriate to CPD policy. Via economic infrastructure and human capital undertakings, CPD has *good* economic development performance. As noted earlier, and enumerated in Table 2, the predominant use of CPD has been for economic development activities. The remaining one-third of CPD efforts have been for "social dividend" purposes; this is consistent with the Alberta Heritage Fund legislative mandate.

There have been Commercial (CMID) and Energy (EID) Investment Divisions since 1980. The economic impact of these divisions has been virtually zero, thus the economic development performance is *poor*. If an endowment-policy* approach had been taken for Alberta Heritage Fund, the CID would have been pivotal instead of token in importance. The primary CMID/EID evaluation is that of lost opportunity. From any perspective CMID should be much, much larger. Building on an Alberta strength of hydrocarbon resources supply, and noting that Canada is not energy *self-sufficient*, EID could have been a vital cog in a wheel of AHF impact on Alberta economic development. Instead, EID is empty.

As revealed by Table 1, the residual has been very large c ver the years, even after the 1979 transfers. The cash management function is very

---

* Endowment fiancial management assigns top priority to maintaining purchasing power of a capital base and secondary emphasis to longer-term growth; about 5 percent is left for annual spending.

important, but does not contribute to economic development on behalf of Alberta Heritage Fund. Over the last five years, about one-quarter of Alberta Heritage Fund financial assets has been held in this residual. For the last decade, the provincial government budget has taken all the Alberta Heritage Fund revenue. As any portfolio manager knows, current revenue can be enhanced, but at some longer-term yield sacrifice. The foregoing reflects a shift in policy from "strengthen and diversify economy" to "rainy day revenue source."

Conclusion

The background and rationale for the Alberta Heritage Fund has been outlined in detail. The data composition of the Alberta Heritage Fund has been presented. The Fund could be evaluated from several perspectives, including those of Canadian unity impact and resources endowment management. Economic development impact is the concluding focus of this paper.

There is a need for economic restructuring in Alberta—from prosperous and unstable to the economic sustainability of prosperity with stability. Economic restructuring requires capital, with concurrent risks. As a source of capital, the Alberta Heritage Fund has potential to meet capital needs in three major ways. Economic infrastructure is costly but vital to economic development. Human capital can be imported, but a preferable policy is to make jurisdictional improvements in educational and training facilities and programs. Each of these ways is costly, both in initial expenditure outlays and future operating costs.

The third way of the Alberta Heritage Fund capital deployment potential is risk-taking. This type of economic development initiative is politically risky for governments; successes tend to be ignored, while risk-attendant failures receive strong political and media focus. There are both financial and political risks.

The Alberta Heritage Fund size is modest. By contrast, two sets of perceptions resulted in difficulties during the 1980s. The Alberta Heritage Fund's existence resulted in Alberta-bashing by some others in Canada; thus the National Energy Program was easier (politically) to impose, and hardened Alberta attitudes that persist to this day. A misperception of the Alberta Heritage Fund's size led Albertans to hold falsely high expectations of how the Fund could "buy solutions" to economic and other problems. Yet, given its modest size, it is important to evaluate the economic development effectiveness of the Alberta Heritage Fund's policy and management.

Each Alberta Heritage Fund division has been assessed. Only the Capital Projects Division (CPD) gets high marks; its contribution to economic development is one primarily to economic infrastructure and human capital instruments of improvements. In addition, CPD holds a venture capital item of $200 million. However, it is to be noted that CPD cannot exceed 20 percent of the Alberta Heritage Fund.

What about the other 80 percent? As noted earlier, by legislative intent and policy design CID is not applicable to the Alberta economic development issue. A similar comment could be made about the "Cash and Marketable Securities" residual category, except it is questionable why there are such large holdings in this form.

Substantial economic development potential could be expected of the Alberta Investment Division (AID), Commercial Investment Division (CMID) and Energy Investment Division (EID).CMID and EID have been virtually unused, so the evaluation of each is poor. Up to now, the potential of these two divisions has been lost.

AID performance has been poor for different reasons. The AID holdings always have been very large. Little economic development use has been made of the division. Even the Syncrude project, while fully appropriate to Alberta economic development, came about as project salvage (with cost escalations and the loss of an original megaproject partner) rather than by economic policy initiative. The predominant AID role has been as in-house banker for Alberta Crown corporations.

Despite the strong and positive impact of CPD, the *overall* Alberta Heritage Fund economic performance has been *weak*. Opportunities have been lost regarding the AID, CMID and EID windows for improvements in economic sustainability. A parliamentary governance point is in order: the Alberta Heritage Fund division requiring legislative accountability (CPD) gets high marks, while the Alberta Heritage Fund divisions managed by the bureaucracy performed poorly. For years disparate groups (business, labour, academics) have urged an Alberta Heritage Fund policy review, and advised the Alberta Government to have the Alberta Heritage Fund managed by an arms-length commission or board with open accountability to the public. Today this seems to be needed more than ever.

References

Alberta. *Heritage Fund Reports*, quarterly and annual 1976/77—1990/91. Edmonton: Alberta Treasury.

──────. 1984. *Proposals For An Industrial And Science Strategy For Albertans, 1985 to 1990*. Edmonton.

──────. 1992. *Budget*. Edmonton: Alberta Treasury.

Boothe, Paul, ed. 1992. *Alberta and the Economics Of Constitutional Change*. Edmonton: University of Alberta, Western Centre for Economic Research, Western Studies in Economic Policy #3.

Canada. 1985. *Report of the Royal Commission on the Economic Union and Development Prospects For Canada* ("Macdonald Commission Report"). Ottawa: Ministry of Supply and Services.

Economic Council of Canada. 1984. *Western Transition*. Ottawa.

Macdonald Commission [Report]. *See* Canada 1985.

Mansell, Robert L., and Michael B. Percy. 1990. *Strength in Adversity: A Study Of The Alberta Economy*. Edmonton: University of Alberta, Western Centre for Economic Research, Western Studies in Economic Policy #1.

Mumey, Glen. 1992. *The Alberta Heritage Fund in 1991*. Edmonton: University of Alberta, Western Centre for Economic Research, Information Bulletin #7.

Warrack, Allan A. 1985. The Alberta Heritage Fund: A Force For Canadian Unity? Paper presented to the Canadian Studies Conference, University of Edinburgh, Scotland, April.

──────. 1992. Managing Megaproject Analysis and Decision Making. Paper presented to the Western Regional Science Association, Tahoe, California. February.

PIERRE MOHNEN AND THIJS TEN RAA

How Much Could Canada Gain from Free Trade?

In the current debates about trade liberalization, whether in the current Uruguay Round of the General Agreement Of Tariffs and Trade (GATT) talks or the negotiations leading to the North American Free Trade Agreement (NAFTA), free trade arguments collide with protectionist arguments, leaving the non-specialist quite perplexed (*see* the excellent discussion of protectionism in Bhagwati 1988).

Our intention in this paper is to provide a list of the benefits in order of magnitude Canada could reap from free trade, and at the same time to pinpoint the areas in which Canada would have to specialize in such a free trade world order.

Theoretical Background to the Free Trade Debate

Traditional economic theory says that each country should specialize in the products where it has a comparative advantage and then exchange those products against other products in which some other country has a competitive edge. In so doing everybody would be better off by sharing each other's strengths.

To explain the notion of comparative advantage, take two countries, Canada and Israel, and two products, cigarettes and oranges. Suppose, for the sake of argument, that the two products require only labour as a factor of production. Canada can produce four units of cigarettes or two units of oranges per hour; Israel can produce six units of cigarettes or twelve units of oranges per hour. Notice that Israel is more efficient in both lines of production; it has an absolute advantage in both commodities. However, if Canada shifted one hour of labour from the production of oranges to that of cigarettes, it would reduce the output of oranges by two units and increase the output of cigarettes by four units. Conversely, if Israel shifted half an hour from cigarettes to oranges, it would increase its output of oranges by six units and reduce its output of cigarettes by three units. Hence if Canada specialized a bit more in cigarettes and Israel a bit more in oranges, both countries could, to their mutual benefit, raise the production of oranges by four units and that of cigarettes by one unit. So Canada is said to have a comparative advantage in producing cigarettes and Israel a comparative advantage in producing oranges.

In terms of real prices or opportunity cost, one unit of oranges sells for two units of cigarettes in Canada and for half a unit of cigarettes in Israel. Hence the price of oranges in terms of cigarettes is lower in Israel; conversely the price of cigarettes in terms of oranges is lower in Canada. Thus the location of comparative advantage can be revealed by the domestic prices in this simple example with only one input. Of course, for both countries to gain from specializing and trading with each other, the trading price (the so-called terms of trade) has to lie in between the two domestic prices.

There can be several sources of comparative advantage. The domestic prices can differ because of differences in technology (the Ricardian theory), differences in factor endowments (the Hecksher-Ohlin theory) and differences in taste. The taste-endowment-technology trio constitutes the classical foundation of comparative advantage and…the consequent benefits from free trade.

The new theory of international trade emphasizes the notions of returns to scale, imperfect competition, product differentiation and strategic behaviour. Differences in domestic prices, and hence incentives to trade, can be due to economies of scale, be they internal to the firm (i.e., related to its size) or external to the firm (such as economies of proximity), to differences in market structure (more monopoly power and hence higher prices in one country than in the other one), to differences in quality (product differentiation), to government intervention in the form of taxes, tariffs, subsidies or to strategic aspects such as dumping (i.e., exporting abroad at prices that lie below marginal cost) or research and development (which can alter the direction of comparative advantage in the long run). Some of these differences, notably in market structure, are related to the fundamentals of the economy—endowments, technology and preferences—in other branches of the economic literature.

The Model

Our analysis concentrates on the traditional sources of comparative advantage directly, i.e., those that a country derives from its endowments, its preferences and its technology as compared to the rest of the world.

We take the Canadian economy as it was in 1980, dividing it up into 29 sectors and 92 commodities and recognizing three primary inputs (labour, capital and the prevailing deficit in the balance of trade). We exploit the rich information contained in the input-output tables of the Canadian economy, and in particular we pay explicit attention to the interindustry flows of goods and services. Each sector can be active in the production of various commodities. Hence, contrary to the usual input-output analysis, we do not assimilate sectors with commodities, although at our level of aggregation there is a correspondence between the two (Table 1). Commodities are

Table 1
Sector and Commodity Aggregation

	29 sectors	50 sectors	92 commodities
1.	Agricultural and related services	1	1–3
2.	Fishing & trapping	2	5, 6
3.	Logging and forestry	3	4
4.	Mining, quarrying and oil wells	4–7	7–12, **13**
5.	Food	8	14–22
6.	Beverage	9	23, 24
7.	Tobacco products	10	25, 26
8.	Plastic products	12	29
9.	Rubber and leather products	11, 13	27, 28, 30
10.	Textile and clothing	14, 15	31–35
11.	Wood	16	36–38
12.	Furniture and fixtures	17	39
13.	Paper and allied products	18	40–42
14.	Printing, publishing and allied	19	43,**44**
15.	Primary metals	20	45–49
16.	Fabricated metal products	21	50–52
17.	Machinery	22	53, 54
18.	Transportation equipment	23	55–57
19.	Electrical and electronic products	24	58, 59
20.	Non-metallic mineral products	25	60, 61
21.	Refined petroleum and coal	26	62, 63
22.	Chemicals and chemical products	27	64–67
23.	Other manufacturing	28	68, 69
24.	Construction	29	**70–72**
25.	Transportation and communication	30–33	73–77
26.	Electric power and gas	34	78, **79**
27.	Wholesale and retail trade	35, 36	80, **81**
28.	Finance, insurance and real estate	37–40	82, 83
29.	Community, business, personnel serv.	41–50	84–87,**88**,89,90,**91**,92

Source: Statistics Canada. 1987, M-classification.
Note: Figures in bold represent non-tradables.

produced to satisfy the demand for intermediate inputs from the various sectors and to meet the domestic and foreign final demands. The technologies of production of the various commodities by the various sectors are explicitly given by the observed flows of outputs and purchases of inputs across sectors. The preferences are given by the observed commodity composition of domestic final demand (consumption plus investment) or, alternatively, by the commodity composition of domestic consumption or domestic investment. The endowments of the Canadian economy in the three primary inputs are given by the total labour force (measured in terms of yearly person-hours), the sum of the sectoral capital stocks available and the overall trade deficit in 1980.

The potential efficiency gain from free trade is measured by the percentage increase in domestic final demand that Canada could achieve by specializing in the production of certain commodities and allocating its inputs optimally across sectors. In doing so, the central planners would have to keep in mind that they cannot use more than Canada's available stocks of labour and capital (which are supposed to be perfectly mobile across sectors and immobile across national boundaries), that they cannot import more than allowed by the prevailing trade deficit (in a fixed-exchange-rate world, one could think of a constraint in the availability of foreign currencies) and that the production of each commodity has to be sufficient to meet the various demands for it. The variables the planners can influence to attain these objectives are the activity levels in each sector and the net exports of all tradable commodities. A formal presentation of the model is contained in the appendix, together with a brief description of the data sources.

The reader should notice that we perform a so-called activity analysis, that is, we allow for an expansion or a contraction of all activities in a given sector (e.g., a 10 percent increase of all commodity productions and purchases and of all primary input uses in a given sector) but exclude any output or factor substitutions. The advantage of this approach is that we do not have to make any particular assumptions regarding the technology of production of a certain commodity or in a given sector in order to construct an input-output coefficient matrix that circumvents negative technical coefficients. Moreover, we are not bound to have as many sectors as commodities. The reason is that we do not work with coefficients but directly with commodity flows.

The objective is to increase all domestic final demand components by the same percentage. To allow for alternative representations of preferences, we also perform the analysis by maximizing domestic final demand and keeping fixed the structure of domestic consumption or domestic investment. We make the assumption that Canada is a small, open economy, implying that it cannot manipulate the world prices. The assumption is probably not too severe overall for a country like Canada, although for particular commodities Canada might have some monopoly power on the world stage. As a consequence of this assumption, the world prices are exogenous—not affected by the solution of our problems. Whatever pattern of trade Canada decides to adopt, it will not affect the prices it faces on the world market. For simplicity, we assume the exchange rate between the Canadian dollar and all foreign currencies to be equal to one.

The model of this paper is similar to the one used in ten Raa and Mohnen (1994), with one major difference. There the objective was to maximize foreign earnings, domestic final demand being exogenous. Here the objective is more realistic, namely maximizing the amount of domestic final demand, making it endogenous by the same token. Since the new objective is domestic final demand, a balance of trade constraint has to be added to prevent the unrealistic solution of infinite imports in order to maximize today's well-being.

The approach we pursue combines the general equilibrium analysis of input-output models with the neoclassical feature of resource substitution. The substitution is the result of intersectoral shifts of labour and capital. The optimal increase in final demand that we obtain under free trade is due to the absence of any trade barrier but also to an optimal allocation of resources across sectors and to the fullest possible utilization of available resources within sectors. However, as we proved in ten Raa and Mohnen (1994), the 1980 Canadian economy cannot boost or maintain its net exports in all commodities simultaneously. This condition also holds in the present case. Hence, Canada is a truly open economy that cannot improve its efficiency without changing its prevailing trade structure.

Interpretation of the Results

The resolution of our model determines simultaneously the activity levels of each sector, the percentage increase in the objective function, the commodity net exports and the shadow prices of each constraint in the problem. The shadow prices of commodities and factor inputs would prevail under ideal conditions of perfect competition. In Table 2 we present the activity levels and in Table 3 the shadow prices under the three preference structures we consider. These three preference structures correspond to three scenarios. In each case we maximize domestic final

Table 2
Activity Levels in Three Alternative Free Trade Scenarios

Sector	Preference structure		
	domestic absorption	domestic consumption	domestic investment
1.	0.00	0.00	0.00
2.	0.00	0.00	0.00
3.	0.00	0.00	0.00
4.	5.80	5.67	2.93
5.	0.00	0.00	0.00
6.	0.00	0.00	0.00
7.	30.65	37.87	0.00
8.	0.00	0.00	0.00
9.	0.00	0.00	0.00
10.	0.00	0.00	0.00
11.	0.00	0.00	0.00
12.	0.00	0.00	0.00
13.	0.00	0.00	0.00
14.	1.45	1.51	1.25
15.	0.00	0.00	0.00
16.	0.00	0.00	0.00
17.	14.81	12.07	0.00
18.	0.00	0.00	0.00
19.	0.00	0.00	0.00
20.	0.00	0.00	0.00
21.	0.00	0.00	0.00
22.	0.00	0.00	0.00
23.	0.00	0.00	0.00
24.	1.60	1.62	2.79
25.	0.00	0.00	0.00
26.	1.10	1.13	1.96
27.	1.46	1.52	1.06
28.	1.47	1.53	5.73
29.	1.45	1.51	1.25

domestic absorption   1.47   1.09   0.80
(actual) (1.00)   (0.71)   (0.29)
Note: The actual sectoral activity levels = 1.

demand, but each time we operate under a different commodity composition of final demand. In the first scenario, we increase in the same proportion the domestic final demand for each commodity; in the second scenario,
we increase in the same proportion the domestic consumption for each
commodity, keeping the domestic investments at their prevailing levels; in
the third scenario, we increase the domestic investment for each commodity in the same proportion, keeping the domestic consumptions at their

prevailing levels. In Table 4 we report the optimal net exports generated by our model.

The numbers in Table 2 indicate the optimal activity levels in each sector and in the objective function for each of the three scenarios. Notice that the actual levels of sectoral activity correspond to a value of one, whereas for the objective function the actual level is one for the first scenario and 0.71 and 0.29 for the other two scenarios, corresponding respectively to the shares of consumption and investment in domestic final demand. By a theorem of linear programming, we know that there will be as many active sectors as binding constraints. Binding constraints are characterized by non-zero shadow prices in Table 3. In the first two scenarios, there are seven binding non-tradability constraints, reflecting the impossibility to satisfy the domestic (final and intermediate) demand for the non-tradables via imports. In the last scenario there are five non-tradability constraints. In all three cases the endowment constraints on the three primary inputs (labour, capital and the foreign trade balance) are binding. Hence, we have ten active sectors (including domestic absorption) in the first two scenarios and eight in the third scenario. The first two scenarios yield similar qualitative and quantitative results. As we shall see, those of the third scenario are somewhat different.

Table 3
Shadow Prices in Three Alternative Free Trade Scenarios

Non-tradable Commodity		Preference structure	
	domestic absorption	domestic consumption	domestic investment
13.	0.00	0.00	0.00
44.	1.48	1.20	1.77
70.[1]	0.00	0.00	3.05
72.	6.57	5.31	0.00
79.	11.10	8.98	15.83
81.	2.04	1.65	2.14
82.	0.42	0.34	0.00
88.	2.68	2.17	0.00
91.	0.00	0.00	0.00
92.	2.47	2.00	5.52
wage ($/hour)	1.53	1.24	1.28
rental rate	0.18	0.15	0.27
PPP[2]	1.04	0.84	0.97

[1] Commodity constraint 71, being perfectly collinear with commodity constraint 70, has been dropped.
[2] PPP=purchasing power parity, i.e. domestic price/foreign price.

In addition to the sectors producing non-tradables, mining, quarrying and oil wells (4), tobacco products (7) and machinery (17) are active in the first two scenarios. The same result was found in ten Raa and Mohnen (1994). Those sectors, in bold print, primarily produce the commodities in which Canada turns out to have a comparative advantage (see Table 4); in other words, those in which Canada would specialize in a free trade world and from which it would earn the foreign exchange needed to import all the other commodities it needs in order to maximize its objective function. For example, if Canada was maximizing its domestic final demand, it would increase its 1980 production of all commodities by six times in sector 4, by 30 times in sector 7 and by 15 times in sector 1. These figures are big. But remember, in a perfectly competitive world it would specialize in only a few tradable commodities and produce those for itself and for the rest of the world. Under the investment structure of preference, again sector 4, but now also sectors 26 (transportation and communication) and 28 (finance, insurance and real estate), display a much higher activity than the prevailing one. Sector 24 cannot be considered a sector of comparative advantage, since it only produces non-tradables. And, as will become clearer when we examine table 4, sectors 27 and 29 are also active mostly because of their non-tradable commodities. We notice that the number of sectors of specialization equals the number of primary inputs. Indeed, the economy will need three sectors to use up its labour, capital and allowed trade deficit. Since imports below the allowed deficit can increase final demand at no cost, the deficit will always reach its upper boundary.

In 1980, Canada could have increased by 47 percent the value of its domestic absorption in a free trade world. By comparing the value of the objective function under the three scenarios, we see that a lower efficiency is obtained by concentrating only on consumption (an increase of 38 percent in the value of domestic absorption) and a higher efficiency by concentrating only on investment (a comparable increase of 51 percent). Hence, of the two, the preference structure implicit in investment is more conducive to growth.

The numbers in Table 3 indicate the shadow prices of the relevant constraints under free trade. As can be shown from the so-called complementary slackness conditions of linear programming (*see* ten Raa and Mohnen 1994) on one hand, the shadow price of each constraint equilibrates the supply and demand corresponding to that constraint and, on the other hand, a sector will be active only when at the equilibrium shadow prices it breaks even. In other words, a shadow price indicates how much more the economy could consume and invest (in fixed ratios) and hence would be ready to pay to have one additional unit of the item under constraint. Non-tradables have to be produced at home and require resources to be put aside for their production. According to our model, in 1980 Canada would have paid $1.48 to have one additional unit of "services to mining," $6.57 for "repair construction," $11.10 for "other utilities" and so on. If there was no secondary production in the sectors producing those goods, these shadow prices would correspond to their unit cost of production.

The shadow price of the labour constraint reveals that one more hour of labour would only fetch a wage rate of $1.53 in the first scenario and even less in the other two. One dollar of capital would be worth a rental rate of 18 cents in the first scenario, but 27 cents in the last scenario. The shadow price of the balance of trade reflects the domestic price of one additional dollar of deficit. Since world market prices are exogenous, the domestic prices of all tradables must equal their world prices, converted in purchasing power parity. Since consumption and/or investment must increase in fixed ratios, additional consumption and/or investment implies additional production of non-tradables and hence diversion of resources from the production of tradables. Therefore the value of the tradables can differ from one. From the so-called dual constraints of linear programming, it can be shown that the weighted sum of all commodity prices equals one, the weights being the shares of each commodity in final demand (consumption or investment respectively). The shadow price of the balance of trade constraint can thus be interpreted as the purchasing power parity (PPP) of all tradable goods in Canada vis-à-vis the rest of the world; in other words, the average Canadian price over the average world price for those goods. If all commodities were tradable, domestic prices would have to match world prices for all commodities and the PPP would be equal to one. Our results indicate that the Canadian PPP in 1980 was higher for investment goods than for consumption goods.

In Table 4, we report the actual and optimal net exports by commodity under the first and the last scenarios only. The optimal net exports under the second scenario are very close to those under the first one and are therefore not reported. The commodities where optimal net exports exceed their actual level by a substantial margin are those in which Canada has a comparative advantage—those in which it would specialize under free trade given its endowment, technology and preferences as of 1980. They are indicated in bold print. Those are the tradable commodities produced by the sectors in bold print in Table 2 (the first scenario), the products of mining (7 to 12), tobacco (25, 26) and machinery (53, 54), and in the last

Table 4
Net Exports in Three Alternative Free Trade Scenarios
(millions of dollars)

Commodity	Actual net exports	Preference structure	
		domestic absorption	domestic investment
1. Grains	3764.2	654.3	1281.1
2. Live animals	169.0	-993.0	-653.8
3. Other agricultural products	-287.8	-11034.8	-2670.4
4. Forestry products	10.1	-210.0	-176.2
5. Fish landings	55.0	-61.3	-24.4
6. Hunting and trapping products	-3.2	-0.1	-0.1
7. Iron ores and concentrate	879.3	9150.4	4433.3
8. Other metal. ores and concentrates	-3014.7	28975.3	12209.6
9. Coal	-328.4	4064.9	1282.1
10. Crude mineral oils	-4974.2	55776.0	27997.0
11. Natural gas	3775.6	31904.4	15360.5
12. Non-metallic minerals	733.3	9364.6	4182.5
13. Services incidental to mining	0.0	10258.2	382.4
14. Meat products	292.5	-8577.9	-6316.9
15. Dairy products	73.8	-5035.0	-3533.0
16. Fish products	-320.3	-2200.2	-1487.6
17. Fruits and vegetables preparations	-401.6	-2855.5	-1957.0
18. Feeds	42.1	-426.5	-338.1
19. Flour, wheat, meal and other cereals	-29.7	-472.0	-368.7
20. Breakfast cereal and bakery products	4.7	-2715.1	-1936.3
21. Sugar	3.3	-390.7	-317.1
22. Misc. food products	-512.2	-4040.9	-2740.3
23. Soft drinks	-10.7	-1368.0	-961.3
24. Alcoholic beverages	22.8	-2876.1	-1855.7
25. Tobacco processed unmanufactured	26.0	2255.9	-139.7
26. Cigarettes and tobacco mfg.	-15.7	26406.7	-901.1
27. Tires and tubes	-170.0	-249.3	-242.3
28. Other rubber products	-199.0	-2862.2	-1315.9
29. Plastic fabricated products	-435.6	-2144.3	-2962.9
30. Leather and leather products	-449.0	-1677.1	-1092.0
31. Yarn and man-made fibres	-329.9	-56.6	-4.7
32. Fabrics	-781.7	-482.6	-337.4
33. Other textile products	-316.0	-2208.7	-2404.2
34. Hosiery and knitted wear	-347.7	-1870.5	-1294.0
35. Clothing and accessories	-456.1	-5588.2	-3679.6
36. Lumber and timber	3090.7	-1084.6	-1794.0
37. Veneer and plywood	109.6	-674.5	-1125.3
38. Other wood fabricated materials	367.7	-2457.7	-4136.4
39. Furniture and fixtures	-90.5	-3471.3	-3449.8
40. Pulp	3570.9	138.9	122.3
41. Newsprint and other paper stock	3975.9	-2378.1	-1741.8
42. Paper products	-328.4	-6442.7	-2765.1
43. Printing and publishing	-583.5	-761.4	-412.4

44.	Advertising, print media	0.0	0.0	0.0
45.	Iron and steel products	417.0	-13621.0	-4336.6
46.	Aluminum products	-424.4	-3240.1	-1502.7
47.	Copper and copper alloy products	903.4	-503.7	146.0
48.	Nickel products	1038.9	-460.6	-725.1
49.	Other non-ferrous metal products	999.3	232.2	688.3
50.	Boilers, tanks and plates	-24.1	-989.7	-1547.1
51.	Fabricated structural metal products	147.6	-3354.2	-5180.1
52.	Other metal fabricated products	-1678.0	-8131.7	-10486.2
53.	Agricultural machinery	-1208.5	**13692.0**	-6124.0
54.	Other industrial machinery	-5535.0	**31548.1**	-24791.7
55.	Motor vehicles	923.9	-11475.5	-15765.6
56.	Motor vehicle parts	-3795.4	-3527.0	-605.2
57.	Other transport equipment	89.6	-4233.3	-6745.4
58.	Appliances and receivers, household	-1465.9	-2176.4	-3332.9
59.	Other electrical products	-1692.7	-8158.7	-15864.3
60.	Cement and concrete products	94.7	-2537.5	-4205.0
61.	Other non-metallic mineral products	-637.9	-3120.4	-3910.2
62.	Gasoline and fuel oil	326.2	-13529.1	-10959.7
63.	Other petroleum and coal products	1271.0	5106.8	1683.4
64.	Industrial chemicals	-2038.5	-4047.4	-2878.8
65.	Fertilizers	-64.1	4386.1	1929.7
66.	Pharmaceuticals	-300.5	-1643.3	-1217.0
67.	Other chemical products	-1157.9	-5654.4	-4637.7
68.	Scientific equipment	-1806.6	-3965.9	-4111.5
69.	Other manufactured products	-295.7	-3971.4	-3343.3
70.	Residential construction	0.0	1860.6	0.0
71.	Non-residential construction	0.0	3785.2	148.6
72.	Repair construction	0.0	0.0	2384.2
73.	Pipeline transportation	153.6	-865.0	-710.9
74.	Transportation and storage	610.2	-27321.5	-22233.5
75.	Radio and television broadcasting	-10.1	-1991.1	-1626.4
76.	Telephone and telegraph	-48.7	-8324.5	-8785.7
77.	Postal services	14.8	-1811.1	-2047.2
78.	Electric power	807.5	-1080.7	**7711.7**
79.	Other utilities	0.0	0.0	0.0
80.	Wholesale margins	2170.6	3093.0	-7010.8
81.	Retail margins	0.0	0.0	0.0
82.	Imputed rent owner occupied dwellings	0.0	0.0	93610.2
83.	Other finance, ins., real estate	-753.9	-20307.2	**143124.1**
84.	Business services	-1205.1	-3015.1	-10978.0
85.	Education services	32.6	34.0	229.8
86.	Health services	-16.5	-135.6	1494.0
87.	Amusement and recreation services	-150.3	22.0	621.9
88.	Accommodation and food services	0.0	0.0	2877.3
89.	Other personal and misc. services	-90.9	2424.8	5269.0
90.	Transportation margins	3413.0	7223.6	6625.6
91.	Supplies for office, lab. and cafeteria	0.0	808.5	1203.1
92.	Travel, advertising and promotion	0.0	0.0	0.0

Note: Figures in bold print locate comparative advantages.

scenario, the commodities of the mining industry (7 to 12); electric power (78); and finance, insurance and real estate (83). The other commodities with net exports in excess of actual exports are either non-tradables or by-products of non-tradables. For all other commodities either there is a slight net export (lower than actual) or a substantially larger trade deficit than observed in 1980. Because of the assumed absence of output substitution, some non-tradable commodities (e.g., commodity 13) get produced beyond demand. For those commodities there is a slack and hence a zero shadow price (see table 3). In 1980, Canada was far away from its optimal trade pattern, which explains the magnitude of potential efficiency it could achieve. Of course, in actuality there are many constraints we have not incorporated in our analysis and, moreover, decisions are taken at an individual level and not by a central planning bureau.

Conclusion

New trade theorists can come up with strong arguments for protectionism, to give the domestic industry a head-start advantage or increase it to enable it to compete with economies of scale on the world stage (*see* Krugman 1987). But the same features emphasized by the new trade theory (imperfect competition, economies of scale and strategic behaviour) can also be used to make a strong case for free trade. The extension of the market will allow firms to specialize within sectors and reap economies of scale and the increased competition from foreign producers will decrease the producers' monopoly power and push prices down.

In this paper, we abstract from these modern arguments for free trade, without denying their pertinence. Our view is simply that the basic elements of taste, endowment and technology are important on their own and should not be swept under the carpet. While we recognize that certain hypotheses we have made regarding technology and market structure are unrealistic, we want to point out that some of these hypotheses are likely to yield conservative estimates of the gains from free trade. The absence of economies of scale, of product heterogeneity, of factor and output substitution and of international factor mobility only add more rigidity to the system, which would otherwise be able to yield even bigger efficiency gains. True, as Harris and Cox (1984) have shown for the Canadian economy, the existence of returns to scale and monopoly power would produce a different picture of specialization. Nevertheless, we found it worthwhile to find out what specialization would occur in Canada in a world of perfect competition, where proper account is taken of the demand for intermediate inputs and the existence of secondary products.

We have conducted an intersectoral, general equilibrium, open economy analysis of the benefits from free trade and the identification of Canadian comparative advantage. Similar studies have been conducted by Williams (1978) and ten Raa and Mohnen (1994). In contrast to Williams (1978), we do not casually classify commodities as import–competing or exportable, but rather let the analysis reveal their identity. Compared to our previous study, we here allow the level of consumption to be endogenous.

We conclude that under conditions of perfect competition and on the basis of its endowments, its technology and the preferences revealed by its domestic final demand or consumption structure, in 1980 Canada had a comparative advantage in mining, quarrying and oil wells, in tobacco and in machinery. Under the preferences implicit in its investment structure, the comparative advantage would have been in mining, electric power and finance, insurance and real estate. In free trade, it could have increased its total final demand by 46 percent. This estimate of the gains from free trade is bigger than those generally reported in the literature. Of course, it only pertains to the year 1980. It would be interesting to examine how much the results would differ over time. *A priori*, we do not believe that 1980 was such an exceptional year in terms of production or final demand structure, nor that the endowments, the preferences and the technology change rapidly over time.

Appendix

A. The Formal Model

Formally, the basic model underlying our analysis is the following linear problem:

$$\max_{t,s} \quad e'ft \tag{A1}$$

$$\text{s.t.} \quad (V'_{NT} - U_{NT})s \geq tf_{NT} \tag{A2}$$

$$L's \leq N \tag{A3}$$

$$K'\hat{c}s \leq K'e \tag{A4}$$

$$\pi'[(V'_T - U_T)s - tf_T] \geq BT \tag{A5}$$

$$s \geq 0 \tag{A6}$$

where

U = (mnx) use table, m being the number of commodities and n the number of industries, showing the commodity purchases by the various sectors;

V = (nxm) make table, showing the commodity composition of sectoral production; hence $(V'-U)$ represents the net output table;

f = (mx1) vector of domestic final demand;

e = unity vector of appropriate dimension;

t = scalar;

s = (nx1) scale or activity vector;

L = (nx1) vector of sectoral labour employment;

K = (nx1) vector of sectoral capital stocks;

N = total labour force;

$\hat{c}$ = (nxn) diagonal matrix of capacity utilizations;

π = vector of world prices of tradable commodities;

BT = total balance of trade with the rest of the world;

T (NT) = index denoting tradable (non-tradable) commodities. A vector or a matrix indexed T (NT) is restricted in its line dimension to the tradable (non-tradable) commodities.

The objective function in this basic model is the maximization of total domestic final demand. Notice that t=1 corresponds to the observed level of domestic absorption. Notice also that the objective is just a matter of increasing the overall level of domestic final demand, keeping its commodity composition constant. The first set of inequality restrictions (A2) states that, for each non-tradable commodity, production has to be sufficient to meet domestic intermediate and final demand. Constraints (A3) and (A4)state that the sum of all sectoral employments (capital stocks) cannot exceed the total labour force (capital stock). Notice that all the inputs, labour, capital and intermediate input commodities, are homogeneous and perfectly mobile across sectors. The (A5) constraint states that the sum, over all tradable commodities, of their trade balances must exceed a certain minimum, in this case the observed total trade balance. This last constraint implies a ceiling to total net imports.

When the objective is to maximize domestic final demand by keeping fixed the structure of domestic consumption (domestic investment), then f in the above model represents the vector of consumption (investment) divided by the share of domestic consumption (investment) in domestic final demand and t becomes t times that same share. The observed level of domestic final demand now corresponds to t = the observed share of consumption (investment). The remainder of domestic absorption is exogenously added to the RHS of (A2) and the total value of its tradables at world prices to the RHS of (A5).

B.   The Data

We studied the Canadian economy of 1980. The use, make and final demand tables are directly taken from Statistics Canada (1987). For the sources and constructions of the sectoral labour flows, the total labour force, the sectoral capital stocks and capital utilization rates, we refer to ten Raa and Mohnen (1991; 1994). All data are expressed in millions of 1980 Canadian dollars or in thousands of person-hours. The economy is disaggregated into 92 commodities and 29 sectors using the concordance contained in table 1. We are constrained to a 29 sectoral classification by the unavailability of sectoral capital stocks at a finer level of disaggregation. Net exports are given by the sum of columns 26 to 28 of the final demand table of Statistics Canada's input-output tables. Domestic investment is the sum of columns 14 to 23 of the same table. Domestic consumption is measured as the difference between the column total of final demand (column 29) and the sum of domestic investment and net exports. Those commodities that display no net exports are considered non-tradables.

ity composition constant. The first set of inequality restrictions (A2) states that, for each non-tradable commodity, production has to be sufficient to

An FCAR fellowship for the first author and a Royal Netherlands Academy of Sciences senior fellowship for the second author are gratefully acknowledged. This paper grew out of constructive comments received at various conference presentations. The authors also wish to thank Sally Zerker and an anonymous referee for helpful comments.

References

Bhagwati, J. 1988. *Protectionism*. Cambridge, Mass.: MIT Press.

Harris, R., and E. Cox. 1984. *Trade, Industrial Policy and Canadian Manufacturing*. Toronto: University of Toronto Press.

Krugman, P. 1987. Is Free Trade Passé? *The Journal of Economic Perspectives* (2):131–44.

Markusen, J.R., and J.R. Melvin. 1984. *The Theory of International Trade and its Canadian Applications*. Toronto: Butterworths.

Statistics Canada. 1987. *System of National Accounts—The Input-Output Structure of the Canadian Economy 1961–1981*. Ottawa: Minister of Supply and Services.

ten Raa, T., and P. Mohnen. 1991. Domestic Efficiency and Bilateral Trade Gains, with an Application to Canada and Europe. Cahier de recherche 70 du CERPE. Université de Québec à Montréal.

———. 1994. Neoclassical Input-output Analysis. *Regional Science and Urban Economics* 24(Feb.):135–58.

Williams, J.R. 1978. *The Canadian-United States Tariff and Canadian Industry: A Multisectoral Analysis*. Toronto: University of Toronto Press.

PART III
ESSAYS IN CANADIAN ENVIRONMENT

DAVID MORLEY

Introduction

The three papers that constitute this section provide a significant beginning. As Simon Berkowicz points out in the first of the three papers, within
the framework of Canadian Studies little attention has been paid to the
environment. This is not surprising, given the traditional disciplinary and
humanities focus of so much of the work included under this area heading.
Environmental Studies is, by definition, transdisciplinary. It seeks to
address the holistic quality of environment issues. However, the emergence of new perspectives on Canadian Studies (significantly encouraged
by the work of the Israel Association for Canadian Studies), which focus on
the opportunities provided for integrated and comparative approaches to
critical issues, suggests that the connection with Environmental Studies is
a natural and relevant stage in this process.

As part of its evolution, Canadian Studies has to struggle to distinguish
between the straightforward study of Canadian issues and settings and
studies of the particular quality of "Canadianness" that attends such
settings. Similarly, Environmental Studies has to distinguish between the
study of particular environments and the issues associated with them and
approaching an issue through studying and learning environmentally.
The bringing together of these two fields—Canadian Studies and Environmental Studies—suggests a particularly useful area for exploration. The
integrated perspective of Canadian Studies provides a context for examining the way in which environmental issues are being addressed in Canada.
Are there specific qualities of the ways in which environmental issues are
defined and addressed in Canada? In what ways does the combination of
critical environmental issues relevant to Canada make particular demands
on researchers, public institutions, the environmental movement, Cana-

dian business enterprises and so on? Topics such as the nature of environmental politics in Canada, the nature and effectiveness of environmental legislation in various jurisdictions and the Canadian response to issues like global warming could all be legitimate areas of Canadian Studies activity in the environmental field.

The three papers that make up this section of the book demonstrate an initial stage in the incorporation of environmental work into Canadian Studies. Each paper focuses on environmental issues in the Canadian context. To a lesser degree they also explore the particularly Canadian nature of the situation under discussion.

Simon Berkowicz's paper on the "Implications of Climatic Change for Canada" does go beyond the direct consideration of the effects of climatic change on Canada. He recognizes that the potential effects of global change related to increases in atmospheric CO_2 "are far-reaching and go beyond the bounds of purely environmental issues." This implies that the implications are a function of the interaction between the environmental change forces and Canadian society. The outcomes of such questioning will extend a physical science perspective of Canadian environments into the study of the unique Canadian responses and potential futures they are likely to generate. This is a useful direction for a Canadian Studies approach to the environment. Berkowicz examines the impact of climatic change on water, agriculture, forests, fishing, energy, transportation and tourism. His concern with the particular institutional responses to these situations provides an initial basis for assessing the Canadian environmental milieu. Interesting points raised are the way in which the Royal Society of Canada's Global Change program has established a multidisciplinary research network aimed at communicating results to policy makers, the need for improved water management, the possibility of long-distance water diversions from Canada to the United States (there appears to be a distinct possibility that this is allowed under the recently signed North America Free Trade Agreement—NAFTA) and the massive costs of the construction of coastal barriers as a result of predicted sea-level rises (this in an era of greatly reduced government spending).

The main point here seems to be that from an environmental science point of view the main issues likely to be raised are concerned with improving the scientific basis for climate-warming scenarios for Canada. For example, Lawford in his paper on "Land Surface Climate Processes and Canada's Water Resources" in this section indicates that the warming process could "also produce feedback effects to the atmosphere that may either accelerate or slow climatic change." His conclusions are therefore that since "land surface climate processes are not…effectively considered in global climate models…it is appropriate for Canada to place an emphasis on research related to the linkages between…biomes and the atmosphere." This is undoubtedly a valid conclusion. However, with regard to evolving Canadian Studies' perspectives of the environment, Berkowicz's conclusions seem very pertinent—the relevance of global-warming scenarios, "given the uncertainty of some of the predictions," is translated into such questions as: "What policies have to be implemented? How will the larger and wealthier provinces react?" Such questions link the outcomes of the continuing scientific research (from Canada and elsewhere) with the social, political and institutional capacities within the Canadian setting. The implication is that this is potentially a field of major interest for Canadian Studies. Indeed, perhaps Canadian Studies can be seen as a particularly useful framework for these questions to be considered in an integrated way among scientists, social scientists, politicians, environmental activists, the business community and other key stakeholders in the process of developing policy and implementation strategies in this critical, but highly uncertain area.

In this context, both Berkowicz and Lawford's papers provide considerable material for Canadian Studies researchers interested in the impact of environmental changes on Canadian society. Both authors focus on the impacts of global warming and their conclusions on water supplies, increased risks of prairie droughts, soil salinization, agriculture and forest cover show that in all cases it is implicit that fundamental questions be raised regarding how to respond to these possible levels of change. Issues such as the regional and international (U.S.–Canada) politics, the drought-proofing of the Canadian prairies, changing farming practices in relation to groundwater resources, the implementation of modern environmental monitoring programs and the use of the federal government's Green Plan underline the need for the kind of integrating research suggested by a Canadian Studies approach to the environment.

Atkinson's paper on "Environmental Impact Assessment in Canada" contributes a careful review of the emergence of environmental impact assessment (EIA) and an evaluation of its application in different parts of the country. The generally "weak" outcomes of much EIA application raise many important questions regarding the long-term potential contribution of this approach to the impact of development on the natural environment in the Canadian political and institutional setting. Here is a major area for the extensive application of integrated and comparative Canadian Studies approaches to environmental issues.

Atkinson's final page begins to address these issues, quoting Holling's approach to "ecology as 'a science of surprises' in a world where the natural state is one of non-equilibrium with an emphasis on uncertainty, surprise, and discontinuities." Later on the same page the author suggests that baseline scientific data and the increased understanding of natural systems will be the critical determinants of the future role of EIA. However, if we accept Holling's prescient statement of the currently popular chaos-theory view of change, then scientific achievement alone will not be enough. Institutions and individuals will have to learn what is occurring at the same pace as the scientists. They will link that knowledge to the realities and opportunities of current societal attitudes. This seems to be the "stuff" of the work of Canadian Studies in this field. Which is just what Atkinson says in his last lines—"we must be prepared for surprises...[and have to]...rely on an interdisciplinary approach, predicting and preparing for a range of outcomes, based on a knowledge of local [Canadian] priorities, and not divorced from day-to-day issues."

SIMON M. BERKOWICZ

Implications of Climatic Change for Canada: An Overview

A perusal of the contents of Canadian Studies journals published in Canada shows that almost all of the contributors have focused on economic, human, cultural and social aspects with little attention paid to the environment. For example, since its inception in 1966, the *Journal of Canadian Studies* has published only a handful of articles on Canada's physical environment (Gillis 1986; Payne and Graham 1987; van West 1989). The *International Journal of Canadian Studies*, established in 1990, has done somewhat better (Rees 1991; Hamley 1991).

One topic that has not been covered in Canadian Studies journals is that of global climate change. As a result of increased atmospheric CO_2 levels, mean global temperatures may increase by 1.5-4.5°C by the year 2050 (Houghton et al. 1990; IGBP 1990). The potential effects upon Canada are far-reaching and go beyond the bounds of purely environmental issues. Changes to Canada's economy will be felt immediately by Canadian society. Figure 1 provides a general regional breakdown of some of the main impacts projected for Canada, as summarized by Phillips (1990, 153). In terms of ecological changes, Rizzo (1988) and Rizzo and Wiken (1992) have assessed Canada's sensitivity to climate change (Figure 2). Their climate change models predicted major shifts northwards in ecological boundaries, and included the development of a semi-desert region in the most southwestern part of the Prairie provinces.

Caution, of course, must be maintained with regard to climate change forecasts. The most recent publication put out by the prestigious Intergovernmental Panel on Climate Change states that despite a rise in global surface air temperature of 0.3-0.6°C over the past 100 years, "the size of this warming is broadly consistent with predictions of climate models, but it is

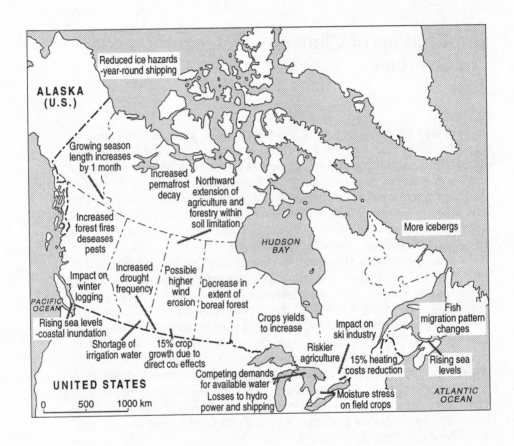

Figure 1: Potential impacts for a changed climate across Canada

After:Phillips 1990

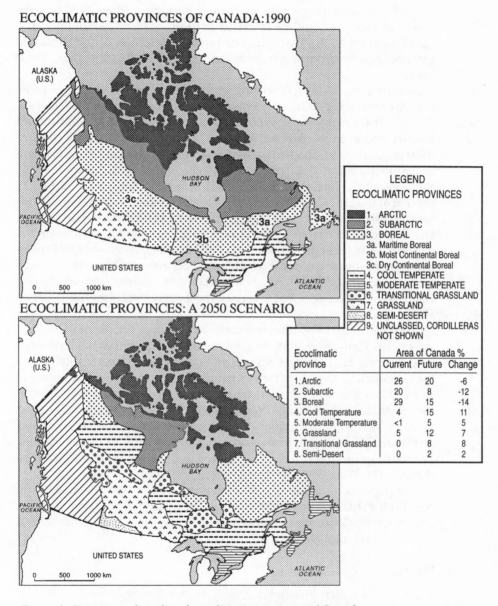

Figure 2: Existing and predicted ecoclimatic provinces of Canada

After: Rizzo 1988

also of the same magnitude as natural climatic variability. Thus the observed increase could be largely due to this natural variability." The Panel went on to say that "the unequivocal detection of the enhanced greenhouse effect from observations is not likely for a decade or more"(IPCC 1992).

Nevertheless, those specializing in Canadian Studies should become familiar with the published literature and forecasts for North America. Changes that can influence water resources and water use, agriculture and forestry and even recreational activities, can combine to exert a tremendous impact upon Canadian society, economy and environment; this will undoubtedly affect both policy and decision-makers (Changnon 1987; Williams 1989; Henderson-Sellers 1991). One must consider that over 21 percent of the 1981 Canadian labour force (1.44 million) worked in agriculture, forestry and related industries (Canada 1989). The importance attached to climate change by the American government is reflected in the request of the American Congress in 1987 that the Environmental Protection Agency investigate what possible impacts the greenhouse effect could have on the United States. As a result, a comprehensive document of over 400 pages was prepared that covered almost every facet (Smith and Tirpak 1989).

Since the mid-1980s, climate change has become a topic of increasing interest in Canada at both the university and government level. The Atmospheric Environment Service of Environment Canada established the Canadian Climate Program focusing on climate change and potential impacts for Canada. In addition, the Royal Society of Canada (RSC) initiated the Canadian Global Change Program (RSC 1992). The program is designed to serve as a multidisciplinary network for coordinating research and communicating results, ideas and recommendations to policy-makers. Canadian geographers have also commenced studies on climate change (Kemp 1991; Woo 1991; 1992).

This paper summarizes some of the work that has been carried out to date for Canada and highlights many of the predicted positive and negative outcomes. Due to the wide variety of material, selected topics reflecting the main issues are presented below.

Water

Much of Canadian economic activity is dependent on water. Marine transport depends on water levels, hydroelectric power is dependent on streamflow, agriculture is dependent on soil moisture and irrigation, industries need water and water must be provided for human consumption. The implications of climate change for Canada's water resources are far-reaching (Lewis 1989). In general it is believed that winter rainfall will increase as a whole across Canada, but that the snow season will be shorter. Spring snowmelt and runoff will occur earlier and be reduced. Rainfall during the growing season will stay almost the same or be reduced in southern Canada. This could have profound effects on Canadian lakes, streams and rivers.

Several hydrological variables will be affected by climatic change.

1. Average annual runoff
This variable is important to the water balance of a watershed. A reduction in runoff can be especially severe in semi–arid areas. A Colorado River basin study calculated that a 2°C increase in annual mean temperature combined with a + or -10 percent change in annual precipitation would reduce annual runoff by 30 percent (Williams 1989).

2. Runoff variability
The frequency of wet and dry years affects soil moisture, drought and flood planning.

3. Seasonal runoff
Some regions rely upon runoff from snowmelt. A change in precipitation from snow to rain could affect the amount of runoff received during the spring.

The Prairie region is already prone to drought (Jones 1990), and an increase in both the frequency of drought and dust storms is forecast (Wheaton 1990; Wheaton and Chakravarti 1990). There is also concern that climate change could cause heavy snowfalls leading to heavy spring flooding, or the opposite, whereby little winter snow is followed by a dry spring (Lawford 1990). The semi-arid southwestern parts of the Prairies are at risk from a decline in water resources (Byrne et al. 1989). The Saskatchewan River sub-basin has been studied for possible effects of climate change. Increased summer warming of up to 9°C could decrease the water supply to the watershed and, together with increased irrigation withdrawals, affect hydroelectric plants downstream. However, climate change models are problematic and the level of certainty of these predictions is low (Cohen et al. 1989). Nevertheless, engineers must take into account that a decrease in rain coupled with higher temperatures could mean that existing reservoirs would have to be increased in size to maintain their original capacity.

The response to such changes may lie in improved water resource management. Federal agricultural policies may shift to encourage the growth of less water-dependent crops and the increased use of recycled sewage water. Water pricing policy may need to be revised in accordance with drought hazard and water availability.

Water resources are also potential sources of contention where they cross international borders. Reduced precipitation and runoff into major river basins may have serious consequences for agricultural production and freshwater quality. The distribution of Colorado River water between the USA and Mexico is a good example where political conflicts already exist and where climate change is likely to exacerbate the situation (Gleick 1988). There are virtually no disputes between Canada and the U.S. regarding water movement. About 60 percent of runoff in Canada is carried by rivers flowing northwards. Thirty years ago the possibility of long-distance water diversions from Canada to United States arid lands, especially southern California, was first aired (Tinney and Quinn 1969). It appears highly unlikely, however, that the U.S. would pressure Canada into such a project if climate changes reduced water resources in the western United States.

Water Level Changes

Coastal Waters

On the face of it, a change by up to 1 m does not seem to be much. Canada is, however, a nation with about 250,000 km of coastline with several major cities and hundreds of villages located on it. The potential effects for Canada are not as apparent as, say, for Holland—a nation that is particularly vulnerable to sea-level rise. There the cost of raising protective dykes, arresting dune erosion and minimizing the intrusion of saltwater has been assessed as being in the order of tens of billions of guilders (den Elzen and Rotmans 1992).

A number of Canada's coastal towns and cities, however, may yet be subject to partial inundation, flooding and saltwater intrusion into groundwater. The cost of constructing coastal barriers and levees and elevating structures such as bridges and roads could be tremendous. Martec Ltd. (1987) predicted for Saint John, New Brunswick, that a 1 m rise by the year 2050 would change the probability of a 1:100 year level for storm surge and river flooding to 1:20 years. Rail and road systems in parts of the city would become inundated, especially industrial facilities near the harbour. The New Brunswick power plant in east Saint John is vulnerable to a storm surge.

Charlottetown, Prince Edward Island, would have similar problems as those of Saint John (Lane and Associates 1988) with periodic flooding of parts of the city. The cost of changing water works, wastewater systems, waterfronts and industrial facilities is estimated to be in the order of C$5 billion. This will certainly force the city to consider developing a policy now for the use of future land development in the city. Lower Vancouver, British Columbia, and towns near the Fraser River Delta, which presently have flooding problems, will require investment for protective barriers.

The Great Lakes
Scenarios for the Great Lakes suggest that mean water levels could drop by 30–80 cm (Cohen and Allsop 1988). Smith (1991), however, found that water levels could drop by as much as 2.5 m. Extremely low lake levels would occur four out of five years due to climate change (Sanderson 1987). This would have important implications for navigation and shipping. Higher temperatures would also increase municipal water use (Cohen 1987.)

Agriculture

Canada is a major food producer and exporter of grains (Canada 1990a). Warmer temperatures would have a mixed effect on Canada. In southern Québec, central Ontario and southern Saskatchewan, increased multicropping and the cultivation of higher-yield crops would be possible.

A number of studies have been published on agriculture in the Prairies (Stewart 1986; 1990). The most in-depth study has been carried out by Williams et al. (1988). It focused on Saskatchewan and projected that the annual temperature of Saskatchewan would rise by about 5°C, with the growing season extended by 5 to 15 percent (about 50 days) with an 18 percent increase in precipitation. However, an increase in potential evapotranspiration would have the effect of making the region drier. Drought frequency would be increased by a factor of 3 to 10. Monetary losses could easily exceed C$1 billion with thousands of agricultural-based jobs lost, not including any spinoff effects on the economy from reduced need for support industries (Cohen et al. 1992). Canada's largest export crop, wheat, accounts for C$3.5 billion per year, and barley exports add a further 600 million (Smit 1989). The extent of Canada's future export markets will be linked to changes in climate in other exporting countries.

Ontario agriculture will improve but may suffer more from shifts in extremes of climate and long–term climatic variability (Brklacich and Smit 1992). Corn and soybean crops may be at risk due to drought. Possible losses of $C170 million per year in agricultural production for Ontario could occur (Smit 1987). In southern Québec, the length of the growing season could increase by about 1 to 2 months (Singh 1988). New Brunswick's situation would become like the existing condition in the Niagara peninsula.

Cultivation in the northern regions of Canada will remain restricted as the soils are presently marginal and cannot be modified as rapidly as the climate changes. Only certain valleys of the Mackenzie district and Yukon would have soil of sufficient quality for agriculture. With an increased growing season, it is projected that the Yellowknife and Whitehorse growing season would be similar to that of present conditions near Edmonton, which lies 1000 km to the south.

Forests

Except for the Prairie grasslands and the cold northern tundra, Canada is mainly covered by trees. Not surprisingly, the boreal forest biome plays an important role in the national economy, especially with regard to timber, wildlife and recreation. Its sheer size makes it a high-risk target for the potential impacts of climate change. The forest industry today is Canada's largest. It employs, directly and indirectly, 280,000 people and generates $45 billion in revenues (Hengeveld 1991).

In western Canada, a shift northwards by 100–700 km of the upper northern boundary of the boreal forest will be accompanied by a 250–900 km shift northwards from the present southern edge of the boreal forest (Wheaton and Singh 1989). The Canadian Global Change Program (CGCP) of the Royal Society of Canada, together with interested Canadian government departments, is contributing to the study of the boreal forest through a major interdisciplinary scientific effort (RSC 1990).

The combination of warmer and longer growing seasons, together with milder winters, is expected to lead to improved productivity. The yield from Québec's forests could increase by 50 to 100 percent. This would be offset, however, by a shift northwards and eastwards of Prairie grasslands due to a lowering of soil moisture. In western Canada, potential biomass productivity could increase by up to 50 percent (Wheaton and Singh 1989). Increased summer temperatures will bring an increase in the likely occurrence of forest fires and insect epidemics (Suffling 1992).

Fishing

Fishing in Atlantic Canada may change as sea surface temperatures could increase by 2–3°C. Fish life cycles and migrations will likely be affected and a northward shift of the most commercially valuable fish species is anticipated (Stokoe et al. 1990). In addition, the aquaculture industry could grow and there would be a longer inshore fishing season.

In the Great Lakes, 30 new species may be able to invade and overtake resident species. In northern Canada, permafrost melt could disturb the fish habitat. In the Pacific region, warming of Pacific waters could increase populations of species such as tuna, hake and squid that migrate from the south (CCPB 1991).

The Arctic and Northern Canada

It is predicted that Arctic summers will be warmer and that winter temperatures could increase by up to 16°C (Maxwell and Barrie 1989). Sea-ice thickness would be reduced by 35 percent from the present 2.5 m Canadian average and ice-free summers would occur in the Arctic islands. There would be a reduction in mean winter snowfall and in the snow season south of 60° latitude, but an increase in sub-arctic snowfall. Improved climatic conditions would be conducive to a northwards expansion of settlements. The removal and/or melting of the permafrost layer near the surface, however, would have a great effect on pipelines, rail lines and roads, in addition to contributing to residential construction problems.

The biological impacts are of importance as this region contains large and very delicate ecosystems. The permafrost line would shift from 200 to 600 km further north and would eventually lead to a corresponding migration of coniferous forest by 200-300 km. The tundra would accordingly shrink in area. There would be a 30 to 40 percent increase in growing degree days and the frost-free period could be lengthened by 20 to 40 percent.

Energy and Energy Conservation

The Canadian government's decision to reduce CO_2 emissions nation-wide as outlined in the Green Plan (Canada. 1990b), will require fuel substitution for coal and oil and greater efficiency in energy use. Canada presently has one of the world's highest per capita use of energy. According to Bruce (1991), Canada no longer has the lead it did in renewable energy and conservation technologies. Such technologies will have an international market and lead to a huge growth industry.

In eastern Canada the average annual temperature could increase by 4°C. In the Great Lakes region this temperature change, coupled with increased domestic water use and reduced runoff, would lower the existing output of hydroelectric stations by over 4150 gigawatt hours of power generation. Replacement cost by nuclear and fossil fuel generation was estimated to be over C$110 million in 1984 (Sanderson 1987). In Québec, however, an increase of hydroelectric generation capacity by about 9.3 x 1012 w/hr is projected due to an increase in precipitation and runoff (Singh 1988). Similarly, in Labrador a 35 percent increase in runoff water is predicted, which would greatly augment its hydropower potential. Warmer temperatures in the Great Lakes region would offset the increased use of air conditioners in summer due to reduced winter heating needs (Bhartendu and Cohen 1987). In Québec, Montréal and Québec City heating requirements would be reduced by 25 and 35 percent, respectively (Singh 1988).

Due to a general increase in both air and water temperatures, offshore oil and gas exploration drilling problems related to ice formation could be greatly reduced, though iceberg problems could develop.

Transportation and Infrastructure

In northern Canada the possibility will develop for settlements to expand northwards. This would entail an extension of transportation services and systems. Permafrost decay, however, will affect roads, rail lines and oil and gas pipelines (Maxwell and Barrie 1989). Their maintenance and construction will be more difficult. Abandonment of the port of Churchill and the rail line for grain export may prove costly if, due to climate change, grain production moves northwards and a much extended navigation season in Hudson Bay and Hudson Strait keeps the port open longer (IBI Group 1990). In the Arctic, marine transportation could increase by 6 to 8 weeks, but rough seas and icebergs would be more prevalent.

Ice-free conditions in the Great Lakes and Gulf of Saint Lawrence that would permit an almost year-long shipping season are predicted (Assel 1991). Lower Great Lakes water levels, however, may require adjustment to harbour facilities due to reduced drafts. Large ships may be forced to travel with reduced payloads. Shipping costs of iron ore, grain, coal and limestone could increase by about 30 percent (Sanderson 1987). Lake Erie ports would have to reduce cargoes by 5 to 27 percent (Smith 1991). On the Canadian coastline, harbours and channels would be deeper. Construction of new bridges would have to bear in mind the marine traffic to pass under them in the future.

Tourism and Recreation

Throughout the world, tourism and related outdoor recreational activities have become an important source of regional and national income. To date little attention has been focused on their sensitivity to climate change (Smith 1990).

Increased temperatures and reduced snowfall would reduce the number of ski-days in southern Québec by 50 to 70 percent (Lamothe and Periard 1988). In particular, there may not be sufficient snow available for the critical Christmas to New Year period. They calculated that each ski-day in Québec brought in C$34 (1981 values) per person into the Québec economy. The skiing industry in Québec in the early 1980s generated 12,500 jobs and C$205 million in annual revenue. The situation in Ontario is bleaker as the ski season will be greatly reduced and possibly eliminated in the South Georgian Bay region (Wall 1988). Losses of about C$37 million of skier spending would occur (1985 values).

Virtually ice-free Great Lakes bays and harbours would curtail winter recreational activity or even eliminate it (Assel 1991). But every cloud has its silver lining. Summer recreational activities such as water skiing and camping would have the potential to increase. In Québec, the number of golf-days would increase by 50 percent and add to the present C$250 million per year industry (Kemp 1991).

The selection and management of Canada's national parks are primarily based on biophysical factors and ecological principles. Thus climate change can have an input in the future selection of parks and their size and boundaries. Prince Albert National Park, for example, could experience a warmer and drier climate in future (Wall 1989). Its boreal forest will likely be reduced in favour of grassland that is more tolerant to this kind of climatic regime. Accordingly, the unique and special features of the park will shift northwards.

Conclusion

This paper has provided an overview of the potential effects of climatic change on Canada, according to published studies and projections. One question to be posed to Canadian Studies specialists is the extent to which climate warming scenarios for Canada are applicable or relevant to their research, for that research to help Canada prepare for the predicted consequences. What policies will have to be implemented? How will the larger and wealthier provinces react? Given the uncertainty of some of the predictions, what strategies could be adopted without too great an expense?

How will Canada's economy be linked to climate changes around the world? For example, improved agricultural conditions outside Canada may reduce the need for many nations to import grains and related food products or may cause some countries to turn to closer and less expensive markets. If the Arctic waters become more navigable, will Canada be forced to display her sovereignty by increasing or augmenting her security presence?

It is clear that the subject of climate change in Canada will become of increasing interest to those specializing in Canadian Studies.

Bibliography

Assel, R.A. 1991. Implications of CO_2 Global Warming on Great Lakes Ice Cover. *Climate Change* 18:377–93.

Bhartendu, S., and S.J. Cohen. 1987. Impact of CO_2 -induced Climate Change on Residential Heating and Cooling Energy Requirements in Ontario, Canada. *Energy and Buildings* 10:99–108.

Brklacich, M., and B. Smit. 1992. Implications of Changes in Climatic Averages and Variability on Food Production Opportunities in Ontario, Canada. *Climatic Change* 20:1–21.

Bruce, J.P. 1991. Myths and Realities of Global Climate Change. *Ecodecision* 1(1):89–92.

Byrne, J.M., R. Barendregt and D. Schaffer. 1989. Assessing Potential Climate Change Impacts on Water Supply and Demand in Southern Alberta. *Canadian Water Resources Journal* 4(14):5–15.

Canada. 1989. Department of the Environment. *Resources and Jobs: The Vital Connection*. Ottawa: Environment Canada, Sustainable Development Branch, Fact Sheet 89-1.

———. 1990a. Ministry of Agriculture. *Agriculture Factfinder*. Ottawa: Communications Branch, Agriculture Canada, Publ. 5251/E.

———. 1990b. *Canada's Green Plan*. Ottawa: Canadian Government Publishing Centre, Cat. # En21-94/1990E.

CCELC (Canada Committee on Ecological Land Classification). 1989. *Ecoclimatic Regions of Canada*. Ottawa: Environment Canada Wildlife Service. Ecological Land Classification Series, No. 23.

CCPB (Canadian Climate Program Board). 1991. Climate Change and Canadian Impacts: The Scientific Perspective. *Climate Change Digest* CCD 91–01. Downsview, Ont.: Atmospheric Environment Service.

Changnon, S.A., Jr. 1987. An Assessment of Climate Change, Water Resources, and Policy Research. *Water International* 12:69–76.

Cohen, S.J. 1987. Projected Increases in Municipal Water Use in the Great Lakes Due to CO2-induced Climatic Change. *Water Resources Bulletin* 23:91–101.

Cohen, S.J., and T.R. Allsop. 1988. The Potential Impacts of a Scenario of CO_2 -induced Climatic Change on Ontario, Canada. *Journal of Climate* 1:669–81.

Cohen, S.J., P. Louie, and L. Welsh. 1989. *Possible Impacts of Climatic Warming Scenarios on Water Resources in the Saskatchewan River Sub-basin.* Saskatoon, Sask: Canadian Climate Centre report No. 89-9 (unpublished).

Cohen, S.J., E. Wheaton and J. Masterton. 1992. *Impacts of Climatic Change Scenarios in the Prairie Provinces: a Case Study from Canada.* Saskatoon: Saskatoon Research Council Publ. No. E-2900-4-D-92.

den Elzen, M.G.J. and J. Rotmans. 1992. The Socio-economic Impact of Sea-level Rise on The Netherlands: A Study of Possible Scenarios. *Climatic Change* 20:169-95.

Gillis, R.P. 1986. Rivers of Sawdust: The Battle Over Industrial Pollution in Canada, 1865-1903. *Journal of Canadian Studies* 21(1):84–103.

Gleick, P.H. 1988. The Effects of Future Climatic Changes on International Water Resources; The Colorado River, the United States, and Mexico. *Policy Sciences* 21:23–39.

Hamley, W. 1991. Economic Development and Environmental Preservation: The Case of The James Bay Hydroelectric Power Plants, Québec. *International Journal of Canadian Studies* 4(Fall):29–48.

Henderson-Sellers, A. 1991. Policy Advice on Greenhouse-induced Climatic Change: The Scientist's Dilemma. *Progress in Physical Geography* 15:53–70.

Hengeveld, H. 1991. *Understanding Atmospheric Change.* Ottawa: Environment Canada, State of Environment Report No. 91-2.

Houghton, J.T., C.J. Jenkins and J.J. Ephraums eds. 1990. *Climate Change: The IPCC Scientific Assessment.* Report of the United Nations Environment Programme, Intergovernmental Panel on Climate Change (IPCC). Cambridge, Mass.: Cambridge Univ. Press.

IBI Group. 1990. The Implications of Long-term Climatic Changes on Transportation in Canada. *Climate Change Digest.* Downsview, Ont.: Atmospheric Environment Service CCD 90-02.

IGBP (International Geosphere-Biosphere Programme). 1990. *The International Geosphere-Biosphere Programme: A Study of Global Change.* Global Change, Report #12. Stockholm: Royal Swedish Academy of Sciences.

IPCC (Intergovernmental Panel on Climate Change). 1992. *Scientific Assessment of Climate Change*-1992 IPCC Supplement. Cambridge, Mass.: Cambridge University Press.

Jones, K.H. 1990. Drought on the Prairies. In *Symposium on the Impacts of Climatic Change and Variability on the Great Plains.* 125-129. Waterloo, Ont.: University of Waterloo, Department of Geography, Occasional Paper No. 12.

Kemp, D. 1991. The Greenhouse Effect and Global Warming: A Canadian Perspective. *Geography* 76:121–30.

Lamothe and Periard. 1988. Consultants in Climatology with the collaboration of Professor Joseph Litynsky. Implications of Climate Change for Downhill Skiing in Québec. *Climate Change Digest* CCD 88-03. Downsview, Ont.: Atmospheric Environment Service.

Lane, P. and Associates Ltd., Halifax, N.S. 1988. Preliminary Study on the Possible Impacts of a One-metre Rise in Sea-level at Charlottetown, P.E.I. *Climate Change Digest* CCD 88-02. Downsview, Ont.: Atmospheric Environment Service.

Lawford, R.G. 1990. Climate Change and Water Supply and Demand in Western Canada. In *Climate Change: Implications for Water and Ecological Resources*, Waterloo, Ont.: University of Waterloo, Department of Geography, Occasional Paper No. 11.

Lewis, J.E. 1989. Climatic Change and its Effects on Water Resources for Canada: A Review. *Canadian Water Resources Journal* 14:34–55.

Martec Ltd. 1987. Effects of a One-metre rise in Mean Sea-level at Saint John, New Brunswick, and the Lower Reaches of the Saint John River. *Climate Change Digest* CCD 87-04. Downsview, Ont.: Atmospheric Environment Service.

Maxwell, J.B., and L.A. Barrie. 1989. Atmospheric and Climatic Changes in the Arctic and Antarctic. *Ambio* 18(1):42–49.

Payne, R.J. and R. Graham. 1987. An Assessment of Northern Land Use Planning in Canada. *Journal of Canadian Studies* 22(3):35–49.

Phillips, D. 1990. *The Climates of Canada*. Environment Canada publ. # En56-1/1990E. Ottawa: Canadian Government Publishing Centre.

Rees, W.E. 1991. Conserving National Capital: The Key to Sustainable Development. *International Journal of Canadian Studies* 4(Fall):7–27.

Rizzo, B. 1988. The Sensitivity of Canada's Ecosystems to Climate Change. *Canada Committee on Ecological Land Classification Newsletter* 17:10–12

Rizzo, B., and E.B. Wiken. 1992. Assessing the Sensitivity of Canada's Ecosystems to Climatic Change. *Climatic Change* 21:37–45.

RSC (Royal Society of Canada). 1990. Boreal Ecosystems-atmosphere Study. Canadian Global Change study, report # 5. Ottawa: Royal Society of Canada.

———. 1992. *Canadian Global Change Program*. Ottawa: Royal Society of Canada.

Sanderson, M. 1987. Implications of Climate Change for Navigation and Power Generation in the Great Lakes. *Climate Change Digest* CCD 87-03. Downsview, Ont.: Atmospheric Environment Service.

Singh, B. 1988. The Implications of Climate Change for Natural Resources in Québec. *Climate Change Digest* CCD 88-08. Downsview, Ont.: Atmospheric Environment Service.

Smit, B. 1987. Implications of Climatic Change for Agriculture in Ontario. *Climate Change Digest* CCD 88-02. Downsview, Ont.: Atmospheric Environment Service.

———. 1989. Climate Warming and Canada's Comparative Position in Agriculture. *Climate Change Digest* CCD 89-01. Downsview, Ont.: Atmospheric Environment Service.

Smith, J.B. 1991. The Potential Impacts of Climate Change on the Great Lakes. *Bulletin, American Meteorological Society* 72:21–28.

Smith, J.B. and D. Tirpak, eds. 1989. *The Potential Effects of Global Climate Change on the United States*. Report to Congress. Washington, D.C.: U.S. Environmental

Protection Agency, Office of Policy, Planning and Evaluation, Office of Research and Development.

Smith, K. 1990. *Tourism and Climate Change*. Land Use Policy 7:176–80.

Stewart, R.B. 1986. Climatic Change: Implications for the Prairies. *Transactions of the Royal Society of Canada* Series V (1):67–96.

———. 1990. Climatic Change and Agricultural Production in the Canadian Prairies. In *Symposium on the Impacts of Climatic Change and Variability on the Great Plains*. Waterloo, Ont: University of Waterloo, Department of Geography, Occasional Paper No. 12.

Stokoe, P., M. LeBlanc, C. Larson, M. Manzer and P. Manuel. 1990. Implications of Climate Change for Small Coastal Communities in Atlantic Canada. *Climate Change Digest* CCD 90-01. Downsview, Ont.: Atmospheric Environment Service.

Suffling, R. 1992. Climate Change and Boreal Forest Fires in Fennoscandia and Central Canada. *Catena Suppl* 22:111–32.

Tinney, E.R. and F.J. Quinn. 1969. Canadian Waters and Arid Lands. In *Arid Lands in Perspective*, edited by W.G. McGinnies and B.J. Goldman. Tucson: University of Arizona Press.

van West, J.J. 1989. Ecological and Economic Dependence in a Great Lakes Community-based Fishery: Fishermen in the Smelt Fisheries of Port Dover, Ontario. *Journal of Canadian Studies* 24:95–115.

Wall, G. 1988. Implications of Climatic Change for Tourism and Recreation in Ontario. *Climate Change Digest* CCD 88-05. Downsview, Ont.: Atmospheric Environment Service.

———. 1989. Implications of Climatic Change for Prince Albert National Park, Saskatchewan. *Climate Change Digest* CCD 89-03. Downsview, Ont.: Atmospheric Environment Service.

Wheaton, E.E. 1990. Frequency and Severity of Drought and Dust Storms. *Canadian Journal of Agricultural Economics* 38:695–700.

Wheaton, E.E., and A.K. Chakravarti. 1990. Dust Storms in the Canadian Prairies. *International Journal of Climatology* 10:829–837.

Wheaton, E.E. and T. Singh. 1989. Exploring the Implications of Climatic Change for the Boreal Forest and Forestry Economics of Western Canada. *Climate Change Digest* CCD 89-02. Downsview, Ont.: Atmospheric Environment Service.

Williams, G.D.V., R.A. Fautley, K.H. Jones, R.B. Stewart and E.E. Wheaton. 1988. Estimating Effects of Climatic Change on Agriculture in Saskatchewan, Canada. In *The Impact of Climatic Variations on Agriculture*, Vol. 1, edited by M.L. Parry, T.R. Carter and N.T. Konjin. Kluwer: Dordrecht.

Williams, P. 1989. Adapting Water Resources Management to Global Climate Change. *Climatic Change* 15:83–93.

Woo, M.K. 1991. The Canadian Association of Geographers and the Global Change Programme. *Canadian Geographer* 35:88–90.

———. 1992. Focus: Assessing the Regional Impacts of Global Warming. *Canadian Geographer* 36:66.

R. G. LAWFORD

Land Surface Climate Processes and Canada's Water Resources

Land surface climate processes have a controlling influence on Canada's water resources and determine the net effect of land surfaces on global climate. Canada is a large country with 7.5 percent of the earth's land surface within its boundaries. Its land base stretches from a latitude of 45° N in the South to 87° N in the North—almost one-eighth of the circumference of the globe. It extends East-West from 51.5° W to 140° W. Given this large land area and Canada's wide range of climate regimes, it is not surprising that its land surface climate processes have a significant influence on the climate that extends far beyond Canada's boundaries. A map of Canada showing the regions and locations referred to in this paper is included as Figure 1.

Other statistics help to illustrate the global significance of Canada's land processes. Almost 43.8% of Canada's surface is covered with forest, another 23.1% is covered with tundra and 12.8% is covered with wetlands. In terms of the earth's total area of these biomes, Canada has 10.7% of the earth's forests, 29.3% of its tundra and 25.0% of its wetlands. In addition, Canada has 36% of the surface area of the earth's freshwater lakes. Given these statistics Canadians have an abiding interest in understanding how these biomes affect the nation's climate and water resources. In addition, 72% of Canada's land area has a mean annual surface temperature lower than 0°C. Consequently, Canadians also have concerns about the way in which cold temperatures affect the hydrological cycle.

Canada's Water Resources

Canada's biomes influence the distribution of water resources in a variety of ways. Precipitation distributions are determined by the ability of the

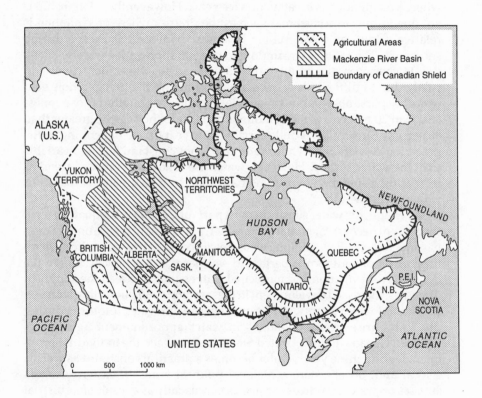

Figure 1: Map of Canada showing the regions and locations referred to in the paper
Source: Lawford 1992

atmosphere's circulation to generate precipitation. Land surface processes in general, and orographic influences in particular, lead to high precipitation totals along Canada's West coast and lower precipitation totals in the Canadian Prairie provinces. In eastern Canada, the distribution of precipitation tends to be more uniform, with the largest amounts where the influence of the Atlantic Ocean is greatest. The month with the heaviest precipitation also varies: monthly totals are highest in July on the Canadian Prairies and in November or December on the West coast.

Runoff is generally correlated with precipitation, with greater runoff where precipitation is greater and vice versa. However the relationship is not one-to-one; in some areas such as the Prairies where precipitation is relatively low, overland runoff is almost non-existent except during snowmelt. The ratio of streamflow to precipitation varies widely, partly due to characteristics of the land surface and the vegetation cover and partly due to difficulties in accurately estimating the precipitation field from the sparse observations available. In prairie regions the ratios average less than 20 percent, while in mountainous areas they can be greater than 80 percent. Streamflow is quite variable from year to year depending on the precipitation patterns. While water use is not constant, it is less variable than the water supply. However, water use follows an upward trend as increasing population and industrialization lead to greater demand for water resources.

In general, the water supply in most parts of Canada is adequate to meet the present needs of Canadians. However, water resources are under stress in some regions. For example, water resources are stressed in the agricultural areas of southern Alberta and southern Saskatchewan, where the demands for irrigation and municipal water equal or exceed the supply in dry years. Increased development in these regions will put further stress on the limited water supply. Additional stresses on water resources during dry years arise from obligations in water apportionment agreements between Canada and the United States and between the individual provinces. During these years, water becomes a practical constraint as well as a local and, on occasion, a regional political issue. In eastern Canada stresses on water resources can also occur, usually as a result of industrial demands or the deterioration of water quality from industrial pollution.

Important Land Surface Climate Processes

The distribution of Canadian water resources in both space and time is largely controlled by land surface processes. These processes include precipitation formation, evaporation, evapotranspiration, runoff and water storage mechanisms. Due to Canada's northern location, snow and ice are important components of the hydrological cycle.

The water balance equation governing the land-atmosphere interactions can be written as follows:

$$P - E - R - S = 0$$

where

P - precipitation

E - evaporation

R - runoff

S - storage.

As described in the following paragraphs, the relative importance of each of these terms varies significantly over different time and space scales. Figure 2 summarizes the direction of fluxes between the land surface and the atmosphere in summer and winter.

Precipitation Processes (P)

Precipitation is governed by low-level moisture conditions, atmospheric stability, large-scale atmospheric dynamics and the local influences of topography on the air's vertical motions. The moisture content of the atmosphere is determined by the trajectory over which the air mass moves before it reaches the point where the precipitation forms. In general, air masses that travel over an ocean surface, particularly a relatively warm ocean, are most likely to be saturated.

Precipitation generally forms in cyclones (low pressure systems), frontal systems or localized convective storms. The vertical motions responsible for the formation of precipitation are often induced by large-scale atmospheric convergence patterns, differential surface heating or the mechanical lifting of air as it moves over mountains or large hills. The precipitation that occurs at a given location over the course of a year has one component related to local influences and another component that arises from large-scale dynamics and remote moisture inputs. Although not proven, it seems reasonable to expect that, with the exception of the Canadian Prairies where the local convective regime contributes a significant proportion of the summer precipitation, the large-scale processes are dominant.

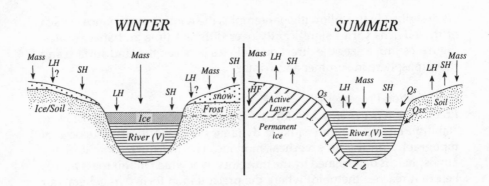

Figure 2: Land surface climate processes that are significant on the Canadian prairies in summer and winter. The terms refer to the followig transfers:
LH   -latent heat transfer
SH   -sensible heat transfer
V   -river discharge
HF   -soil heat flux
QS   -overland runoff
QSS-sub-surface runoff

Source: Lawford 1992

Evaporation Processes (E)

Evaporation and transpiration are the processes whereby moisture enters the atmosphere. Computing evaporation rates in semi-arid environments is an important scientific problem. Although there have been numerous techniques devised for computing evaporative fluxes, there is no consensus on which one is best. In the past, evaporation has been computed by the use of regression equations that rely on observations from evaporation pans and by energy and water budget techniques. The concept of potential evaporation is used to represent the maximum amount of moisture that can be added to the air when it is at a particular temperature. In areas where the surface moisture is available, the actual evaporation rate will approach the potential evaporation rate. However, when the surface is dry, the actual evaporation will be much less than the potential evaporation.

With the anticipated global warming resulting from increasing atmospheric CO_2 concentrations, the potential for the air to hold moisture will increase as will the potential evaporation. In areas where the moisture in the soil is adequate, evaporation will increase. However, in other areas where the soil normally dries out during the course of the summer, the increase in actual evaporation resulting from climatic warming may be minimal. Assessing the rate of transpiration is even more complex because it depends on plant type, plant phenology and the water available at various levels in the soil.

Runoff and Streamflow (R)

In areas where the rainfall is intense or falls on soil surfaces that are saturated, the additional moisture runs off from the surface into a network of gullies, streams and rivers. In some areas, such as the Canadian prairies, runoff is relatively rare except during snowmelt when large amounts of water run off while the ground is still frozen. Most of the summer rainfall infiltrates the soil. Soil water moves laterally and maintains a base flow in many rivers through sub-surface inputs. Internal drainage areas, where no streamflow leaves the area, occur in the agricultural region of the prairies.

Studies of climatic warming suggest its effects on runoff depend on the model used and the area considered. In northeastern Canada, streamflow is expected to increase due to increased precipitation (Singh 1988). However, studies by Cohen et al. (1989) for the prairies and McBean et al. (1991) for British Columbia, suggest that the situation is less clear in western Canada. Figure 3 summarizes the possible effects that a global warming may have on Canada's water resources.

Storage (S)

The storage term consists of two contributing factors: water storage in the soil (soil moisture) and water storage on the surface (snow and ice). Soil moisture controls the rates of latent and sensible heat transfers to the atmosphere and provides the major source of water for plants. Plants draw water from a layer of 0.5–1.5 m depth immediately below the surface. In Canada, another major surface storage component is the snow cover storage (SS). Snow accumulates in the winter with successive snowfalls in below-freezing weather and then melts during the spring months.

Soil Moisture (SM)

Soil moisture provides the link between evaporation and precipitation. Unless the soil is saturated and surface pore spaces are filled with water, rain water infiltrates the upper layer of the soil. If the soil is saturated the rainfall runs off. While some of the water stored in the soil matrix percolates through to the groundwater system, a large proportion of it returns to the atmosphere through direct evaporation from the soil surface and through transpiration by plants. The water holding capacity of soil in a particular area is dependent on soil type. Much of Canada's surface is covered with a shallow layer of soil, or no soil at all, particularly in the Canadian Shield areas and further north; hence the average capacity of the soil to retain moisture is low. However, in the critical agricultural areas of southern Ontario, Québec, the Prairie provinces and in selected areas of British Columbia and the Maritimes, where the soil layers are well developed, the water holding capacities are substantially higher.

Soil moisture has an important feedback effect on the atmosphere since it ultimately controls the proportion of the incoming solar energy that is used for latent heating (evaporation) versus the amount used for sensible heating. If the soil is moist, as much of 90 percent of the incoming energy will be consumed by latent heating. However, unless this soil moisture loss is replenished by precipitation, the surface layer of the soil will dry out in a few days, at which time sensible heating will become more dominant. With the exception of the Canadian prairies where soils dry out to some extent nearly every summer, this condition tends to arise during drought years. On the prairies, where evaporation rates are high and summer precipitation is relatively low, soil salinization can become a problem because of the tendency for the upward migration of saline groundwaters to the surface to compensate for evaporative losses. In winter, soil moisture and evaporation are less important because the ground is frozen and the vegetation is dormant.

Snow and Ice (SS)

The cold temperatures experienced in Canada for six months of each year (and longer in more northern areas) exert a major control on land surface climate processes. The winter snow cover has a high albedo and over the course of the winter can become a large water reservoir. Ice in the soil has an important influence on the rate at which the ground warms in the spring. The winter temperatures also cause the moisture in the soil to freeze, greatly reducing infiltration rates.

Ice obstructs the movement of water in rivers. In larger rivers and streams the flow is maintained under the ice cover throughout the winter; however, in smaller streams at northern latitudes, the water freezes to the stream bed during the winter. During spring breakup, this ice cover weakens as temperatures rise until it breaks up in-situ, or until water and ice from upstream push the weakened ice out of the way. When ice is moving in a channel, localized river hydraulics can cause ice to aggregate in preferred parts of the channel resulting in flow obstructions. The ice cover that forms on Canadian lakes reduces the effects of wind and sunlight on the physical and biological processes of lakes and reservoirs.

Warmer temperatures projected by global climate models (Houghton et al. 1990) will lead to later freezeup and earlier breakup dates thus reducing the length of the period of winter quiescence. The warmer temperatures projected by global climate models may also lead to a shorter snow season and reduced snow accumulations, although it is possible that increased precipitation arising from a northward shift in the jet stream could counteract the effect of the shorter snow season.

Variability And Change In Climate Processes

In Canada there is considerable variability in these land climate processes from season to season and from year to year, particularly for precipitation. Although evaporation is less variable it also undergoes significant seasonal and inter-annual fluctuations. This is most evident on the Canadian prairies where drought conditions occur approximately one year in every four (Bonsal 1991). These droughts affect agriculture, water resources, waterfowl and other areas of the economy. Droughts and floods also occur in most other parts of the country with potentially large damages to structures during floods and significant stresses on water supplies during droughts. Floods can be the result of the rapid melt of heavy snowpacks or ice jams in river channels on the prairies and in the North, rain on snow or heavy rain events in British Columbia and heavy thunderstorms on smaller basins in eastern Canada.

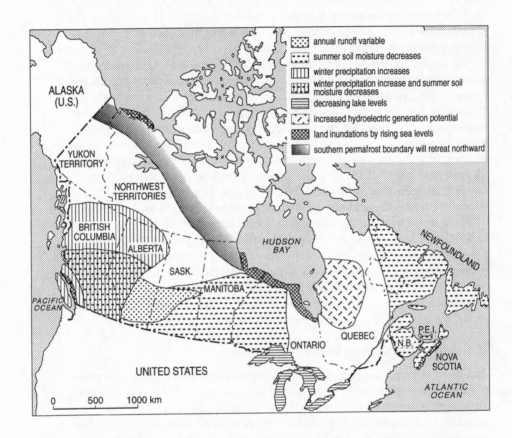

Figure 3: Possible hydrological impacts that may be inferred from recent GCM climate change scenarios

Source: Lawford 1992

Based on the results from global climate models (GCMs) it is widely accepted that the increasing levels of atmospheric carbon dioxide will result in an average global warming of 2.5 to 4.5° C in the next half-century. An increase in temperature will affect those land surface processes that are most temperature sensitive. Changes can be expected in the rain-to-snow ratios resulting from longer periods with above freezing temperatures. Other changes will likely involve earlier thaw dates and later freeze dates for Canadian lakes and rivers, and increases in the length of the growing season that could increase water demand. However, these increases may be partially offset by the increased water use efficiency that characterizes plants in a CO_2-rich environment.

In terms of the integrated effects of changes in land surface processes arising from global warming, it is expected that more frequent and possibly more severe prairie droughts will occur in the future. These droughts would result in very limited water supplies and increased demands for irrigation, and for industrial and domestic water. It is possible due to computational schemes in current GCMs that the evaporative losses have been overestimated, consequently the depletion of soil moisture may not be as dramatic as the current scenarios suggest.

It is also important to consider feedbacks between biological and hydrological processes. Increased moisture stresses may lead to changes in vegetation patterns in some parts of the prairies. For example, moisture stresses are expected to occur along the boundary between the agricultural and forestry areas in central Saskatchewan and Alberta. With warmer temperatures and no significant change in precipitation, it is expected that the southern edge of the forest will slowly die out and be replaced by agriculture. In turn, this change in vegetation cover will alter the evaporative losses in these areas and their vulnerability to drought.

Preparing For The Future

Canadian governments at both the federal and provincial levels have been taking steps to "drought-proof" the Canadian prairies. This has been accomplished through the construction of small on-farm reservoirs, assistance programs for farmers to make better use of groundwater sources and crop insurance programs. Better information and prediction systems are needed to ensure that Canada's water resources are properly managed, particularly in areas where the stresses from climatic fluctuations are likely to be the highest. This will involve the improvement of climate models, the development of seasonal predictions and the more extensive monitoring of water resources using modern technology.

Through the World Meteorological Organization's (WMO) World Climate Research Program and its Global Energy and Water Cycle Experiment (GEWEX), the need to obtain a better understanding of land surface processes is being addressed by the climate modelling community. Through its Green Plan the Canadian government is encouraging several initiatives that deal directly with land surface climate processes. One such initiative, known as the Canadian GEWEX (Global Energy and Water Cycle Experiment) Study, will focus on hydrometeorlogical processes in the Mackenzie River Basin. Through this initiative Canadian scientists hope to gain a better understanding of the cold region land surface climate processes in the hydrological cycle. The Canadian program complements a major international hydrometeorlogical modelling study being carried out in the Mississippi Basin. The Boreal Ecosystem Atmosphere Study (BOREAS) is another international project supported by the Canadian government. It involves the analysis of moisture, heat and carbon dioxide fluxes from small areas at the southern and northern boundaries of the boreal forest. Field sites are being established in the Prince Albert National Park and near Nelson House, Manitoba. Other studies are being planned to look at the links between climatic change and the water resources in the Canadian prairies, the Mackenzie River Basin and the Great Lakes. Many of these studies will make extensive use of the new sources of satellite data which are expected to become available later this decade.

References

Bonsal, B.R. 1991. Possible Teleconnections Between North Pacific Sea Surface Temperatures and Extended Dry Spells and Droughts on the Canadian Prairies, Unpubl. MSc. Thesis, University of Saskatchewan, Saskatoon, Sask.

Cohen, S., P. Louie and L. Welsh. 1989. *Possible Impacts of Climatic Warming Scenarios on Water Resources in the Saskatchewan River Sub-basin*. Saskatoon, Sask: Canadian Climate Centre report No. 89-9. (Unpublished.)

Houghton, J.T., C.J. Jenkins and J.J. Ephraums, eds. 1990. *Climate Change: The IPCC Scientific Assessment*. Report of the United Nations Environment Programme, Intergovernmental Panel on Climate Change (IPCC). Cambridge, Mass.: Cambridge Univ. Press.

Lawford, R.G. 1992. Hydrometeorlogical Indicators of Climatic Change: Issue or Opportunity? In *Proceedings of the Workshop on Using Hydrometric Data to Detect and Monitor Climatic Change*. Saskatoon, Sask.: NHRI Symposium #8.

McBean, G., O. Slaymaker, T. Northcote, P. Lebland and T.S. Parsons. 1991. *Review of Models for Climate Change and Impacts on Hydrology, Coastal Currents and Fisheries in British Columbia*. Saskatoon, Sask.: Canadian Climate Centre, Report No. 91-11. (Unpublished.)

Singh, B. 1988. The Implications of Climate Change for Natural Resources in Québec. *Climate Change Digest* CCD 88-08. Downsview, Ont.: Atmospheric Environment Service.

KEN ATKINSON

Environmental Impact Assessment in Canada: Past Achievements, Future Prospects

Environmental impact assessment (EIA) has become a major concern of governments in North America, the European Community and many other parts of the world (e.g., Israel). Environmental assessments are used in the public and private domains to integrate environmental criteria into decision-making and the development of policy. EIAs are designed to ensure that environmental impacts are considered as early in the planning process as is possible and practicable. If adverse environmental effects are identified, every effort should be made to investigate them, so that the eventual policy or project achieves an appropriate balance among social, economic and environmental goals.

Birth of Environmental Assessment in Canada

Environmental assessment, as a planning tool, has been practised by the Government of Canada since 1973 when an informal process was established by a Cabinet Directive stating that environmental assessment should be carried out on all federal undertakings and activities, where it should be used to predict the potential environmental effects of proposals requiring a federal government decision. As with many other countries, stimulus had come partially from the 1970 U.S. National Environmental Policy Act (NEPA)) and the establishment of the U.S. Environmental Protection Agency. This agency was able to show that the cost of assessing impacts on the environment is not high and represents only a fraction of the capital costs of most projects. In Canada, a second Cabinet directive of 1977 made some procedural adjustments to the 1973 directive, and the processes were further updated in 1984 when the Environmental Assessment and Review Process (EARP) Guidelines were issued by Order-in-Council.

The EARP Process

The EARP Guidelines Authorized the Minister of Environment to ensure that new federal projects, programs and activities were assessed for potential environmental effects early in the planning process and the results taken into account. The office set up to administer the EARP process was the Federal Environmental Assessment Review Office (FEARO), which was separate from the Department of Environment, although the Executive Chairman reported directly to the Minister of Environment.

The EARP process was essentially a self-assessment process. The responsibility for considering the environmental effects lay with the initiating government department, board or agency. Where appropriate, various levels of government agreed to hold a joint review. The EARP process had two stages, an initial assessment and a public review by an EARP panel. The initial assessment was carried out by the initiating government department. If it concluded that there were no adverse environmental effects, there was no further review. If it concluded there were *significant* adverse effects, the proposal was automatically referred to the Minister of Environment for public review by an EARP panel. If the proposal had *some* environmental effects, the assessment by the initiating department continued. The department then decided whether:

1. the proposal could proceed, with changes,
2. further study was required by means of a report, an initial Environmental Evaluation (IEE), to investigate further the nature and significance of the potential effects,
3. the proposal had to be modified for re-assessment,
4. the proposal should be referred to an EARP panel for public review,
5. to reject the proposal.

Once a proposal was referred to the federal Minister of Environment for review by an EARP panel, the terms of reference were drafted by FEARO in consultation with the Minister of the Environment and the Minister of the initiating department. The Minister of Environment appointed members of the Assessment Panel, who would be mostly unbiased experts with special knowledge and experience, chaired by the Executive Chairman of FEARO . The Panel was required to conduct its public information program to advise the public of its review, and to ensure public access to all information prior to a public hearing. The Panel issued guidelines, after public consultation, to the proponent for the preparation of an Environmental Impact Statement (EIS) that, once received by the Panel, was made available to the public. If deficiencies in the EIS were identified by the Panel or the public, the proponent was required to provide additional information.

Once the EIS was acceptable, public hearings, which were of two types, were held. *Community hearings* were held when a rural area was affected by the proposal; the hearings were informal and sought to encourage local residents to express their views. *General hearings* were usually held in larger centres and dealt with the technical aspects of the proposal and its potential impacts. At the end of the public review, the Panel prepared its report of conclusions and recommendations. The Panel Report was submitted to the Ministers of Environment and of the initiating department who arrived at their final decision, often in Cabinet. They were not legally bound by the Panel's Report, which, however, had to be made available to the public. The initiating department had to ensure that any decisions made by the Ministers were incorporated into the design and operation of a proposal, including any monitoring required. There was no provision for appeal against the recommendations of the EARP Panel and the Ministers' decision. The broad outlines of the former EARP under FEARO are illustrated in Figure 1, which has generalized what is clearly a more complex set of procedures.

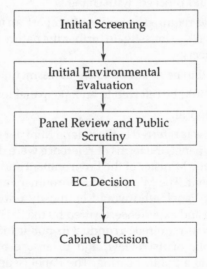

Figure 1: The EARP sequence

The 1991 Reform of EARP

During the 1980s several difficulties were identified with the EARP as it had been operating. One criticism was that the Guidelines allowed the decision on the need for public review by the Review Panel to be made by the Minister responsible for the project and not by the Minister of Environment. As well, the Guidelines did not provide for public participation in the initial assessment part of EARP. In addition, the Guidelines failed to clarify the responsibilities of certain agencies and federal bodies, for example Crown corporations. A number of outstanding issues arose regarding their application in particular cases. Court decisions by the Federal Court of Canada, particularly with regard to the Rafferty/Alameda and Oldman dam projects in the Prairies, have given legal interpretations of the Guidelines Order that broadened the application of EARP beyond what was originally intended when the Guidelines Order was introduced. The Federal Court also overturned a 1990 federal government Order-in-Council exempting the Kemano Completion Project in British Columbia from an environmental assessment review. Economic interests have expressed concern that decisions such as these made the EARP process unpredictable and that such uncertainty can affect economic development adversely. Another impetus to reforming EARP was given by the World Commission on Environment and Development 1987 (The Brundtland Commission) that, in its report, *Our Common Future*, concludes that EIA processes would be more effective if they were mandatory and entrenched in legislation. A series of public meetings was held across Canada in 1987 and 1988, followed by a national consultative workshop; the consultation involved governments, the private sector, Native peoples, environmental and other special interest groups, the legal profession and EIA professionals.

The result of the federal government's deliberations is the Canadian Environmental Assessment Act 1991 (Bill C-78). The new reformed EARP seeks to introduce a consistent, fair and efficient assessment package. It is hoped that the legislation will remove the uncertainty of the old Guidelines. More resources have been made available for environmental assessment across the federal government, and a new agency has been set up—the Canadian Environmental Assessment Agency—that will be independent of Environment Canada and other federal departments and agencies. The reform package covers many aspects of the environmental assessment process. Table 1 draws out the main contrasts between the old

Table 1
The Old and New FEARO

	Old	New
Need for Review	Responsible minister	Environment minister
Scope	No guidelines	Requirements on alternatives, cumulative effects, sustainability
Public Review	Only panels	Mediation and panels, subpoena powers
Transborder Effects	No federal role	Major federal role
Monitoring	Not required	Plans required; proponent must implement
Administration	FEARO office in EC	CEA Agency independent of any department
Mandatory	None	A list
Federal Policies	Discretionary	Required
Indian Lands	Exempt	Land claims must consider
Foreign Aid	No provision	Subject to CEEA

and new FEARO, and Figure 2 shows the sequence of decisions under the new scheme.

In future, the federal government will be required by law to integrate environmental considerations into all its project planning and implementation. The new FEARO provides for joint review panels with the provinces when there is an overlap of responsibility. The Act provides for greater public input at all stages, and participation is encouraged through public hearings, mediation processes and public registries containing project information. A program of participant funding gives assistance to people affected by a project to make their views better known. The range of activities to be encouraged under the general heading of "public participation" is as follows:

• Early ratification
• Public registries
• Mediation
• Public learning
• Public comments
• Reports and follow–up activities
• Annual report
• Participant funding.

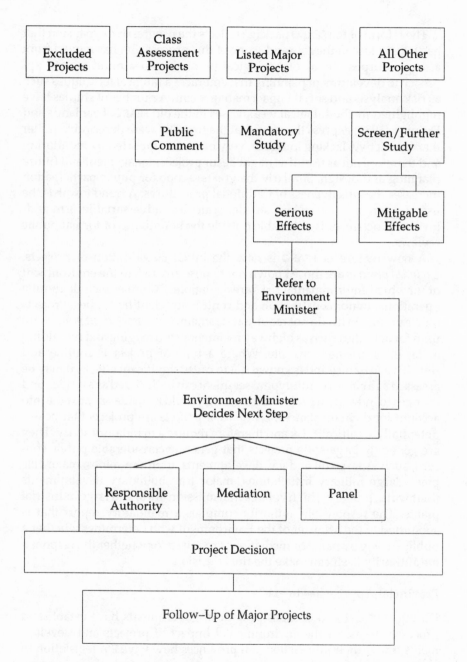

Figure 2: The sequence of decision-making under the new FEARO

The reform of the FEARO package reflects the progressive expansion that has taken place in the role and scope of this process. EIA has moved from a single-purpose focus on ecological prediction to a multi-faceted approach to development planning that embraces a range of techniques such as risk analysis and social impact management. A number of studies have highlighted methodological weaknesses in the old FEARO. Beanlands and Duinker (1983) express the view that the first EISs were descriptive rather than predictive, lacking in rigour, very often unsupported by monitoring and therefore not as useful as might be for project management and future planning and design. Similarly the greater scope for public participation increases the effectiveness of traditional procedures. A trend towards the use of a range of lower-key, smaller scale, less adversarial inform-and-involve procedures is noticeable outside the boundaries of formal public reviews.

A new feature of FEARO is now the initial classification of projects. *Excluded projects* are those known not to pose any risk to the environment or for which environmental risks are negligible. Examples include routine operations, minor construction and controlled scientific studies. Projects on the exclusion list do not require assessment. *Class assessment projects* are used for activities such as highway maintenance, dredging and rebuilding of facilities on the same site. Where a type of project is routine and repetitive in nature and is known not to cause significant effects, it may be assessed as a class. A prototype assessment can be declared as a model, and changes to individual project assessments would be made only to take into account local circumstances. *Listed major projects* are projects that pose a potentially significant risk and therefore require a mandatory study. They are generally large-scale projects that generate considerable public concern, such as large oil and gas developments, uranium mines, major HEP plans, large military installations, major transboundary developments (highways, pipelines, high voltage transmission lines) and large industrial plants. The responsible authority compiles a mandatory report that is submitted to the Minister of the Environment who determines whether a public review by panel or mediation is required, or whether the responsible authority itself can make the final decision.

Provincial Approaches to EIA

During the past two decades provincial governments have established processes to assess the environmental impact of projects and developments under their jurisdiction. All provinces now have EIA legislation in place. One of the best known is the Environmental Assessment Act of Ontario 1975. Ontario was the first province to enact legislation. New-foundland's 1980 Environmental Assessment Act was the first such legis-lation to require private-sector undertakings, as well as those sponsored by government, to be subject to EIA. A recent attempt has been made to rank provincial and federal EARP in terms of their effectiveness, on the basis of 10 evaluation criteria (Smith 1991) (Figure 3). According to this study, three provinces were highly rated: Saskatchewan, Newfoundland and Québec. These provinces were judged to be the best in Canada on the basis of clear, inclusive definitions of the environment, excellent institutional arrange-ments and widespread public participation in the assessment process. Four schemes were described as weak and unacceptable: New Brunswick, PEI, Manitoba and the federal EARP. All four jurisdictions were criticized for lacking effective institutional relationships.

However, EIA is a dynamic and rapidly changing field, and each of these four schemes has been altered or amended since 1990. Any evaluation of the efficiency of EIA is fraught with difficulties and subjective pitfalls. The high rating given to Québec, for example, resulted from a high rating on all criteria, except that of exemptions; the major exemption is the exclusion of the James Bay region from provincial EIA which means that the provisions apply only to southern Québec. It is difficult to sustain faith in any ranking that leads to an anomaly as major as this. Also EIA is a complex, multi-faceted set of procedures whose efficiency cannot possibly be quantified by subjective, "hunch" judgements.

The Future for EIA in Canada

The 1991 Canadian Environmental Assessment Act represents a new direction for EIA in Canada. Similar moves in the provinces mean that a more closely defined set of procedures is now in place for much of the country. The largely administrative and pragmatic procedure of the origi-nal Cabinet Guidelines has been replaced by a new legalistic and sophis-ticated style that owes much to NEPA 1970. Critics of the reforms wonder whether the simple and speedy processes of EARP will be improved by the large bureaucracy implicit in the new FEARO. To repeat an old criticism of NEPA, will it make "a land fit for lawyers to live in" but one which will stifle economic development? Business interests will welcome any moves to reduce the unpredictability of the original FEARO, but will they welcome a process that is potentially time-consuming and, therefore, costly and bureaucratic? Such fears may not be expressed in times of economic

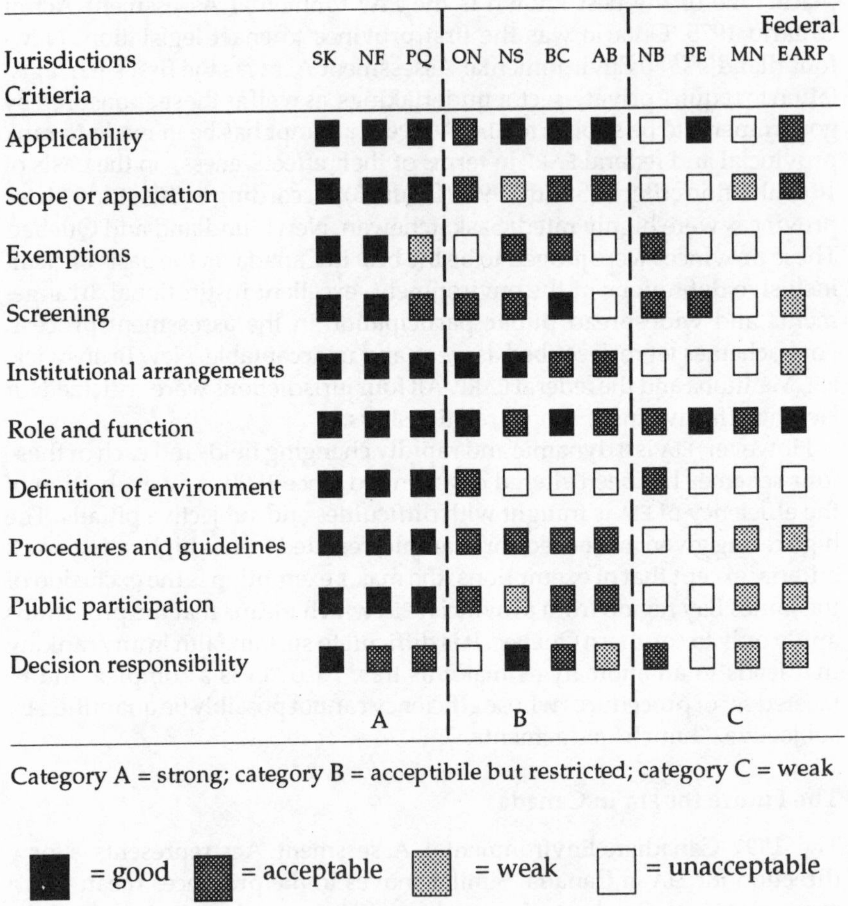

Jurisdictions / Critieria	SK	NF	PQ	ON	NS	BC	AB	NB	PE	MN	Federal EARP
Applicability	■	■	■	▦	■	■	■	□	■	□	▦
Scope or application	■	■	■	▦	░	▦	▦	□	□	░	■
Exemptions	■	■	░	□	▦	▦	□	▦	□	□	□
Screening	■	■	■	▦	■	■	□	▦	■	□	▦
Institutional arrangements	■	■	■	■	■	■	▦	□	□	□	░
Role and function	■	■	■	■	▦	▦	▦	▦	■	■	■
Definition of environment	■	■	■	▦	□	□	□	▦	□	□	□
Procedures and guidelines	■	■	■	▦	▦	▦	▦	□	□	▦	▦
Public participation	■	■	■	▦	░	▦	▦	□	□	▦	▦
Decision responsibility	■	■	■	□	■	▦	▦	■	□	▦	▦
	A			B				C			

Category A = strong; category B = acceptibile but restricted; category C = weak

■ = good   ▦ = acceptable   ░ = weak   □ = unacceptable

Figure 3: The effectiveness of provincial and federal EARP
Source: Smith 1991.

recession and will not be felt until business expansion and development becomes the order of the day.

Views of environmentalists and ecologists on the hew FEARO are likely to be ambivalent too. Holling (1978) is just one among many natural scientists who wonder whether it is wise to place so much faith in EIA in the face of so many unknowns with respect to natural systems. He emphasizes that it is a myth that EIA could ever consider all impacts. Ecology is seen as a "science of surprises" in a world where the natural state is one of non-equilibrium, with emphasis on uncertainty, surprise and discontinuities. Birkes (1988) indicates clearly that the EIS on the James Bay HEP project failed to predict a series of major impacts on natural ecosystems and Native peoples. The unpredicted impacts range from chemical effects, e.g., the increase in methyl mercury in ecosystems to the unpredicted social impact of roads. Birkes concludes, in fact, that five of the six major impacts of James Bay were unpredicted. Dickman (1991) also reports on the failure of an EIA for Polaris mine, Little Cornwallis Island, NWT to predict excessive levels of heavy metals in Garrow Lake, Canada's most northerly hypersaline lake.

The conclusion is emerging that EISs cannot by themselves protect natural systems or the users of those systems. No amount of institutional, administrative and legal reform of EARP can substitute for baseline scientific data and understanding concerning natural systems. Public expectations may well have run ahead of scientific capability during the 1980s. The ability to predict will only improve if a scientific approach to EIA is taken, and one of the biggest challenges for the future is for EIA to provide more useful scientific data to decision-makers. Given the inevitable uncertainties that accompany any development, the best that might be achieved might be to identify "valued ecosystem components" (Beanlands and Duinker 1983) and evaluate impacts under different trajectories, based on an interdisciplinary understanding of these systems. In short, we must be prepared for surprises. Such a preparation will rely on an interdisciplinary approach, predicting and preparing for a range of outcomes, based on a knowledge of local priorities, and not divorced from day-to-day realities.

References

Beanlands, G.E., and P.N. Duinker. 1983. *An Ecological Framework for Environmental Impact Assessment in Canada*. Ottawa: FEARO.

Birkes, F. 1988. The Intrinsic Difficulty of Predicting Impacts: Lessons from the James Bay Hydro Project. *Environmental Impact Assessment Review* 8:201–20.

Dickman, M. 1991. Failure of an EIA to Predict the Impact of Mine Tailings on Canada's Most Northerly Hypersaline Lake. *Environmental Impact Assessment Review* 11:171–80.

Canada. 1990. Ministry of the Environment. *Federal Environmental Assessment: New Directions*. Ottawa: FEARO.

Holling, C.S., ed. 1978. *Adaptive Environmental Assessment and Management*. New York: Wiley.

Smith, L.G. 1991. Canada's Changing Impact Assessment Provisions. *Environmental Impact Assessment Review* 11:5–9.

World Commission on Environment and Development. 1987. *Our Common Future* ("The Brundtland Report"). Oxford: Oxford University Press.

PART IV
ESSAYS IN CANADIAN SOCIETY

Cyril Levitt

Introduction

The four papers contained in this section of the book are contributions from the disciplines of economics, social work and sociology. They cover the economic integration of immigrants, problems of female-headed one-parent Jewish families, long-term care for aging Canadians and racial confrontation. The common theme that unites them is their intense concern with major social problems in Canadian society.

The paper by Chiswick and Miller on language and earnings among immigrants to Canada provides a survey of recent research on the topic and suggests directions for public policy on immigration. Neysmith's study is concerned with the effects of policy on a large sector of the population, aging women, and suggests that there is a fundamental opposition between the rhetoric of care and the willingness on the part of governments to invest in those areas that are most overburdened. Schlesinger's article focuses on a smaller group—Jewish women heading single-parent families and, by means of qualitative and quantitative data, analyzes their situation and outlines the problems that they are facing. Levitt's contribution subjects the oft-repeated charge that Canada is a racist society to scrutiny.

About one in seven residents of Canada is foreign born. Even though some of them are native English- or French-speakers, a large number of them had little facility in one of Canada's two official languages when they arrived in the country, and, as Chiswick and Miller point out, "(l)anguage acquisition is an important part of the economic and social adjustment of immigrants...". The two authors utilize the human capital theory to study the process of language acquisition. According to this theory, economic agents will invest in acquiring language proficiency in order to increase their earning power and maximize their net wealth in the long run.

Which of Canada's two official languages is learned by immigrants is a function of region of residence and of an assessment of the economic benefits that accrue to the immigrant who learns one language as opposed to other languages. Proficiency in English is the nearly universal condition of immigrants in English Canada whereas in Québec bilingualism increases with duration. The empirical evidence on language fluency shows, according to the authors, that an immigrant's official language fluency is related both to efficiency (years of education and age at immigration) and exposure factors (exposure prior to emigration, exposure time in Canada, intensity of exposure in Canada).

In the section of their paper that deals with the empirical evidence on the determinants of earnings, Chiswick and Miller criticize existing studies for failing to consider data for men and for not emphasizing the foreign-born. They could not have known at the time of the writing of their paper of the excellent study written by Arnold DeSilva for the Economic Council of Canada in the spring of 1992 on the earnings of immigrants to Canada that showed that, by and large, immigrants eventually catch up to and even surpass the earnings of the native-born.

The policy implication that the authors suggest in their conclusion relates to the selection of immigrants by Canadian immigration authorities. In the interests of rapid and successful adjustment and integration of new immigrants to Canada, those who can be expected to learn quickly one or both of Canada's official languages should clearly be given preference.

The contribution by Neysmith on aging women in Canada is less optimistic. Focusing on Old Age Security and its supplements and the system of long term care, the author arrives at the conclusion that large numbers of older women do not receive equitable benefits from the existing arrangements. Since pension benefits are to a large extent a function of length of employment in the labour force and of the income level of the employee, many women find that they do not receive the same level of benefits as men or as women who have husbands with high pensions. In May of 1991, for example, the average payment to women from the Canada/Québec Pension Plan was less than two-thirds of the average payment to qualifying males.

Although Canada has a national health care system, most of the elements of long-term, chronic care programs are not covered by it. These programs fall largely to the provincial governments and there is a wide variability in quality and level of support across the country. There are two elements to each of these programs—formal, institutionally based initiatives and informal home care undertaken by family members and friends. Using a recent report on the state of the system in Manitoba as a harbinger of things to come elsewhere in the country, Neysmith argues that "Home care was rapidly turning into a hospital replacement service, even though the program had neither the human nor financial resources to undertake this type of care. The report documents pressures for home care to assume even more of a hospital replacement function in the future."

In Manitoba, the informal, home care component of the system had already been responsible for over 80 percent of care. Soaring institutional costs were pushing the government to force even more of the burden upon informal kin and friendship networks, while hospitals and other relatively well-funded institutions were clamouring for more of the ever-diminishing resources.

Neysmith suggests that this thrust by government to put the burden of long-term care on the overburdened home-care component is based upon outmoded assumptions concerning women's unpaid care-giving role in family and society. We see here a classical case of the struggle between economic priorities established by governments and the ideology of women's and citizen's rights. This is a political struggle, as the author suggests, and it appears that during the current political climate governments may be successful in their efforts at cutting costs at the expense of family members, especially females, caring for the elderly.

Schlesinger's paper on female-headed one-parent families is based upon a study of 55 such families in Toronto and seeks to present a picture of the typical lives of women in this situation. Policy implications, especially with regard to the involvement of Jewish Community Services, are secondary. The focus is not on the negative aspects of the situation, although these are clearly brought out. The interviewers were favourably impressed with these women who presented themselves as a thoughtful and articulate group on the whole. There is significant material on the emotional stresses of their situation, but there was general agreement that the financial burdens were the cause of their severest difficulties. The author organizes the comments of the respondents in four lists that provide a concise summary of the text. Perhaps the most important in a practical sense is the fourth list, which offers advice to new Jewish single parents. This advice is broken down into three categories—informal and formal support system, attitude and legalities, and children.

In his paper, Levitt asks the rhetorical question: "Is Canada a racist country?" Written at the time of a race riot in Toronto (May 1992), the article reviews the current literature on race relations in Canada, which ranges from topics such as violence and discrimination to economic opportunity and social mobility. The author shows that Canada has made great strides forward to develop a multicultural society that works and that provides a climate of tolerance and acceptance of racial and ethnic minorities. The most recent evidence, which Levitt has included in his review, shows that immigrants, even members of visible minorities, are upwardly mobile and ultimately overtake Canadians born in the country. Recognizing the futility of comparisons between democratic countries concerning the degree of racism practised, Levitt concludes by citing the words of Howard McCready, a black Member of Parliament for the New Democratic Party, that "Canada is the least racist country on earth."

Even considered collectively, the four papers in this section do not cover all the aspects of Canadian social problems. And yet, they portray a concern with some of the most significant issues in Canadian life today. Immigration, (health) care, racism and the state of family life are major focuses of political and social concern. In the aftermath of one of the most critical elections in Canadian history, one that promises to be a watershed for future development, it is these issues that are among those at the top of the national agenda.

BARRY R. CHISWICK AND PAUL W. MILLER

Language and Earnings Among Immigrants in Canada: A Survey

According to the 1991 Census of Canada, 16 percent of the population is foreign born. The national origins of these immigrants are diverse, and the majority will acquire skills in one or both of the official languages, English and French, after arrival in Canada. Language acquisition is an important part of the economic and social adjustment of immigrants in Canada.

The unique situation of Canada with respect to language has an important bearing on the adjustments of immigrants in Canada. Canada is a dual-language country. English and French are official languages at the federal level, although there are differences across the provinces. French is the official language of Québec, English and French are the official languages of Manitoba and New Brunswick, and English is the official language elsewhere in Canada (de Vries 1986). At a practical level, French is the dominant language in Québec, and English is the dominant language in the other nine provinces. Immigrants in Québec and elsewhere in Canada are faced with a choice of English monolingualism, French monolingualism, bilingualism in the official languages or learning neither language.

Analysis of language proficiency among immigrants in Canada has been presented in a number of studies, including Richmond and Kalbach (1980), de Vries and Vallee (1980) and Chiswick and Miller (1992, 1993a). The impact of language skills on earnings has been analyzed by Meng (1987), Abbott and Beach (1987) and Chiswick and Miller (1988, 1992), among others. While there are differences across these studies, they are all grounded in human capital theory. A brief review of this theory is presented to provide a basis for the interpretation of the empirical findings related to language acquisition, language choice and the effect of language on labour market earnings. Following the overview of the empirical research, a summary and conclusion will outline the major policy implications.

Theoretical Framework

Language Acquisition
Breton (1978a, 1978b) and Chiswick and Miller (1992, 1993b) have outlined a model of the acquisition of language skills that follows the traditional human capital literature. In this model, economic agents are viewed as investing in language capital in order to maximize their net wealth. Thus, language acquisition depends on the costs and benefits associated with the learning of the language. The costs of acquiring a language vary across individuals.

Part of the cost differences in language acquisition will arise because some individuals are more able in the learning process, and hence more efficient at this type of capital formation. Efficiency is defined in Chiswick and Miller (1993b) as "the extent to which a given amount of destination language exposure produces language fluency." Efficiency in language capital creation will be related to age at migration, educational attainment and motive for migration (e.g., refugees may have less efficiency in acquiring dominant language skills). Part of the cost differentials may also arise from family background factors. Grenier and Vaillancourt (1983), for example, propose that the cost of acquiring language capital, or the funds to finance the investment, will be lower in more affluent families.

Exposure to the destination language also matters (Chiswick and Miller 1993b). Circumstances favourable to learning a language include the use of the language within the family (e.g., children learning English at school may pass on language skills to parents). Regional patterns are also important, including the frequency with which languages are spoken in the area and regional policies that foster the use of the particular language. As a result, it would appear to be easier to acquire fluency in both English and French in Québec than in the rest of Canada. Exposure has three components: exposure prior to immigration, time units of exposure in the destination and the intensity of exposure per unit of time in the destination.*

The benefits from the acquisition of a second language may be monetary or non-monetary, and they accrue over time. A major economic benefit is the higher wage that individuals proficient in a dominant language (or those who are bilingual) may command. The wage premium may arise from higher productivity in the current job, a factor associated with the

---

* Breton (1978a, 2) attributes language skills, in part, to non-economic factors. He writes that "those who are lucky are simply placed in circumstances that make learning easier." By definition, the analysis of the determinants of "luck" is beyond the scope of social science.

ability to communicate in the workplace (Tainer 1988). Some language groups could, however, achieve a higher wage through having greater choice of regional locations and types of jobs.

The model applied by Chiswick and Miller (1992) includes variables for age at migration and educational attainment as efficiency variables, and includes as exposure variables duration of residence in Canada, birthplace, location of residence, family circumstances (e.g., marital status, whether married to a Canadian-born person, whether children are present) and the minority group language concentration of the location where the individual lives. The minority group language concentration measure is hypothesized to capture the effects of an environment in which more people converse in the immigrant's first language.

Language Choice

Language choice in dual-language Canada refers to the decision by immigrants to be English monolinguals, French monolinguals, bilingual in the official languages or not fluent in the official languages. The major determinant is likely to be the dominant language of the region of residence. A dominant language will tend to emerge in a multi-language environment as a cost-effective means of facilitating communication. There is likely to be a positive relationship between the dominance of a language and the economic benefits from learning it relative to the benefits from learning other languages. The large social, cultural and economic impact of the United States on Canada, as well as the large share of English Canada in Canadian life, gives English a competitive advantage over French for dominance.

Although both French and English are widely used in Québec, French is generally referred to as the dominant language. Elsewhere in Canada, English is the dominant language. Consequently, the return to learning English for a monolingual French worker would be higher in English Canada than in Québec (Breton 1978a). Similarly, the role of English as a dominant language implies that the return to a monolingual English worker from learning a second language will generally be small.

Chiswick and Miller (1993a) model language choice using the same explanatory variables as for language acquisition. In this analysis only non-official languages are treated as minority languages in the definition of the minority group. (Treating French as a minority language in English Canada and treating English as a minority language in Québec does not have a major impact on the findings.)

Earnings

Models of immigrant earnings typically focus on three related issues: the motive for migration, the degree of skill transferability and the economic adjustment of immigrants in the destination. A model incorporating these issues is developed in Chiswick (1978, 1979), and summarized in Chiswick and Miller (1988, 1992).

The two motives for migration generally distinguished are economic and non-economic. Economic immigrants are attracted to the destination country by expectations of economic advancement. Migration decisions for non-economic migrants are not based primarily on differences in labour-market opportunities between the origin and the destination countries. Non-economic migrants leave their country of origin for various reasons, including political or religious persecution (refugees), ideological concerns and family reunification. Because non-economic migrants are not self-selected for economic success in the destination, they are expected to have a lower attainment and a more difficult adjustment.

The skill transferability issue attracted most attention in the early literature (see Chiswick 1978). Skill transferability refers to the degree to which skills obtained in the country of origin are productive in the country of destination. As outlined in Chiswick and Miller (1988), the skills relevant to immigrant labour-market status include job-specific skills (formal on-the-job training, apprenticeships, certification, licences) and general skills such as schooling and language. The smaller the degree to which these skills are transferable between countries, the greater would be the decline in economic status between the pre-immigration and post-immigration jobs, and the greater would be the incentive to invest to overcome particular skill deficiencies, such as language difficulties. Language skills may be improved through formal language programs although, due to the lack of data on formal training programs, the emphasis in applied research has been on the informal determinants of language skills, including learning-by-doing.

Chiswick and Miller (1992) model earnings as a function of standard skill and demographic variables (educational attainment, labour-market experience, duration in the destination, weeks worked, marital status, citizenship, location of residence, birthplace) and dominant language fluency. The variables for duration of residence, citizenship and proficiency in the dominant language capture the primary dimensions of the economic adjustment process among immigrants. (To the extent that current educational attainment includes post-migration schooling, this too is part of the adjustment process (Chiswick and Miller 1994).) The relationship between earnings and duration of residence reflects learning about the institutions and idiosyncrasies of the labour market of the host country, cultural adjustment factors, the development of networks of labour-market contacts and investments in destination-specific human capital skills.

While acquiring citizenship is usually thought of as a measure of political or civic adjustment or assimilation, it also has economic dimensions. Citizenship would be expected to be associated with monetary and non-monetary rewards sufficient to offset the monetary and non-monetary costs (Yung 1992). The costs of citizenship include obtaining sufficient official language skill to pass the examination and, depending on the country of origin, the forfeiture of citizenship in the birthplace. Benefits include expanded job opportunities and higher earnings, and greater rights to sponsor the immigration of family members. Naturalization reflects a commitment to the host country and may be associated with greater investments in skills specific to the destination.

Learning the language of the host country also reflects a commitment to the adopted country and an adaptation to the circumstances of that country. It may provide access to better jobs, or make the individual more productive, and hence be associated with higher earnings. The interaction between duration of residence and language skills in the earnings equation has been a focus of recent studies of immigrant wage adjustment.

Empirical Evidence on Language Fluency

The majority of studies of dominant-language skills in Canada have been based on cross-tabulations. Examples include Richmond and Kalbach (1980) and de Vries and Vallee (1980), and summary details are contained in Table 1. Recently, multivariate approaches that have been successfully applied in other types of labour-market analysis have been used in the study of language capital. Chiswick and Miller (1992) present an analysis of the factors associated with variations in dominant language fluency in Canada based on the 1981 Census. Their encompassing study shows, directly, that an immigrant's official language fluency is related to both efficiency and exposure factors and indirectly, that the expected wage gains associated with dominant language skills affect the language capital investment decision. The major features of their study are summarized in Table 1.

The efficiency factors that affect language proficiency are years of education and age at arrival. Each additional year of education is associated

Table 1: Summary of Major Studies of Dominant Language Skills among Immigrants in Canada

Study	Primary Data Sets	Populations Studied	Primary Methodology	Dependent Variable	Explanatory Variables	Major Findings
Richmond & Kalbach (1980)	Census of Canada, 1971; Dept. of Manpower and Immigration Survey	Total population; Foreign-born; by Québec, English-Canada	Cross-tabulations of home language, official language	Birthplace, period of immigration, language skills, ethnic origin, sex	• Immigrants from western and eastern Europe have relatively high language skills; immigrants from southern Europe have a relatively low level of language skills • Language skills differ upon arrival in Canada and those (e.g., southern Europeans) possessing the fewest skills at arrival experience the most rapid improvement in their official language fluency
de Vries & Vallee (1980)	Census of Canada, 1971	Total population by province	Cross-tabulations of various language characteristics	Province, location, sex, age, education, birthplace, ethnic origin, years since migration	• Propensity to be bilingual in official languages negatively correlated with the relative density of mother tongue • Better educated more likely to be fluent in both languages • Official bilingualism less prevalent among older age groups • Immigrants who arrive as youths more likely to become English monolinguals

Study	Primary Data Sets	Populations Studied	Primary Methodology	Dependent Variable	Explanatory Variable	Major Findings
Chiswick & Miller (1992)	Census of Canada, 1981	Employed 25–64 year-old foreign-born workers	Binary probability models	Binary measure of official language fluency	Education, age, years since migration, marital status, residence in CMA, province, minority language concentration, birthplace	• Official language fluency increases with years of education and duration in Canada • Official language fluency decreases with age at arrival, foreign marriage and minority-language concentration • Official language fluency varies with country of origin in accordance with the extent to which one of Canada's official languages was used in the origin country
Chiswick & Miller (1993a)	Census of Canada, 1981	Employed 25–64 year-old foreign-born workers	Multinomial logit	Four categories: English only, French only, both English and French, neither English nor French	Education, age, years since migration, marital status, residence in CMA, province, minority language concentration, birthplace	• Learning English is the dominant feature of the immigrant experience • An older age at migration is associated with a higher proportion speaking only French and a lower proportion bilingual • English skills increase with years since migration • The better educated have a greater propensity to be bilingual

with about a one percentage point improvement in the proportion of immigrants fluent in English or French. The positive impact of a higher level of education may arise because the more educated have a greater mastery of their first language, are more efficient in learning new concepts, or were exposed to English or French in the curriculum in the higher levels of schooling in their country of origin. There is a strong negative relationship between age at immigration and dominant language fluency. This relationship is presumably reflecting, in large part, the diminution of the ability to acquire language skills with age (see Long 1990).

The exposure factors examined by Chiswick and Miller (1992) may be discussed in terms of exposure prior to migration, time units of exposure in Canada and the intensity of exposure per unit of time in Canada. The main variables capturing exposure prior to migration are the birthplace variables. These have been constructed in empirical analyses so as to identify countries where English and/or French have been used as the primary language or as a lingua franca. For example, the Asian countries have been categorized as "Chinese-Asia" and "Other-Asia," with the defining characteristic being the experience most of the countries in the latter group had with English or French during American, British and French colonial administrations or occupations.

Among the immigrants from Asia, those of Chinese origin have a rate of dominant language proficiency 10 percentage points lower than immigrants from other Asian countries and from English- and French-speaking countries, other variables the same. The language deficiency of the Chinese-Asians is also consistent with the greater linguistic distance between Chinese and the official languages of Canada. Southern Europeans also have a lower level of language skills; their rate of dominant language proficiency is 6 percentage points lower than that of immigrants from English- and French-speaking countries. Eastern European and western European immigrants have only slightly lower levels of language skills (1.4 and 1.1 percentage points, respectively) than otherwise similar immigrants from English- or French-speaking countries.

Time units of exposure in Canada are measured by the number of years since migration, which has a non-linear effect on official language proficiency: language skills improve, albeit at a decreasing rate, with years spent in Canada. There is, for example, a 10 percentage point difference in the rates of dominant language proficiency of a recent arrival and a comparable immigrant with the mean duration of residence (19 years) in Canada. The process of adjustment captured by the duration variable continues for at least 35 years.

Three variables were considered by Chiswick and Miller (1992) to measure the effect of the intensity of exposure per unit of time in Canada. Two of these capture home-environment factors, that is, marital characteristics and the presence of children in the household. The third is a measure of the concentration in the region of residence of speakers of the immigrant's minority first language. This latter variable captures social- and work-environment factors. The findings reveal that children do not affect language outcomes among men in Canada. This contrasts with the study of the U.S. and Israel where children are important to understanding variations in dominant language fluency. This difference may be associated with the higher overall level of dominant language fluency in Canada, which may lessen the importance of the exposure to the dominant language that parents gain through children. The result for Canada is similar to that reported for Australia (see Chiswick and Miller 1993b).

Similarly, marital status per se does not exercise an independent influence on language skills. However, where the individual married the current spouse prior to migration (and therefore where they presumably share the same first language) there is a statistically significant reduction in the probability of dominant language fluency. The foreign marriage variable may reflect language usage within the home. It may, however, also reflect a greater propensity to identify with the country of origin through both retaining their first language and eschewing the official languages of Canada.

The estimated effect of the language enclave variable is sizeable. It shows that if a region has a concentration of people speaking the same non-dominant home language as the respondent, which is 5 percentage points above the national average, the respondent's probability of being fluent in a dominant language would fall by 9 percentage points. Being able to communicate in a non-dominant language presumably provides a shelter against having to learn English or French. The adverse effect of a language enclave, however, is not neutral. It is more intense during the initial years in the destination, for less educated immigrants and for those who immigrated as adults. These are the very immigrants with the lowest level of language fluency.

The effects of these explanatory variables do not arise from subtle differences by country of origin. The study of the dominant language attainment process within the major birthplace groups yields a pattern of results consistent with the aggregate analysis. Education, age at migration, years since migration, foreign marriage and minority language concentration variables exercise important influences on dominant language fluency within country of birth categories. The larger impact of the human capital variables (education and duration in Canada) for birthplace regions with lower initial levels of dominant-language proficiency emerges as a major finding of the disaggregated analysis.

Empirical Evidence on Language Choice

Language choice in Canada has been an issue of considerable importance in empirical research. In an early study, Lieberson (1970) noted that among immigrants who are neither English nor French speakers, there is a clear tendency to adopt English as the spoken language. That is, English is the dominant language with regard to assimilation for immigrants. In large part this is attributable to the tendency of immigrants to locate in the English-speaking parts of Canada. That is, while the decision by immigrants regarding region of residence in Canada is influenced by economic factors, it is also influenced by the language of the immigrant and the province.

The language choice issue is developed in a formal model advanced in Chiswick and Miller (1993a). They distinguish among four language states: monolingual English speakers, monolingual French speakers, bilingual in the official languages and fluent in neither English nor French. Separate analyses are conducted for Québec and the rest of Canada.

The analysis has several major findings that help clarify the process of language acquisition described in the previous section. An older age at migration is associated with less fluency in the dominant languages, and this appears as a greater proportion reporting fluency in neither language and, in Québec, a smaller portion bilingual. Immigrants arriving in Canada at a later age also have an increased probability of speaking only French rather than only English. De Vries and Vallee (1980) also report that language use among immigrants is related to age at arrival, the most striking feature of the data being that those who arrived as youth tended to become unilingual English in higher proportions than others.

Fluency in the dominant languages increases with duration of residence in Canada, and the pattern of improvement in language skills differs by major language group. English language skills are nearly universal in English Canada, and there is only a slight increase with duration. In Québec, however, English fluency rises sharply with duration, largely as a consequence of a transformation of French-only speakers into English-French bilinguals.

Education plays an important role in the determination of language choice, and its effects differ between English-speaking Canada and Québec.

In the rest of Canada higher levels of schooling are primarily associated with a rise in bilingualism, with a decline in the proportion who are monolingual English or lacking fluency in both English and French. In Québec, higher levels of schooling are also associated with a pronounced increase in bilingualism, but with a sharp decline in French monolingualism. Note, however, that fluency in English rises in both regions with schooling level.

Linguistic distance between the language of the immigrants' country of origin and the official languages influences language choice. Thus, immigrants from France, and to a lesser extent Italy and Portugal, are much more likely to speak French but not English if they live in Québec. In English-speaking Canada nearly all of the immigrants from other parts of Europe, Asia and Central and South America speak English when they learn one of the official languages. Among immigrants from the same countries living in Québec, however, many speak only French or are English-French bilingual speakers.

Finally, it is noted that there are separate provincial effects in English Canada. Residence in the Eastern provinces is associated with a higher level of bilingualism, relative to speaking only English, than is the case in Ontario. In the provinces west of Ontario, however, the proportion speaking only English is significantly larger, at the expense of the bilingual and neither language categories.

Empirical Evidence on the Determinants of Earnings

There have been a number of studies that have adopted the human capital approach to investigate the links between language and earnings in Canada, including Veltman et al. (1979), Boulet (1980), Kuch and Haessel (1979), Abbott and Beach (1987), Meng (1987) and Chiswick and Miller (1988, 1992). These studies have been conducted exclusively on data for adult men. They have generally used information on first language, the usual language spoken at home, language spoken at work, knowledge of the official languages, and location in various ways to construct language variables that permit evaluation of the economic returns to language transfer (e.g., the learning of English by a Francophone), current language skills (e.g., the knowledge of at least one of the official languages) and language choice (e.g., knowledge of English, of French, or of English and French). In the study of immigrants, it is current language skills and choice that are most relevant to economic adjustment, and it is apparent that this information needs to be interacted with location to differentiate between residents of Québec and other parts of Canada.

Few of the Canadian studies on the relationship between earnings and language skills have an emphasis on the foreign born. The few exceptions examine either the economic returns to official language fluency (Chiswick and Miller 1992) or to official language choice (Abbott and Beach 1987, Meng 1987, Chiswick and Miller 1988). Table 2 contains relevant summary details.

Human Capital and Demographic Variables

Education and on-the-job training are both associated with substantial increases in earnings among adult, male, foreign-born workers in Canada. Thus, earnings increase by between 4 and 5 percent with each additional year of education, and by around 1.5 percent with each additional year of labour-market experience in the country of origin (evaluated at 10 years of experience). Labour-market experience in Canada is associated with an earnings premium compared with experience prior to migration. Evaluated at 10 years residence in Canada, the premium for Canadian over foreign experience is around 1.7 percent per year. Even after 20 years of residence in Canada, an extra year of Canadian labour-market experience tends to be worth one percentage point more in earnings than experience in the country of origin. All studies report that weekly earnings do not vary much with respect to the number of weeks worked, a 1 percent increase in weeks worked results in an increase in annual earnings of around 1 percent.

Region of residence affects earnings, with both size of location and province being important factors. Residents of census metropolitan areas have earnings slightly higher than workers who live outside the major cities. The earnings of immigrants in Québec are about 5 percent lower than in Ontario, and the earnings of residents of the Prairie provinces and British Columbia are about 10 percent higher than in Ontario.

Country of origin is very important for understanding variations in earnings in the Canadian labour market (Chiswick and Miller 1992). Each birthplace group has earnings significantly lower than the earnings of immigrants from Britain, *ceteris paribus*. The ranking in terms of decreasing earnings is: Britain, France, U.S., Africa, western Europe, southern Europe, Ireland, eastern Europe, West Indies, other Asia, South and Central America, Chinese-Asia. At the lowest end of the spectrum, the earnings of immigrants from South and Central America and Chinese-Asia are around 30 percentage points lower than for immigrants from Britain.

The earnings of immigrants who have become Canadian citizens are 7 percent higher than for non-citizens, when other variables remain the same (Chiswick and Miller 1992; Yung 1992). This sizeable earnings premium may reflect, in part, the use of citizenship status as a screen for access to higher paying jobs, explicit barriers to alien employment or the greater motivation and commitment to living in Canada of individuals taking out citizenship.

Earnings and Language Fluency
The average annual earnings of adult male immigrant workers in Canada who are fluent in a dominant language are 49 percent higher than the earnings of immigrant workers who lack this skill (Chiswick and Miller 1992). Those who possess dominant language skills are also relatively well endowed in most other skills that are associated with higher earnings. Their average level of schooling is 11.8 years and their average duration of residence in Canada is 19.7 years, compared to the averages of 7.1 and 11.9 years, respectively, for workers who lack fluency in a dominant language. While workers who lack dominant language fluency have more years of total labour-market experience (34 compared to 26), two-thirds of this experience was accumulated prior to immigration because they immigrated at an older age.

When allowance is made for these differences in other forms of human capital, individuals who are proficient in a dominant language have earnings 12.2 percentage points higher than male immigrants who lack this skill (Chiswick and Miller 1992). When the comparison is between men who lack proficiency in a dominant language and English-French bilinguals, the earnings disadvantage of the former group is 19 percent (Chiswick and Miller 1988). The inclusion of the dominant language proficiency variable has a negligible impact on the effects of other variables on earnings. In particular, the partial effect on earnings of years since migration is not affected in any material way (see Abbott and Beach 1987; Chiswick and Miller 1988; 1992). It appears, therefore, that the effect on earnings of duration of residence in Canada is largely due to unmeasured factors rather than measured language fluency.

The evidence also suggests that those who have a greater economic incentive to acquire fluency have a higher degree of fluency. That is, the acquisition of language capital appears to be responsive to the economic incentives for acquiring language skills.

Table 2: Summary of Selected Studies of the Impact of Language Skills on the Earnings of Immigrants in Canada

Study	Primary Data Sets	Populations Studied	Dependent Variable	Independent Variables	Definition of Language Variables	Major Findings
Meng (1987)	1973 Job Mobility Survey	22–64-year old males with positive weeks worked and earnings in 1972; non-students; by birthplace	Natural log of annual earnings	Education, experience, weeks worked, full-time, self-employment, work history, province, size of residence, language, marital status, religion, birthplace, years since migration, family background variables	3 groups for first spoken language, E, F, O 3 groups for current language practice, E, F, B	• Results for language variables not reported, but years since migration a significant determinant of earnings in equations that control for language
Abbott & Beach (1987)	1973 Job Mobility Survey	22–64-year old males with positive weeks worked and earnings in 1972	Natural log of annual earnings in 1972	Education, experience, weeks worked, usual hours, province, size of residence, language, marital status, occupation, birthplace, years since migration, age at migration, family background variables	3 groups for first spoken language E, F, O 3 groups for language in first job, E, F, B, O 3 groups for language in current job, E, F, B, O	• Language in current job more important that first spoken language or language in first job • Return to bilingualism for native French speakers exceeds return for native English speakers • Results not specific to foreign born • Little change in years since migration-earnings relationship following inclusion of language variables

Study	Primary Data Sets	Populations Studied	Dependent Variable	Independent Variables	Definition of Language Variables	Major Findings
Chiswick & Miller (1988)	Census of Canada, 1981	Males, aged 25–64 with positive earnings; by birthplace	Natural log of annual earnings	Education, experience, weeks worked, marital status, employment status, residence in CMA, province, language, ethnic origin, duration of residence	Six groups combining official language and province: F only, non-Québec; F only, Québec; E only, non-Québec; E only, Québec; B, neither E nor F	• Return to bilingualism for English and French foreign-born monolinguals in Québec but only to foreign-born English monolinguals in English-Canada • Large reduction in earnings associated with dominant language deficiency among foreign-born • Addition of language variables results in minor reduction in impact of duration of residence variables
Chiswick & Miller (1992)	Census of Canada, 1981	Employed foreign-born males aged 25–64	Natural log of annual earnings	Education, experience, weeks worked, marital status, residence in CMA, province, language fluency, birthplace, duration of residence	Binary variable recording whether the respondent could speak E or F well enough to conduct a conversation	• Individuals who are proficient in a dominant language have earnings 12.2 percent higher than individuals who lack this skill • Inclusion of language variable has a negligible impact on all other estimated co-efficients

Note: E =English; F=French; O=language other than English or French; B=Bilingual in the official languages

Earnings and Language Choice

The returns to language choice are examined in Chiswick and Miller (1988). They argue that it is important to differentiate between residents of Québec and English Canada. Hence, the earnings positions of six language groups are considered: bilinguals, English monolinguals resident in Québec, French monolinguals resident in Québec, English monolinguals resident in English Canada, French monolinguals resident in English Canada, and individuals who lack fluency in English or French.

French, English and other monolinguals resident in Québec have lower earnings than bilinguals. Compared to English-French bilinguals in Québec, the earnings disadvantage for French monolinguals is 14 percentage points, that of their English monolingual counterparts is 10 percentage points, and that of other monolinguals in 19 percentage points. Another way of looking at these results is that the ranking in terms of earnings in Québec is English-French bilinguals, English monolinguals, French monolinguals and other language monolinguals.

Among residents of English-speaking Canada, the earnings of French monolinguals and bilinguals do not differ significantly, while the earnings of English monolinguals are around 6 percentage points lower than bilinguals, and the earnings of other language monolinguals are 19 percentage points lower than bilinguals. Hence, while the learning of English or French by those lacking official language skills results in higher earnings in English Canada, bilingualism results in higher earnings only for English monolinguals.

Conclusion

The empirical analyses surveyed in this paper demonstrate that the fluency of immigrants in one of the two official languages in Canada can be related to efficiency, exposure and economic incentive factors. Language skills of immigrants in Canada are of course related to their exposure to English and French in their country of origin. Official language fluency, however, also rises with years of education and with the number of years of residence in Canada. It declines with age at migration, foreign marriage (i.e., marriage prior to migration) and with a greater minority-language concentration of the area of residence. Language skills are shown to be determined endogenously with earnings: immigrants who acquire official language fluency are those with the greatest economic incentive to do so.

Immigrants to Canada appear to select an official language to learn in accordance with a human capital model of language choice. Thus, immigrants tend to select the language that is closer to their first language (which lowers the cost of obtaining dominant language fluency), and that is closer to the language that predominated in their region of residence (which lowers the costs and increases the economic benefits of learning the language). For example, in English Canada, nearly all immigrants speak English but not French, with the exception of those from Romance language countries. Among immigrants from the same countries living in Québec, however, many speak only French or are English-French bilinguals. Immigrants tend to choose the language with the broader labour market. Consequently, English is viewed as the dominant language in the immigrant adjustment process in Canada.

The research shows that earnings differ across language groups, but that there are important differences between Québec and the rest of Canada. Immigrants who are able to carry on a conversation in English or French have earnings that are around 12 percent higher than immigrants who do not possess proficiency in an official language, other measured variables the same. There is a premium to bilingualism, although this differs between Québec and English Canada. Generally Anglophones are better situated in the labour market than Francophones.

The empirical results demonstrate that if the successful economic adjustment of immigrants is an important policy objective, there will be benefits from selecting immigrants who have, or who can be expected to acquire quickly, official language skills. Many groups of immigrants (e.g., the young, and better educated) fall into the latter category. As immigrants respond positively to the economic incentives for fluency, it can be argued that effects to shelter them from the economic consequences of inadequate proficiency will be counterproductive. It is also apparent that for Québec to be successful in promoting French language fluency among the immigrants it selects, it should focus on those with pre-existing French or other Romance language skills.

References

Abbott, Michael G. and Charles M. Beach. 1987. Immigrant Earnings Differentials and Cohort Effects in Canada. Kingston, Ont.: Queen's University, Institute for Economic Research, Discussion Paper No. 705.

Boulet, Jac-André. 1980. *Language and Earnings in Montréal*. Hull: Canadian Government Publishing Centre.

Breton, Albert. 1978a. *Bilingualism: An Economic Approach*. Montréal: C.D. Howe Research Institute.

———. 1978b. Nationalism and Language Policies. *Canadian Journal of Economics* 11(4):656–68.

Chiswick, Barry R. 1978. The Effect of Americanization on the Earnings of Foreign-Born Men. *Journal of Political Economy* 85(5):897–921.

———. 1979. The Economic Progress of Immigrants: Some Apparently Universal Patterns. In *Contemporary Economic Problems*, edited by William Fellner. Washington DC: American Enterprise Institute.

Chiswick, Barry R., and Paul W. Miller. 1988. Earnings in Canada: The Roles of Immigrant Generation, French Ethnicity and Language. *Research in Population Economics* 6:183–224.

———. 1992. Language in the Immigrant Labour Market. In *Immigration, Language and Ethnicity: Canada and the United States*, edited by Barry R. Chiswick. Washington DC: American Enterprise Institute.

———. 1993a. Language Choice Among Immigrants in a Multi-Lingual Destination. Chicago: University of Illinois at Chicago, Department of Economics.

———. 1993b. The Endogeneity Between Language and Earnings: An International Analysis. Chicago: University of Illinois at Chicago, Department of Economics. Mimeographed.

———. 1994 (forthcoming). The Determinants of Post-Migration Investments in Education. *Economics of Education Review*.

Grenier, G., and F. Vaillancourt. 1983. An Economic Perspective on Learning a Second Language. *Journal of Multilingual and Multicultural Development* 4(6):471–83.

Kuch, P., and W. Haessel. 1979. *An Analysis of Earnings in Canada*. Ottawa: Statistics Canada.

Lieberson, Stanley. 1970. *Language and Ethnic Relations in Canada*. New York: John Wiley.

Long, Michael H. 1990. Maturational Constraints on Language Development. *Studies in Second Language Acquisition* 12(3):251–85.

Meng, Ronald. 1987. The Earnings of Canadian Immigrants and Native-born Males. *Applied Economics* 19:1107–19.

Richmond, A.H., and W.E. Kalbach. 1980. *Factors in the Adjustment of Immigrants and their Descendants*. Ottawa: Statistics Canada.

Tainer, Evelina. 1988. English Language Proficiency and Earnings among Foreign-Born Men. *Journal of Human Resources* 23(1):108–22.

Veltman, Calvin, Jac-André Boulet, and Charles Castonguay. 1979. The Economic Context of Bilingualism and Language Transfer in the Montreal Metropolitan Area. *Canadian Journal of Economics* 13(2):468–79.

de Vries, John. 1986. *Towards a Sociology of Languages in Canada*. Québec: International Centre for Research on Bilingualism.

de Vries, John, and Frank G. Vallee. 1980. *Language Use in Canada*. Ottawa: Statistics Canada.

Yung, Juliana. 1992. The Economic Determinants of Naturalization: The Case of Canada. Ph.D. dis., Chicago: University of Illinois at Chicago, Department of Economics.

SHEILA M. NEYSMITH

Developing Policies That Support Aging Women: An Examination of the Canadian Situation

This paper examines the interaction of pension and home-care policy in the lives of Canadian women. It juxtaposes benefits flowing to women from these public resources to those flowing from private resources, in particular, those of family-based care. In doing so, the analysis questions policies that are presented as gender neutral; policies that assume that ensuring individuals' claims are processed under "equal terms and conditions" will result in equitable outcomes. Pension benefits and health care are usually discussed in isolation as two separate areas of expertise—and indeed each is sufficiently complicated to warrant this. This isolation, however, makes their interactive impact on particular segments of the population less visible.

One of the themes that ran through this conference was the effect of the Canadian version of federalism on various policy arenas. Nowhere are the dynamics of this more apparent than in the policies that affect elderly persons. Pension and health care authority tend to fall under federal and provincial jurisdictions respectively—although not exclusively. This adds a level of complexity, not to mention political sensitivity, to the discussion. Although a valid concern in its own right, a preoccupation with federal–provincial relations can distract from other issues of equity—in particular those of gender justice, which address quite a different set of concerns.

Old Age Income Security

The Canadian old age security system is not only multi-tiered, it also reflects several principles of eligibility.

- The Old Age Security (OAS) pension is a right of citizenship; it is universal and paid for out of general revenue with about three million beneficiaries.

- On top of this foundation, about half the population over 65 qualify for some part of the Guaranteed Income Supplement (GIS), a federal income tested program; there are additional provincial top-ups.

- The other component of the public system is the Canada/Québec Pension Plan (CPP/QPP) that covers all members of the labour force. Employee and employer contribute to it; benefits reflect an individual's earnings record up to a yearly maximum. About two-thirds of those now over 65 receive some benefits.

- Occupational pension coverage varies considerably across industrial sectors; about 40 percent currently receive some income from this source.

- Finally, Registered Retirement Savings Plans (RRSPs) are a tax-deductible savings scheme available to individuals with sufficient discretionary income to take advantage of them during their years in the labour force.

As Canadians we are rather proud of several aspects of this system. Its foundation is universal; the public part is indexed four times a year; during the eighties we had several major pension reviews that resulted in making occupational pensions more portable, decreased their vesting require-

Table 1
Canadian Retirement Income System

Level one	Beneficiaries	Eligibility
Old Age Security 65+	2.9 million	Universal pending clawbacks
Guaranteed Income		
Supplement 65+	1.4 million	Income-based
Spouse's Allowance 60–64	135,000	Income-based
Provincial/Territorial		
Supplements mostly 65+	430,000	Income-based
Level two	Contributors	Pensioners
Canada Pension Plan	8.9 million	1.6 million
Québec pension Plan	2.9 million	0.5 million
TOTAL	11.8 million	2.1 million
Level three	Plan Members in Labour Force	Retired Beneficiaries
Occupational Pension Plans	4.7 million	1.2 million
Registered Retirement		
Savings Plans	3.2 million	332,000?

Source: National Council of Welfare 1989. Appendix A.

ments and allowed for pension entitlements to be split upon marriage breakdown.

These positives notwithstanding, there is considerable variation across the population in terms of benefits received from the various parts of the system. On the one hand, over 40 percent of the elderly population is hovering at the poverty line (Grenon and Bernard 1989). On the other hand, benefits can be substantial for those who have steady and good incomes during their working years. Because a major part of pension benefits are geared to one's track record in the labour force, women do about as well financially in their old age as they did when younger—not too well. Only women with continuous activity in above average paying jobs can feel secure about having incomes in their old age that are above the guaranteed minimum. In other words, financial independence is assured only for those with employment patterns similar to those of men; for many women such assurance is possible only if they happened to have had husbands with occupational pension benefits.

Thus, it is not surprising that in May 1991 women received an average of $295.00 from the Canada/Québec Pension Plan compared to $500.00 for men. At that time the maximum Guaranteed Income Supplement benefit was $387.00 per month. The Canada/Québec Pension Plan is now some 25-years-old. It is an interesting historical footnote that at the time of its inception, the CPP/QPP was seen as replacing the need for the income-tested GIS. Unfortunately, the earning capacity in women's jobs is such that they still do better on income-tested schemes than on those that reflect their life-long salary paths.

I want to juxtapose these financial facts of aging women's lives against some assumptions that underlie the design of our long-term care policies.

Canadian Long-term Care

I will focus on long-term care, particularly home care, because chronic care, and home care programs in particular, will be *the* focus of policy debates in the next few years as health care directions are reviewed. The outcome of this debate will have significant impact on the welfare of women as care receivers, as informal caregivers and as paid service providers.

When people laud the Canadian health care system they are usually referring to those services covered by the *Canada Health Act*. Its reputation is based on the five principles that underlie it: public administration, comprehensiveness, universality, portability and accessability. Unfortunately, only traditional medical services are covered. These are defined specifically as goods and services that are *medically* necessary and distributed by *licensed medical practitioners* and *organizations* for the purpose of maintaining health, preventing disease and diagnosing and treating injury, illness or disability (Section 2).

This wording effectively excludes those services that make up the bulk of home-based care. Despite some federal–provincial cost sharing arrangements, Canada does not have a national long-term care program based on legislation similar to the Canada Health Act. The latter program is able to utilize funding as a mechanism for ensuring access to covered services across the country. Although all provinces have long-term care programs, their organization, coverage and funding patterns differ—as does the language used to describe their various components.

Provincial long-term care policy statements present a variety of reasons for promoting home care as a desirable policy direction. However, its rapid expansion in the second half of the eighties was driven by spiralling costs— and even worse predictions of a continued reliance on institutionally based care—that by international standards are rather high in Canada.

About 7 percent of Canada's population over 65 is in some kind of institutional care; this rises to 35.6 percent for those over 85 (Forbes et al. 1987, 37). These figures are higher than those for the United Kingdom and the United States. There is, however, considerable provincial variability. For example, among the 85-and-over group the rate is 30 percent in Nova Scotia, 41 percent in Ontario, and 50.5 percent in Alberta (Stone and Frenken 1988). These figures raise questions about the organization of our long-term care systems as well as the cost implications of the current set-up. My concern, however, is that the development of home-care programs has been so pushed by cost that it has crippled their potential as a creative alternative for meeting the needs of elderly persons.

A major review of the Canadian long-term care system in 1989 described it as:

1. having very little systematic data; fragmented, with too many players "doing their own thing"; national level co-operation seems elusive.

2. community based programs are threatened by having fallen into the pit of cost-effectiveness analysis; too large a proportion of what we know about home care deals with its impact, for better or for worse (and it's usually for worse) on health care costs.

3. the orientation of community based services is threatened because medical and hospital based interests, who are the most powerful players in Canadian health care, increasingly seek to develop initiatives in the area. (Marshall 1989, 87–91)

In the last couple of years the larger provinces have undertaken reviews of the health and social service programs that are heavily used by elderly persons (British Columbia 1989; Alberta 1988; Price Waterhouse 1988; Ontario 1990; Québec 1985). Despite considerable variation in the breadth and depth of these assessments, it is fair to say that the issue of cost control was a major theme in all of them.

To the outside observer, Québec and Manitoba would seem to have the most integrated long-term care systems. Although specific organizational features differ, and many would argue that they are imbedded in differing philosophies of provincial responsibilities and community-based care, in both provinces a central authority ensures province–wide coverage while decentralized delivery structures permit considerable local variability.

Ontario, which accounts for about one-third of the country's population, has one of the most fragmented arrangements. Ontario has argued that the size and mix of its population warrants a "decentralized" system. Most informed sources suggest that the current system is decentralized by default, not by design. In addition, Ontario's laissez-faire approach to long-term care has resulted in home-care services remaining undeveloped while costs have escalated on the institutional side of the ledger. Within the long-term care system most monies go to nursing home and chronic care beds; only 23 percent of the total is spent on in-home or community services (Ontario 1990, 8).

In recent years the Ministry of Health has been facing enormous pressures to contain costs as federal transfer funds have shrunk. It was within this atmosphere of fiscal restraint that an interministerial committee was appointed to develop an integrated province-wide system of long-term care. A major policy paper has been released that outlines future directions in this area (Ontario 1990). Not surprisingly, the focus was on the coordination, not the expansion of home care; issues of efficiency and cost control permeate the paper.

At the other extreme is Manitoba's long-term care program, which has been in operation since the early seventies. In a national comparative assessment done in 1987 it was noted that Manitoba's scheme had one of the highest per capita costs in the country. For example, in 1985 the per capita costs were: Manitoba, $20.38; Ontario, $15.05; Saskatchewan, $11.64; New Brunswick, $11.38 (Canada 1987).

Shortly after the release of these figures Manitoba engaged a group of outside consultants to conduct a thorough evaluation of its services. This study is of interest because it captures the contradictions shaping the development of long-term care policy across the country. The study revealed that clients using home care were much sicker than in earlier years. In fact, home care was rapidly turning into a hospital replacement service, even though the program had neither the human nor financial resources to undertake this type of care. The report documents pressures for home care to assume even more of a hospital replacement function in the future (Price Waterhouse 1988, 30).

In addition to these broad concerns about the purpose of a home-care service, the specific issue of whether or not the program was too expensive was addressed. The home-care budget had averaged an annual growth of 19 percent over the last 12 years. However, this was accompanied by a growth in cases, and in units of service per case, and it offered a richer set of services than that available in other provinces (Price Waterhouse 1988, 26). There was concern that administrative costs were so low that efficiency might suffer.

Finally, the overall growth of costs was found to be comparable to those of other provinces. For example, Ontario and British Columbia averaged cost growths of 24 and 19 percent, respectively, during the same period. Recently instituted spending ceilings in Alberta and Saskatchewan on most components of their home-care programs probably explain why their costs are now lower than in previous years. Manitoba's program administrative costs are lowest: 17 percent—compared to 23 percent in Ontario.

The Manitoba system has acquired a fair international reputation over the years for the quality of its services (see Kane and Kane 1985 for details). It also apparently meets an accountant's and taxpayer's demand for better services at lower cost. Yet the recommendations from this evaluation endorse policy directions that are consistent with those appearing in assessments of other provincial long-term care schemes: above all contain costs. There is not even a suggestion that, in order to be consistent with policy statements, home-care services ought to be expanding and that resources for doing this could be diverted from the high cost institutional sector.

It is only if home-care costs are examined in isolation from other components of the health care system that the recommendations made in the report are tenable. The report

1. recommended that housekeeping, meals-on-wheels and cleaning should be provided on a fee-for-service basis under non-profit auspices. Since

these would be on a sliding scale, and if we assume that 40 percent of Manitoba's elderly qualify for an income supplement (see earlier GIS figures), only pennies would be saved.

2. noted that while 51 percent of the clientele lives alone, and 30 percent resides with an aging spouse, 75 percent had family living in the same city. While the age of the adult relatives is unknown, it is possible that family can assume responsibility for all or part of the elderly client's needs (e.g. house cleaning, maintenance, financial management, transportation). Regions where clients lack close family proximity may need to be prepared to provide more support services than in other regions. (Price Waterhouse 1988, 72)

In sum, cost will not be controlled by redirecting resources from one part of the health care system to another, but by expanding family-based care. Such recommendations do not reflect the fact that families *already* provide over 80 percent of care!

Perhaps most disturbing in such evaluations is the underlying "blaming-the-victim" stance that believes elderly persons overuse services. Canadian data are consistent with international comparisons showing that an aging population per se is not a significant factor in rising health care budgets (Pfaff 1990, 20; Evans 1990, 121). Contrary to the facts, since elderly individuals are the primary users of home care, these programs are particularly vulnerable to charges of overspending. In an overview of home-care programs across the country, Evelyn Shapiro, a community health scientist who has tracked the Manitoba system since its inception, concluded:

> The irony of the current situation is that, although home care is more often "under the microscope" than the "big spenders," its program directors are generally further from the centre of power within the provinces' decision-making process than the high cost health sectors. (Shapiro 1988, 43)

In a review of models of community-care programs in the United States and Canada, Marshall (1989) noted that, contrary to the rhetoric, most reviewers of cost-effectiveness research found little support for home care being cheaper; he also asked why home care had to be defended on cost grounds when institutional programs are judged by criteria having to do with their purpose.

Our home-care programs are still based on residualist welfare models. They assume that the family is the "natural" or socially given channel through which an individual's need for care is properly met. Only when this breaks down or is not available should the state intervene. This expectation of the informal care system operates at the same time that pension benefits, beyond a guaranteed minimum, rest on earnings from paid work. It is women's labour-force patterns that are primarily shaped by expectations that they will care for dependent family members whether they be young or old.

I would now like to take a closer look at the so-called "informal care system" from which we are expecting major contributions.

An Examination of Informal Care

Studies show that for every aged person in an institution there are approximately two equally impaired elderly persons living in private homes who remain there by virtue of the critical role played by informal support systems (Rowe 1985). Data from the Canadian Health and Activity Survey (Statistics Canada 1986) found that 45.5 percent of seniors over age 85 report some disability. (Disability was defined as a limitation that was not alleviated by a technical aid and had lasted or was expected to last for at least six months.)

In a 1987 national survey of Canadians over 65, respondents were queried about the assistance they received with those types of activities for which services do exist in some communities (Stone 1988, 53-54). Some of the findings were:

- by their mid-70s even persons reporting good health were needing help with grocery shopping;
- that the majority of services were provided by informal sources;
- that reliance on formal organizations, however, rises with age for those living alone, and one-third of women over 80 live alone;
- that for those over 80, about half of men and 1 in 5 women received help with housework and meal preparation. Spouses and then daughters were the helpers; friends and neighbours did very little;
- personal care was not received by many respondents.

Findings from this national survey accord with other Canadian smaller-scale studies on patterns of help. They also support studies showing home-care users are older, and have more functional incapacities, a less positive assessment of their health and a smaller informal network than comparable groups of non-service users. Home-care users tend to receive as much or more informal help as do non-users; however their assistants (helpers) are less likely to be located in the home. (Chappell 1985; Beland 1984; 1985). For instance, in a random sample from one province of persons with functional impairments, over half received help only from the informal system (Chappell and Blandford 1991).

Most provincial home-care policies have statements declaring their support of family caregivers. What is more difficult to find out is exactly how this is put into practice allowing us to evaluate its impact.

Furthermore, a generalized commitment to supporting caregivers begs the question of who these people are: we know that a substantial group are elderly spouses, both men and women (Stone 1988; Green 1988; Stone, Cafferata and Sangl 1987). Such caregivers provide the most consistent care, and resist institutional placement longer, regardless of their spouse's level of disability. We know that the situation of caregiving elderly spouses is qualitatively different from that of caregiving provided inter-generationally. The former are usually old themselves but the care they give tends to be embedded within an intimate relationship that can give it a meaning not possible in other familial situations.

There is also mounting evidence, however, that men and women experience the conditions of caregiving quite differently (Horowitz 1985; Brody et al. 1990; Pruchno and Resch 1989; Stoller 1990). Some of these differences are around the dimensions of physical and mental deterioration emphasized, assumptions about authority, task management, and the use of social supports (Miller 1990, 97). Intergenerational caregivers are primarily daughters who fit parental care into their other family responsibilities and employment commitments. To group them all as caregivers masks these differences.

In addition, research focusing on care by family members does not address the situation of several other subgroups of elderly. Fifteen percent of ever-married Canadians and 9 percent of those who have never married do not have children. It is no accident that such persons are disproportionately represented among service users and institutional residents.

Finally, extended family, friends and neighbours respond to emergency situations; they do not provide the type of continuous involvement that frail persons require. It is misleading to suggest that they can supply essential services. Including them as part of the informal sector serves more of an ideological than service function—it pumps up the illusion of substance when in fact the informal sector is the care provided by an elderly spouse and/or a harried daughter.

Despite these data, existing services assume a familial model of care is the model of choice. In other words, the fact that families provide 80 percent of care has been transformed into the normative assumption that this approach is the most desirable. It is recognized that in some cases this preferred model cannot be realized because of strain on the caregiver and / or the lack of an appropriate individual in the social network of the elderly person. Services are then developed to fill in these gaps; however, these documents constantly reaffirm the expectation that it is the responsibility of families to provide daily care (Rosenthal and Neysmith 1990).

Shoring up the Caregiver

Over the last few years Canadian service providers have become more aware of the economic and emotional costs borne by informal caregivers, most of whom are women. Efforts have been made to provide help with some of the daily routine. However, as Hooyman (1991) has argued, the cost-effectiveness of these programs is often evaluated by whether they prolong the caring relationship, not the caregiver's well-being. Interventions aimed at enhancing self-esteem and self-efficacy may in fact imply that personal inadequacy is the source of caregiver burnout. Training programs that promote efficiency and better time management in task performance have been promoted as a presumed antidote to stress. It is interesting that the correlation between lower stress and task management has been primarily associated with male caregivers, yet it is women who are the focus of these programs.

However, no matter how efficiently one might learn to change a bed, this does not deal with the stress of having to do it several times a night. Whatever short-term benefits may accrue by focusing on individual stress, familial responsibility is reinforced rather than challenged. Such programs are limited in their potential to alter the structural imbalance of care responsibilities. To put it graphically, we are concentrating on rescuing individuals from drowning downstream rather than going upstream to see who pushed them in in the first place!

Canadian research substantiates research in other countries showing that people with similar conditions receive different services depending on where, and with whom, they happen to live (Beland 1989). In fact in Canada, as in Australia and the UK, caregivers have now become part of the service unit—sometimes as co-clients or co-workers—consumers in their own right (Twigg 1990). One of the consequences of this model is that *need* is det ermined at the point of assessment, albeit usually in terms of service availability, but *provision* is based on an assessment of the person *and* the family's ability to provide service.

Research on various aspects of family obligation shows clearly that family support is there but one does not have a right to it as a citizen. Reliance on kin is seen as a safety net, a last resort, something to fall back on in an emergency (Finch 1989). This does not agree with the assumptions underlying the rationing of most of our services.

An unspoken corollary of this de facto familial model of care is that caregiving should not cost. Traditionally, caring for others is women's work. This largely explains why it is undervalued and underpaid. It is interesting that despite such public underestimation of the job, women who provide the services view the work itself differently. My own research on home-care workers supports that of others showing high job satisfaction on the intrinsic components of the job (Neysmith and Nichols 1989). However, the turnover rate is also high. Across the country it is over 50 percent per annum, primarily because of low wages.

Our ambivalence about paying for care is a real if somewhat underplayed component of the home-care discussion. One of the results of current attitudes is low wages for front line home-care providers who are primarily women. There seems to be an assumption that caring for strangers is the same as caring for family members and should be done on an altruistic basis; otherwise it will attract "the wrong kind of people." This is quite different from the criterion that we use in other skilled jobs where the dictum is to pay a decent salary in order to attract "good people." For example, in the male-dominated, service professions there is no doubt that the maxim "you get what you pay for" prevails. Most people do not question the motives of physicians or lawyers when they demand high fees (Leat and Gay 1987, 62). Payment and care are not antithetical—payment does not negate caring, just as non-payment does not guarantee it.

The unpaid, related caregiver is in an even more precarious position than the paid care provider. She does not have the option of quitting. I choose these words carefully because caring for family members is not something that women choose to do in the context of weighing alternatives, imputing opportunity costs for various courses of action and deciding on a course of action reflecting economic rationalism. (If they did there would not be an informal care system.) Rather, research in Canada, Britain and the U.S. documents how women are socialized to care, and are well aware of the costs and benefits that accrue to them. However, it has also become clear that this work is invisible when done within the family context (Baines et al. 1991; Abel and Nelson 1990; Ungerson 1990).

I would argue that until the needs of frail elderly persons become unhooked from ideological presuppositions of family responsibility, the prognosis is poor for improving the quantity and quality of, as well as remuneration for, this type of labour. Throughout their lives it is women, rather than men, who find themselves doing aspects of both private and public caring labour. Ironically, their longer life expectancies means that women are more likely to be the recipient of lower incomes and rationed services resulting from the unpaid labour that they performed in their earlier years—a graphic instance of the social creation of dependency.

Conclusion

Theories of justice are centrally concerned with whether, how and why persons should be treated differently from one another. They are about which initial or acquired characteristics or positions in society legitimize differential treatment of persons by social institutions, laws and customs. They are about how and whether and to what extent beginnings should affect outcomes (Okin 1989, 8).

In this paper, Canadian pension and home-care policies were analyzed to see how well they promote gender-based justice. On international comparisons our policies measure up quite well but their benefits do not flow equitably to all sectors of our population. In fact, they place many women in a precarious position. Theory and practices imbedded in our pension and long-term care programs actually reinforce the bias against women that exist separately within each.

Family obligations are viewed by the state in a different way than are financial obligations. In the latter the concept of citizenship underlies an individual's right to sufficient resources for survival; the claims that people make to secure these is upon the community as a whole, not the family. (Historically this was not always so but the welfare state idea has led to a stand that people have a right to the means of subsistence as citizens no matter what their personal past or present circumstances.)

However, when it comes to the rights and obligations of caring for physically dependent elderly persons, the individual gets attached to a family that then tempers her/his claim on public goods and services. This allows services to be restricted in a way that cannot be done when we are addressing pension entitlements. Whatever the hue and cry about the amount of these, payments are made if a person qualifies. Not so home care—here the availability of kin to do caring modifies the assessment of need that forms the basis of service allocation.

Thus in Canadian long-term care policy one finds strong statements about a commitment to support family caregivers. However, these statements are always imbedded within overriding concerns of financial constraints (Rosenthal and Neysmith 1990). Absent from these documents is a serious discussion of how resources might be redistributed within the total health care budget—not just capping the growth of institutional beds. It seems that the real meaning of supporting the family is supporting private (family) responsibility for care of the elderly rather than public (collective) responsibility.

The interpretation of need is a very political act; not the obvious or given that is often presented as we debate the pros and cons of various assessment instruments. Most important is our understanding of what are family obligations, citizen rights and social justice, and who shapes the discourse. If Canadians seriously propose to develop a social model of care that is also just, we will have to build in a level of service guarantee that is grounded in public, not private responsibility, where the old person is viewed as a citizen with rights as well as responsibilities rather than as a dependent family member.

I wonder what possibilities might open up if Canada were to adopt a version of the Scandinavian policy (Hokensted and Johansson 1990, 255) that states there should be sufficient home care to ensure that no family is forced to substitute informal care for formal care.

Bibliography

Abel, E., and M. Nelson, eds. 1990. Circles of Care: *Work and Identity in Women's Lives*. Albany: State University of New York Press.

Alberta. 1988. *A New Vision for Long-term Care: Meeting the Need*. Edmonton.

Baines, C., P. Evans, and S. Neysmith. eds. 1991. *Women's Caring: A Feminist Perspective on Social Welfare*. Toronto: McClelland & Stewart.

Beland, F. 1984. The Family and Adults 65 Years of Age and Over: Co-residency and the Receipt of Help. *Canadian Review of Sociology and Anthropology* 21:302–17.

———. 1985. Who Are Those Most Likely to Be Institutionalized: The Elderly Who Receive Comprehensive Home Care Services or Those Who Do Not? *Social Science and Medicine* 2:347–54.

———. 1989. Patterns of Health and Social Service Utilization. *Canadian Journal on Aging* 8(1):19–33.

British Columbia. Minister of Health and Minister Responsible for Seniors. 1989. *Towards a Better Age: Strategies for Improving the Lives of Senior British Columbians*. Victoria.

Brody, E., N. Dempsey and R. Pruchno. 1990. Mental Health of Sons and Daughters of the Institutionalized Aged. *The Gerontologist* 30(2):212–19.

Canada. 1985. Department of Health and Welfare. *Profiles on Home Care/Home Support Programs*. Ottawa: Health Services and Promotion Branch.

———. 1986. Department of Health and Welfare. *Achieving Health for All: A Framework for Health Promotion*. Ottawa.

———. 1987. Department of Health and Welfare. *National Health Expenditures in Canada 1975–1985*. Ottawa.

———.1988. Federal/Provincial/Territorial Sub-Committee on Long-Term Care. *Description of Long-Term Care Services in Provinces and Territories of Canada*. Final Report. Ottawa.

Chappell, N. 1985. Social Support and the Receipt of Home Care Services. *The Gerontologist* 25(1):47–54.

Chappell, N., and A. Blandford. 1991. Informal and Formal Care: Exploring the Complementarity. *Ageing and Society* 11:299–317.

Daatland, Svein. 1990. What Are Families For? On Family Solidarity and Preference for Help. *Ageing and Society* 10 (Part 1, March):1–16.

Evans, R. 1990. Tension, Compression, and Shear: Directions, Stresses, and Outcomes of Health Care Cost Control. *Journal of Health Politics, Policy and Law* 15(1):101–28.

Finch, J. 1989. *Family Obligations and Social Change*. Cambridge: Polity Press.

Forbes, W., J. Jackson and A. Kraus. 1987. *Institutionalization of the Elderly in Canada*. Toronto: Butterworths.

Green, H. 1988. *Informal Carers*. London: OPCS, HMSO.

Grenon, André, and Marie-Luce Bernard. 1989. *The Financial Situation of Canadian Pensioners. Pension Survey 1987*. Research Note Income Security Prog. Ottawa: Health and Welfare Canada.

Hokensted, M., and L. Johansson. 1990. Caregiving for the Elderly in Sweden: Program Challenges and Policy Initiatives. In *Aging and Caregiving: Theory, Research and Policy*, edited by D. Biegel and A. Blum. Newbury Park: Sage Publications.

Hooyman, N. 1991. *Family Caregiving to the Elderly*. Special Lecture at the University of Melbourne, Melbourne, Victoria, Australia, August 29.

Horowitz, A. 1985. Sons and Daughters as Caregivers to Older Parents: Differences in Role Performance and Consequences. *The Gerontologist* 25(6):612–17.

Kane, R., and R. Kane. 1985. *What the United States Can Learn from Canada About Caring for the Elderly: A Will and a Way*. New York: Columbia University Press.

Leat, D., and P. Gay. 1987. *Paying for Care: A Study of Policy and Practice in Paid Care Schemes*. London: Policy Studies Institute.

Marshall, Victor. 1989. *Models for Community-Based Long Term Care: An Analytic Review*. Prepared for Aging Policy Section, Health Policy Division, Policy, Planning and Information Branch, Health and Welfare Canada. Ottawa.

Miller, B. 1990. Gender Differences in Spouse Management of the Caregiver Role. In *Circles of Care: Work and Identity in Women's Lives,* edited by E. Abel and M. Nelson. New York: SUNY Press.

National Council of Welfare. 1989. *A Pension Primer.* Ottawa: Minister of Supply and Services.

Neysmith, S., and B. Nichols. 1989. Home-help: Who Pays When Care-givers Become Care Providers? Paper presented at the Annual Meetings of the Canadian Association on Gerontology. Ottawa.

Okin, S. 1989. *Justice, Gender, and the Family.* New York: Basic Books, Inc.

Ontario. 1990. *Strategies for Change: Comprehensive Reform of Ontario's Long-Term Care Services.* Toronto: Queen's Printer for Ontario.

Pfaff, M. 1990. Differences in Health Care Spending Across Countries: Statistical Evidence. *Journal of Health Politics, Policy and Law* 15(1):1–24

Price Waterhouse. 1988. *Review of the Manitoba Continuing Care Program.* Vol. I. *Executive Summary.* Toronto.

Pruchno, R., and N. Resch. 1989. Husbands and Wives as Caregivers: Antecedents of Depression and Burden. *The Gerontologist* 29(2):159–65.

Québec. 1985. Ministère des Affaires Sociale. *Un Nouvel Age à Partager: Politique du ministère des affaires sociales à l'égard des personnes agées.* Québec: Les Publications du Québec.

Roos, N., E. Shapiro, and L. Roos. 1984. Aging and the Demand for Health Care Services: Which Aged and Whose Demand? *The Gerontologist* 24(1):31–6.

Rosenthal, C., and S. Neysmith. 1990. *Informal Support to Older People: Conclusions, Forecasts, Recommendations and Policy Prescriptions in Recent Policy Deliberations.* A report prepared for Statistics Canada.

Rowe, J. 1985. Health Care of the Elderly. *The New England Journal of Medicine* 312(13):827–35.

Shapiro, E. 1988. *Home Care: Where Is It and Where Should It Be Going?* Paper prepared for a consultation of European and Canadian experts on long-term care with the Elderly Services Branch of the Ministry of Community and Social Services. Toronto.

Statistics Canada. 1986. *The Health and Activity Limitation Survey.* Cat # 41034. Ottawa.

Stoller, E. 1990. Males as Helpers: The Role of Sons, Relatives and Friends. *The Gerontologist* 30(2):228–35.

Stone, L. 1988. *Family and Friendship Ties Among Canada's Seniors: An Introductory Report of Findings from the General Social Survey.* Ottawa: Statistics Canada.

Stone, L., and H. Frenken. 1988. *Canada's Seniors.* Statistics Canada. Cat #98–121. Ottawa.

Stone, R., G. Cafferata, and J. Sangl. 1987. Caregivers of the Frail Elderly: A National Profile. *The Gerontologist* 27:616–26.

Twigg, Julia. 1990. Carers of Elderly People: Models for Analysis. In *Contrasting European Policies for the Care of Older People,* edited by Anne Jamieson and Raymond Illsley. Aldershot: Power Publishing Co. Ltd.

Ungerson, C. 1990. *Gender and Caring: Work and Welfare in Britain and Scandinavia.* Hertfordshire: Harvester Wheatsheaf.

BEN SCHLESINGER

Jewish-Canadian Female-headed One-parent Families

When a man has compassion for others, God has compassion for him.
(Talmud, Bezah, 90a)

During the past decade, Jewish communities in Canada and the United States have expressed concern about the growing number of one-parent families. Waxman (1976) points out that the issue of single-parent families is the most critical family issue facing the Jewish population. The American-Jewish Committee Task Force Report commented:

> In community after community the plight of one-parent families is one of the most, if not the most, urgent item on the agenda of the Jewish community. Most communal institutions, however, have not yet squarely faced up to the matter; they continue to address their service almost exclusively to traditional two-parent families. (1979, 17)

Hofstein adds, "The single parent family is one of the most rapidly developing phenomena of the Jewish communal life. Many of our leaders perceive the single-parent family as a calamitous result of the breakdown of Jewish values" (1978, 229).

Yet, in examining the existing literature, I found only a handful of studies that had investigated Jewish one-parent families headed by a mother who was widowed, divorced, separated or had never married (Schlesinger 1987).

The Sample

In 1990 we completed a study of 55 women who had been active with the Jewish Family and Child Service of Metropolitan Toronto (JF&CS). Most of our subjects were separated and divorced. There were also four widowed and three never-married women.

The mothers averaged 36.5 years old, had two children and had been single parents for five years. Most of the mothers were born in Canada. Twenty-five of the subjects worked full-time and 11 worked part-time. Twenty-four of the mothers owned their own house or apartment. Forty-one of the women owned their own cars. Twenty-two women had at least one university degree. Twenty-seven earned under $10,000, 24 had an annual income range of $20–$40,000 and 4 earned $40–$50,000. They all lived in the Metropolitan Toronto area. The majority had sole custody of the children, and 58 percent received regular support from their spouses. About half of the children had weekly contact with their fathers, while one-quarter had at least monthly contact. Sixty percent of the mothers had at least one parent living in Metropolitan Toronto. The sample had been active with JF&CS primarily for counselling. Nearly one-half of the mothers had received some financial assistance from the agency, and nearly one-quarter used a Big Brother or Big Sister service.

All of the women were interviewed in their own homes, using a questionnaire that contained structured and open-ended questions. This was an exploratory study that used a nonprobabability-availability sample.

Jewish Identity
A little over one-third of the families kept a kosher home, 40 percent kept the Sabbath, and nearly all celebrated High Holidays and Passover. Nearly two-thirds attended synagogue.

One-quarter sent their children to full-day Hebrew schools, while another quarter used part-time Hebrew schools. About 30 percent indicated that they participated in Jewish lectures, seminars and clubs. Seventy-one percent of the women read the *Canadian Jewish News* (a weekly paper) regularly. A little over one-third spoke Hebrew, and 40 percent spoke Yiddish as well as English.

Findings

The open-ended questions allowed the women to share some of their opinions related to being in a Jewish one-parent family.

Positive Aspects
When one thinks of "single-parent families," images of hardship, stress and loneliness may come to mind. Although these images may be the reality for some families, there are also many positive aspects to being part

of such a family as we see from the respondents' answers to the question "What aspects of being a single parent do you enjoy?" The women often enjoyed a close relationship with their children and experienced a sense of freedom. The respondents' comments to that question can be grouped under four general headings.

Decision-Making
• only one boss
• no one to answer to
• being in control of my life
• standing on my own two feet
• sole control of family
• make decision by myself
• can cook what I like
• financial independence

Life With the Children
• more time with the children
• closer relationship with the children
• no conflict and fighting with the children

Social Life/Leisure Time
• come and go as I please
• see whom I wish
• pursue my own interests
• going back to school
• less domestic work

Self-Image
• sense of freedom
• independence
• more positive self-image
• more confidence
• life is more secure
• less stress
• more peace

A 32-year-old separated mother of two said, "I enjoy the feeling of accomplishment as a result of the guidance I give to my children and their appreciation of it." A separated mother of one stated, "The tension and the anxiety have been removed since my husband left the home. It is now a peaceful and happy home." Another divorced woman with five children stated, "I feel good about this, life is more secure. A single woman with children is better off than a married woman with a useless husband—one you cannot even depend on to babysit responsibly. I couldn't trust my husband alone with the kids."

Negative Aspects of Living in a Jewish One-Parent Family

Self/Loneliness
• miss male companionship
• lack of emotional supports
• no one to talk to
• not having positive reinforcements
• holidaying alone
• being alone
• loneliness
• miss sexuality, closeness

Financial and Social Aspects
• only financial support for children
• financial strain
• sole breadwinner
• social life is limited

Parenting
• disciplining of children
• no time for myself
• lots of physical work
• have total responsibility
• to be "all things" to the children
• juggling time
• competing with spouse for children

It becomes evident from these responses that three areas are of major concern to Jewish single parents: the loneliness, the financial burden and the overwhelming responsibility of single-parenting. A divorced mother of two comments, "You cannot really expect to have any courting time or time left over for yourself; there is no relief shift." A divorced mother of three comments, "The total responsibility; I wish their father was more responsible and that they had more contact with him." A 33-year-old separated mother of two said, "If it wasn't for a lack of money I would have not had any problems." Finally, a 38-year-old divorced mother of one comments, "Dealing with loneliness while trying to be a good parent is hard; kids just don't understand the loneliness of the adult."

Responsibilities for Parenting

We asked our respondents which new parenting responsibilities they had acquired.

New Roles
- chief decision-maker
- both mom and dad roles
- chief disciplinarian
- chief reward-giver
- source of emotional strength
- moral teacher
- responsible for amusement and recreation
- supermom

Financial
- handle all the budgeting
- no support
- chief breadwinner
- handling estate

Self
- little time left for self
- 24-hour a day job
- "I feel like I'm sacrificing my life for my children"
- must juggle time around my kids' time
- forced into dependence
- superwoman

Most notably, we found that 17 respondents said that there really wasn't any change, as they had had all parenting responsibilities prior to the divorce or separation. For example, a separated mother of three said, "None, because parenting issues were always mine to deal with. The only changes are ones that are a result of my son's changing needs as he gets older." In another example, a divorced mother of two related the impact single parenting has had on herself, "The difference now is that I'm responsible—I never thought about it in this way when I was married, even though I was doing the same things. It's hard to explain it—before I did it because I had no choice; [now] there's no one else to do it."

The children's fathers had done little things like errands or taking children to appointments whereas it seems that the mothers had the more major responsibilities like disciplining and decision-making. One separated mother of two said, "Driving my children to school is the only new thing I do; I always did everything else when married...." Other respondents referred to the fact that the only new responsibility was financial. A divorced mother of five who is in a low income bracket states, "Really little has changed except that I have total financial responsibility now." A substantial number of women felt that "financial worries" was their major new parenting responsibility. Many respondents referred to having to go back to work, thereby becoming the chief breadwinner in the family. Many worried whether that there would be enough money to take care of the needs of their children and running a house and a car. A 49-year-old widowed mother of one said, "I am now aware of money responsibilities such as...looking after things in the house. Selling this house and buying a new one was a very big thing for me; I had to learn a lot of things."

We noted that the respondents felt acquiring new parenting responsibilities had had a major impact on their own lives. For example, three of the respondents said they were now "on call 24 hours a day." Another said that she had to juggle her schedule according to what her kids were doing. Another respondent, a 32-year-old mother of two felt that being a single parent forced you to learn about things that you didn't know about before, especially financial worries.

Advice to One-Parent Families
The suggestions made by the respondents can be categorized into three general areas. First came the need to have a good support network; second, the need to mobilize one's strengths and keep a positive outlook towards the separation and/or the divorce; and third, suggestions for custody and access arrangements, and the importance of preparing one's children for the break-up without involving them too much in the details of the divorce.

Support System—Informal and Formal
• have a good support system
• find and be with other people in the same situation
• make friends
• be with other people—do not hide
• do not be afraid to ask for help
• obtain counselling
• use Jewish Family and Child Service (JF&CS)

- get a Big Brother at JF&CS
- ask for assistance from all social service agencies
- go out and join a support group
- a "surviving separation" group is helpful
- get busy, get out of the house, do something
- have a good job

Attitude
- do not feel sorry for yourself—don't dwell on the past
- do not be bitter
- be open-minded
- be flexible in your attitude
- be open to ideas and change
- attitude has a lot to do with it
- accept what has happened and go on
- it takes time to adjust
- taking things slow and easy, it will work out
- time eases the pain
- look at your strengths and act on them
- look at singlehood as a new lease on life, not the end of the world
- do not feel guilty

Legalities and Children
- do not stay in a bad marriage for security
- get good legal advice before you separate
- work out custody without lawyers
- try to come to an agreement about custody and access that is fair to all
- prepare your children for the separation
- be honest with your kids as to what is going on without burdening them
- do not spoil your kids
- do not badmouth the other parent

A 37-year-old widow with two children cautioned single parents to "not be bitter because it will not get you anywhere. Accept what has happened to you and go on, if not for yourself, then do it for your children. If you have boys and you are a mother, find a network of role models for them—this is extremely important." Similarly, a 39-year-old separated mother of two said, "Be open-minded, don't dwell on the past and feel sorry for yourself. Be flexible in your attitude. Be open to ideas and change. Attitude has a lot to do with it." A 38-year-old widow with three children suggests that single parents should "Get busy, get a job, get out of the house—do something."

Implications for Family Life Education
It seems evident that ethnicity has not been examined in great detail in the literature related to one-parent families as a variable in understanding this growing family pattern (Schlesinger 1987). In working with Jewish one-parent families, we have to take into consideration the ethno-religious factors that play a part in the lives of many of these families.

We found quite a few items in the literature related to Jewish family life in which the authors preach in an alarming tone about the growing rate of Jewish one-parent families (Schlesinger 1987). But we found almost no real family research studies that look at the lives of these families. What part does "Jewishness" play in handling the shift to a one-parent family? How can the family-life educator involve the various resources in the community such as the synagogue, Jewish community centre, Jewish social agencies and Jewish socio-cultural groups in helping Jewish families? We realize that each family has a different degree of "Jewishness," but we have to explore with the family what part their Jewish identity plays in their lives.

Impressions Gathered during the Study

The interviewers also recorded their impressions of the women themselves in an attempt to present a fuller picture of the participants than is available from statistical information alone.

Participant Profile
The interviewers were impressed by the women whom they interviewed. The women were an open, articulate group who essentially were making the best of a difficult situation. The majority were motivated to participate in the study by the selfless desire to help others who were encountering similar circumstances. Many indicated a keen interest in sharing their experiences with an impartial outsider. A number of women had gained real insight into these experiences through self-reflection and/or therapeutic assistance.

The subjects researched presented themselves to the interviewers in a variety of ways. Particularly noteworthy was the number of women who were described in positive ways. The women in this group were portrayed as "happy," "optimistic," "enjoying life," "good-humoured" and "at peace."

The majority of women appeared to be adjusting well to their renewed singlehood and the responsibilities of single parenthood. Many women were confident and self-sufficient, and competently handled both their

family and public lives. They indicated great initiative and resourcefulness, and appeared in control of their lives.

This emphasis on the positive does not seek to overlook the real difficulties inherent in the loss of a partner or the struggles many of the women
continue to face. Most of the participants labelled the process as "not easy,"
demanding that they work extremely diligently "to put their lives back
together." For some, the resulting tiredness and depression was ongoing,
for others periodic, but it was an affective state with which the majority of
women were familiar. Several women sought to mask a very real loneliness
with hard work and cheerfulness. Others identified continual fluctuations
in mood. The affective experience appeared to reflect the length of the
separation.

Most of the participants spoke of a blow to their self-esteem that many
continued to try to overcome. They felt that the separation had initially had
an impact on their ability to cope with a variety of daily living functions
such as employment and child-rearing. Several respondents expressed a
fear of what the future might bring, particularly anticipating loneliness
when their children had grown up.

For a number of women, an already stressful period was exaggerated by
a messy custody battle. Some retained much bitterness towards their ex-
partner, especially if their separation had been filled with conflict. Other
women, particularly if the decision to end the marriage had been joint, had
successfully overcome some of that bitterness and no longer mourned the
loss of the relationship.

Those women whose loss of a partner was less immediate were able to
identify changes within themselves about which they felt great pride.
Many felt increasingly secure in their abilities that stimulated a heightened
sense of self-worth. Some clearly viewed themselves as surviving on the
basis of their strength, resilience and newly developed skills. Although
recognizing the separation as a painful process, many of the women
viewed its outcome as positive.

Becoming a Single Parent
The respondents felt that since the end of their marriages they had come a
long way in their own personal growth and maturity, and they were
somehow relieved that the marriage was over. Most respondents saw the
separation or divorce as somewhat beneficial for themselves and their
children. One divorced mother of three felt that she was stifled during her
marriage and could now pursue things, for example, a university education or a career, something she could not do before.

A separated mother of two felt that the separation was a positive experience because she was able to find out who she was again, and did not have to be defined by her husband. An interesting comment came from a divorced mother of two. "It was really hard at first experiencing emotions I didn't know I was capable of. The way I feel about myself has changed— I'm more confident and have learned a lot. My kids see me as a person not just 'mommy'." Furthermore, one researcher noted that "many of the women felt that generally not much had changed in how much parenting responsibilities they had." The researcher said, "A pattern has established itself among the women I have interviewed in that their ex-partners play a very small role in the lives of their children and that was the way it was in their marriage also."

Another researcher noted in her impressions that for these women a status change meant a major emotional adjustment, especially in what other people (extended family, friends) thought. It seems that if the women had support and positive reactions from those significant others they were less ashamed and felt less guilty, and if there was some blame and/or pressure (for example, not to separate) the women either felt anger or guilt, particularly because of their children, and had a much more difficult time adjusting. One divorced mother summarized these feelings when she said, "When I first separated it was like a pox on the family." Therefore the conclusion would be that positive support often leads to a more positive or initially easier adjustment to the new status.

One researcher noted in her impressions that finances also had a major impact on the subjects' happiness: the women who were well-off or relatively well-off seemed happier and felt it was easier to be alone than those who had many financial difficulties. One interviewer said the following about a divorced mother of three who had a very low income, had no job skills and was an immigrant: "Subject is very afraid about what the future will hold. She is afraid of being alone because her kids are growing up. She is very uncertain about the future because of her financial problems and problems finding a better job than the one she currently has."

Marriage
The participants' experience of their marriage prior to its dissolution appeared to vary as much as did the women themselves. Many viewed the relationship as "bad" or a "disaster," and as causing them a great deal of pain. These experiences ranged from a lack of love or respect for one another to actual physical abuse. One said, "He would scare the children

by beating me up in front of them and screaming in front of them. He made our life miserable."

Several women described a loss of themselves within marriage "like living in a prison." These participants felt they had lost their independence and freedom. Still others described themselves as continually berated or "put down" by their ex-partners, which led them to question their own adequacy. One woman claimed, "It was a relief to leave even though it was hard. I was relieved I wouldn't be pushed around any more." Many had had little help from their spouses with parenting.

Another participant asserted that she was against people staying together for the sake of the children. She felt that this had been a part of her hesitancy in leaving, which had ultimately exposed her son to a very negative, conflicted emotional environment. One woman stated, "I chose to separate because I got to the point in my marriage where the unhappiness outweighed my fear of going on my own."

Separation and Stress

The majority of the participants, regardless of why they separated, experienced the loss of their partner and transition to single-parenthood as stressful and traumatic. As one woman exclaimed, "I didn't know what stress meant before!" Another felt her "psychological wires had been cut."

Most respondents described a period of adjustment that varied from woman to woman. Some of the participants identified the "terrible struggle" as behind them, while others were still in its midst. As one woman stated, "I live day-to-day with a constant struggle. I try to be optimistic and see the light at the end of the tunnel, but I feel I take one step forward and three back." Another participant claimed, "You often have more growing up to do than you're ready for, even if you're an older parent."

A number of the women spoke of the exceedingly rough, lonely times in the face of the adjustment. One spoke poignantly of waking in the night and hearing a scream: "the scream was inside me." Another participant advised, "You have to live with the attitude that you don't have the choice to quit, or give up, even temporarily."

An aspect of separation that escalated the stress level was the fact that few of the women were on good terms with their ex-spouses. Several remained in heated custody battles over their children. A nun ber of others felt their ex-partner had given them a "raw deal" about which they remained extremely bitter. One woman stated she resented the fact that the presence of their child necessitates some continuing involvement with her ex-husband.

Some of the participants retained a great deal of hostility and anger towards their ex-partners, despite a length of time since the separation, that was occasionally connected to the dramatic change in lifestyle the women were forced to undergo when the separation limited their finances. A few of the respondents remained emotionally engaged with their ex-partners either as a result of this bitterness or because they continued to hope for a reconciliation.

Personal Growth and Resourcefulness

A surprising number of women looked to the experience of separation as providing them with opportunities for personal growth. Several partici-pants revealed that they were forced to learn to do many things on their own which they might otherwise not have learned. Many of the women indicated a real resourcefulness in finding the programs and people whom they needed. Some suggested it took strength and a "swallowing of pride" to approach these resources. One woman prided herself on becoming "an expert on every resource in the city."

The participants agreed, however, that the process of arriving at this new self-awareness and acquiring these abilities had been a difficult one. Numerous respondents agreed that they now felt better about themselves, had become more complete people and, as a result, liked themselves better. Many described themselves as happier, more self-secure and confident than they had been prior to the separation. This newly developed self-esteem and pride appeared to result from their successful handling of their circumstances and a recognition of the gains they had made. One woman quoted her son, "You are strong, Mom. We wouldn't have made it without you." Another participant described herself as looking better and younger since her separation.

Although the majority of women still found single-parenting physically and emotionally draining, it was "still better than being in a bad mar-riage—the lesser of two evils."

Involvement with Children

Many women identified a closer involvement with their children after the loss of their partners. This increasing attachment usually was positive. The respondents indicated great pride in their children and a real enjoyment of their company. A few women stated they enjoyed their child's company more than anyone else's. Participants said that they deeply missed their children when they were on their regular visits with their father.

The majority of the children were described as equally loving and devoted to their mothers. It was clear that, given the circumstances, some women relied on their children for support in addition to companionship. While talking about her dependence on her children, one woman exclaimed, "Sometimes it's hard to know who is the mother."

It was apparent that the source of much of the women's pride was their ability to care for their children independently. Only a few participants worried that they might be becoming too emotionally attached to their children. One woman was particularly concerned about the extent of her loneliness when her child was not at home.

Most of the women spoke of their children's newly developing independence as positive; however, some worried that it might not yet be something with which they were prepared to cope.

A number of the women identified problems with their children, some of which necessitated counselling. They expressed guilt and worry about the damage done to the children by hostility during the separation and the earlier stress within the marriage. Discipline was identified by some, particularly those with teenagers, as a problem. Sole child management on top of the stress connected with loss of a partner was overwhelming for some. A few women labelled themselves as inconsistent in their parenting and blamed their children for "taking advantage of the situation."

Lessened Involvement with Fathers
The concerns mentioned most frequently in connection with their ex-partner's involvement with their children was the extent to which contact between father and children had decreased. Most of the women had arranged regular access to the children of which the fathers did not consistently avail themselves. Several children had no contact with their fathers whatsoever. The participants perceived this lessened involvement as related to the ex-spouses' lack of interest ("when it suits him") or to uncooperativeness with themselves. A few mothers deliberately kept their children from contact with their fathers.

Several women were actively making attempts to improve their relationship with their ex-partner for the sake of the children. One couple was pursuing mediation at JFCS "because we do not talk to each other." One of the participants was very careful about the information she shared with her child about the father. She was concerned that if a person talked negatively about her ex-spouse "a child will have no chance to develop a good relationship with someone when they are older." Some women spoke of unsuccessful efforts to rekindle involvement between the children and their fathers.

A number of the participants had become increasingly concerned about the effects on the children of this limited contact, and the resulting lack of a male role model. Several had sought to compensate for this deficit by utilizing JF&CS Big Brother volunteers or by seeking to involve other family members.

Still other participants were concerned that the children's involvement with their fathers might actually be detrimental. Several speculated that their ex-spouse might be trying to turn their children against them. Commonly described was the father's assumption of the role of "Mr. Happy Times" which relegated the mother to the role of "bad guy" or disciplinarian. One respondent summed up this phenomenon as "the non-custodial parent has the best deal because it's parenting without the nitty-gritty."

On a more positive note, one woman commented that her children actually had a far better father after the marriage was over. "Now they see him on his best behaviour so it's positive."

Separation and the Jewish Woman

The emphasis within the Jewish community on marriage and family life made the loss of a partner particularly difficult for the Jewish woman. One woman termed the community's concept of single-parenthood as "mediaeval." Another participant perceived herself and her family as "outside the mainstream" of Jewish life as a result of her single-parent status. Due to the community's strong couple orientation, women are subtly "made to feel worthless and unimportant without a man."

Several women spoke of the stigma attached to separation within the Jewish community. One elaborated, "Divorce is like death in the family," and advised that the individuals "sit Shiva."* Another said, "There's an attitude that single parents aren't conscientious. Maybe this is so but there are a lot of people who are married who are like that."

Some of the women spoke of the religious divorce (get), which the ex-husband has the sole right to grant. They emphasized that the man should not have sole power of divorce. Several ex-spouses used the get as a weapon by refusing to grant it. One women described the process of obtaining the

---

* The formal period of mourning for a family member.

"kosher *get*" as degrading to women. She had been consulted only once throughout the lengthy process.

The "Rich" Jewish Family—a Stereotype
Several felt that the community attached a stigma to those individuals who fall outside what is believed to be the norm. Some women's experiences with the Jewish community were of very little help to single parents, "almost as though they are embarrassed about the problems."

Those who had experienced financial difficulties stated, "As a poor Jew, you feel you are a burden to the Jewish community in particular." Others identified the community as "snobbish and only caring about those individuals with money." Still another woman described feeling stigmatized because she received family benefits and lived in public housing.

A few respondents related that, although they were proud to be Jews, they experienced the community as a whole as "materialistic and unconcerned about social issues." One woman identified the Jewish single-parent community as "particularly stuck-up—expecting a person to dress and act a certain way." Another participant said she would like to be more active in the Jewish community, but was fearful of the monetary implications, "It's expensive to retain Jewishness."

Lack of Resources
A majority of women identified a lack of necessary resources for single parents and their children. Those participants who had successfully procured essential services labelled the financial demands as burdensome. Several women also defined the process of finding those resources difficult and suggested the compilation of a resource list for single parents.

Availability of both good daycare (particularly subsidized daycare) and reliable babysitters were problems. Social programs and recreation for both single-parent mothers and their children, regardless of age, were identified as sorely needed. Subsidies for those who wished their children to receive a Jewish education were viewed as essential.

Many women indicated interest in attending support groups that would enable them to meet other single parents. Some participants thought that the community should encourage fathers' continued involvement with their children by establishing groups for non-custodial fathers. Services for meeting potential partners other than the derided singles' dances was suggested. Greater involvement by the religious community in the form of outreach might better familiarize leaders with single-parent family circumstances and stimulate the development of necessary services. One woman suggested, "Maybe they could have a *seder** for single parents and on other holidays make provisions for them."

The Jewish Community

The participants' utilization and perceptions of the Jewish community were diverse. Some women were highly critical of its lack of acceptance of single-parent families and resources for that group. Others perceived the community as "generous and good to its members" and had not experienced any connected disappointments. The women ranged from minimal involvement in Jewish life and the community to a strong identification with things Jewish and a high community activity level.

Many participants related a positive reception from all those they had approached within the community. Several women described themselves as not isolated or unaccepted, but made welcome by the community. One participant stated, "Every time I've needed anything, the Jewish community has always been there for me." Another declared, "I think the Jewish community has more programs for single parents than other ethnic/religious groups." One woman identified other women as particularly empathic and helpful.

A number of women suggested religion had been a real source of support. A few participants viewed their rabbi as particularly helpful.

Of those women who had been dissatisfied with aspects of their reception by the Jewish community, several had been forced to turn to other communities for necessary assistance. A few women identified supports for children within the community as particularly absent. However, one participant asserted, "I prefer the kids to be with a mixed group of people, not segregated in Jewish organizations. I think it's important in today's society for people to mix so that they can learn about one another, as this reduces ignorance which is usually the cause of most problems."

Several of the participants were familiar with the Montréal Jewish community to which they compared Toronto's unfavourably. One woman viewed the Toronto community as "breeding isolated people." A number concurred that it was difficult to meet new people and develop friendships in Toronto because most people already have their own long-lasting relationships. Real dissatisfaction with the opportunities available to meet men was cited.

Toronto was again described as less helpful than Montréal with regard to provision of financial assistance to Jewish families with low incomes.

---

* The Passover meal.

The relative wealth of the Toronto Jewish community contributed to a sense of stigmatization of low-income people. Activities were described as expensive, and infrequent discounting limited their accessibility.

Despite the variety of impressions about the Jewish community, however, the majority of the participants did express concern for the community's lack of recognition and absence of concrete assistance to single parents and their children. Several suggested that certain segments of the community (for example, the Orthodox) had even less familiarity with separation than others.

They explained this lack of acknowledgement of separation and the resulting single-parent family by the focus on marriage and the family within Judaism. A number of women suggested this focus results in single-parent families, perceived as breaking the norm, being isolated from the community. Other participants felt that, although the community is beginning to notice the increasing occurrence of family break-up, there remains a negative attitude towards it. One respondent declared, "In the first year of my separation, I felt very different and felt ashamed—I thought people looked at me and said, 'Ooh, she's single.'" This attitude towards singlehood results in some perceived pressure to return to the ex-partner or remarry. This is particularly evident in Jewish religious tradition: "Synagogues cater to families; the single parents feel left out." One woman stated that she felt so out of place as a single, she no longer attends synagogue.

Family Support

Almost all of the women in the study reported that their families provided a great deal of support during the separation and divorce. "I get most of my emotional and financial support from my parents," said one woman. Of those who received little financial support, most stated that they believed their families were willing to provide it, but could not afford to.

One woman told us, "After the separation, I lived for almost two years with my parents and my kids in my parent's two bedroom apartment. It was very difficult. I was lucky to have good parents, not everyone does." Another felt that without her family she would have felt like a "pariah." One's extended family can also play an important part—"I talk to my parents, aunts and cousins a couple of times a day."

A few of the women talked about their relationship with their in-laws. One widow said her in-laws were not supportive and believed this was a result of the settlement of her husband's estate. Another widow also reported less contact with her in-laws who "separated after the death of their son." They do not visit her because her home is a reminder of their dead son. On the other hand, one woman said her in-laws had more positive contact with the children than her ex-husband did, while another said, "I'm closer to my in-laws now than when we were married. They were very supportive during the separation."

Positive Aspects of Separation and Divorce

Many of the respondents identified positive aspects, particularly in the area of personal growth. One divorced mother of two stated that her new-found freedom has allowed her the opportunity to explore new worlds and get to know more about herself. Another said, "I feel a lot of personal growth—both professionally and in maturity."

Separation was described by one young woman "as a time to expand and explore, and to get out into life. I'm having more fun, re-doing my life by creating new memories." She was putting the separation behind her and felt she had symbolically erased her memories of the past year by writing an epitaph to 1986 and burning it on New Year's Eve.

Many expressed a sense of increased confidence and self-esteem. One woman said she feels better about herself since the divorce. She has gone back to school, is in the process of setting up a business and feels more confident and independent. Overall there is less tension in her life. Another reported a more active social life since becoming a single parent. She is an active participant now in the National Council of Jewish Women and is working towards a BA at Glendon College of York University.

One woman told us that raising children as a single parent has its rewards: "One of the best things about being a single parent is that I get to take all the credit and praise for how well the kids have turned out."

Loneliness

Loneliness was a feeling experienced by many of the respondents. A never-married mother preferred to stay in a bad relationship than be alone. She is currently involved with a man who drinks a lot and is temperamental. "I'll never leave him though because I hate being alone."

The interviewers found that the women in the study really just wanted to talk and welcomed the opportunity to relate their stories. Some felt abandoned by their old friends who no longer invited them to dinners since the break-up of their marriages. Others find it difficult to make new friends, "I was extremely disillusioned with the single women I met at the groups I went to…they were petty, competitive, depressed and very down on men, yet all they ever did was complain about not meeting anyone and asked, 'Can you fix me up?'."

On the other hand, one woman was impressed by how supportive women, both married and single, had been to her. Another said that friends include and welcome her no matter what the situation, but feels it is a two-way street—she is also responsible for making an effort to keep in touch.

Lack of Time

As could be expected, the demands made upon single parents means there is little time left over for oneself. A frequent description of the women's lives used by the interviewers was "chaotic." These women are juggling their children's needs, their own needs and, often, the demands of jobs or school. "You have to live with the attitude that you don't have the choice to quit or give up, even temporarily. When you don't have extra support you don't have time off for your own foolishness or recreation."

One woman described parenting two young boys as physically and emotionally draining. She is eagerly anticipating her ex-partner's move back to Toronto as she feels it will relieve some of the parenting burden. The burden is best expressed by one woman who says, "The most difficult thing in being a single parent is accepting that you will have very little time left over for yourself; you must become both mom and dad, but it's difficult trying to explain why you can't be both supermom and superdad combined."

Financial Difficulties

Not surprisingly, finances were one of the main problems for the single parents in this study. "I don't have any problems that money couldn't solve" is a common sentiment. The primary concern of one woman who separated ten years ago is financial. Her lifestyle has changed considerably since becoming head of a one-parent family. "Most of my problems are financial. From the time of my separation, I have lowered my standard of living by about 25–30 percent or more...I had my own home when I was married. I miss having my own home now."

Many are concerned about the future. One says "I don't want to die in poverty."

While some respondents were well-off and lived in $500,000 homes, some women lived in Ontario (public) Housing and received financial assistance from welfare and JF&CS. Many find themselves unable to afford many activities for themselves or their children, such as camps and memberships at the Jewish Community Centre (JCC), that they had been able to afford when married. One angry woman felt there should be discounts offered for recreational and other activities for children so that her son could participate in the same activities as his friends.

Remarriage

Many of the women in this study felt tremendous pressure to remarry, primarily because of our couple-oriented society. "As a single parent you're on the fence—you're not really single and not really a family" in the traditional sense. "Women are made to feel worthless and unimportant if they do not have a man," according to some of the women.

Parents often exert pressure on single parents to remarry. One respondent who had only been separated for six months was in a rush to be remarried. Her parents are urging her to "straighten" herself out by finding a suitable man. A 39-year-old marketing coordinator and mother of two children says, "I have felt pressure to remarry by my mother—'I wish you would find someone to marry so you wouldn't have to work so hard'—Mom is from the old school that you need to have a man to be happy."

For some women the pressure is self-imposed. One young mother feels her life without a man is terrible. Others say they would like to remarry but "it's hard to meet someone." One woman would prefer to remarry than go back to work. She finds it difficult to find employment with only a high school education and is afraid to return to school. Thus, for her, remarriage represents security.

Others are in no hurry to remarry or feel they never will: "I'm beginning to think I won't remarry and that maybe I was never meant to be married." One woman said, "I do not feel any pressure from family or friends to remarry and I have no real interest. If it was important for someone I was involved with and loved to marry, I would, but not until my daughter was out of the house and living on her own." Another woman who was content with her single-parent lifestyle had difficulty understanding why others felt pressured to remarry: "I can't believe that so many women in this day and age can't seem to function on their own and rely so much on a man for their happiness....No one can make you happy, you have to find your own happiness."

Dating in the Jewish Community

Our respondents are quite dissatisfied with the dating scene in the Jewish community. Singles' dances received the greatest amount of criticism. They are regarded as "simply providing opportunities for 'pick-ups.'" One woman, in describing her experiences at two dating parties, said, "They were all over 50...it was a meat market." Another criticism was that "Most social clubs and activities in the Jewish community cater to younger singles." There is also a feeling that men met through dances are not interested in marriage.

It is clear that these women wished that the community would provide alternate means of meeting men. One woman said she would like to see more advertisements for people trying to find mates, while another lamented the fact that there are few "respectable" opportunities to meet someone. "I'm a mother, I don't go to dances."

Another problem cited was the difficulty of meeting men when one has children. "It's difficult to find decent men who are willing to go out with females who are encumbered with children," says one woman who has four teenaged sons. Another said, "Guys would be all over me until they heard I had five kids—then they'd take off like lightning;" or "It's hard to find a man who wants a woman with three children." For yet another woman, the combination of children and a low income makes it difficult to meet men. Her despair is evident when she says, "It's hard to find a man I'd fall in love with. I don't think Canadian men want me because I'm poor and have kids. I'll never marry for money. I don't think I'll find the right person."

A final comment about the difficulties involved in dating: "The worst thing about the Toronto Jewish dating scene is that everyone knows everybody else; others tell you all about a certain man before you can find out anything for yourself."

Jewish Family and Child Service

Responses of the women concerning the services provided by JF&CS were quite varied. Some could not say enough good things about the agency, while others were very disappointed. In general it seemed that one's level of satisfaction with the services provided by JF&CS was determined by the counsellor one had. If one had a counsellor one liked, then comments about the agency were favourable; if one had a bad experience, comments tended to be negative. One person said she depended on her counsellor, while others felt their counsellors did not understand them—"They say they understand but they don't." Some found their workers to be patronizing. In one case a worker advised a woman she would be better off on family benefits than trying to find a job, while another was told that no man wants a woman with three kids. JF&CS was not helpful to one woman whose primary needs were for affordable housing and counselling. She felt the agency was really acting as a referral service, providing her with telephone numbers, when she wanted help in "starting life over from scratch."

Those services found to be the most helpful were Big Brothers, counselling, Picking Up the Pieces (PUTP) and financial assistance. Only one who requested a Big Brother was turned down and that was because her ex-partner continued to be involved with the children.

Counselling was described as most helpful by most of the women. One described her worker as very supportive of her initiative to obtain employment and helped her to obtain daycare. She had high praise for JF&CS both "for providing me with an excellent counsellor and for supplying financial assistance at various times." Her babysitting is subsidized and JF&CS helped with special expenses associated with an accident her daughter had.

Another woman expressed extreme pleasure with both the separation counselling and mediation services she and her ex-spouse used. Another helpful service was PUTP, a program that runs groups for parents and children to help children through the parental separation.

Most of the criticism of JF&CS was directed at the Financial Assistance program, which provides a financial supplement to those receiving welfare, family benefits and/or those on low incomes. While most appreciate the supplement, they found the process of applying and qualifying for it to be difficult. The eligibility requirement was described by one woman as "practically impossible to meet" and that "You have to con them to get any money." Another, who on the whole found the agency to be excellent, complained that the process of obtaining financial assistance was "extremely insensitive and inhuman. The people at welfare and FBA were kinder."

A single parent who expressed interest in adoption encountered difficulties, as she was told she would not be given priority because of her single status. She was furious and contacted the Metropolitan Toronto Children's Aid Society, which was much more open to having single parents adopt. The Jewish Dateline also received criticism as the men met through the services were described by a number of women as "losers."

When asked what services the subjects would like JF&CS to provide, many suggested services that were already offered by the agency, such as a dating service, education groups and so on. This indicates that the agency does not promote itself as well as it could. One woman suggested that JF&CS should launch an extensive outreach program in order to make single parents aware of the services that are available to them. There was one woman who went for over five years without realizing what programs and facilities were in existence for single parents.

Implications of Including Impressions

We chose to include impressions of our interviewees in this research study as an additional source of information. They offer a glimpse of people and lives that cannot be obtained from answers to questionnaires. As social workers we are trained to pay attention not only to what people say, but also to how they say it, how they look and so on. Caution must be exercised when including impressions, though, because they are biased by what the interviewer has chosen to focus on or deems important. In this study, this factor is compounded by the fact that more than one researcher conducted the interviews. On the other hand, the impressions give us an extra dimension of Jewish one-parent families who are headed by women.

We hope that this exploratory study, which is one of the first in Canada, will shed some light on the topic. We also hope that other studies will focus on one-parent families in diverse ethnic and religious groups.

The research team included the following social work students: Rachel Achtman, Terry Biggs, Judith Forman, Elissa Glick, Shirley Lindsay, Pam McKee and Brenda Patterson. Professor Kim Lambert was the research consultant.

References

American-Jewish Committee. 1979. *Sustaining the Jewish Family*. New York: American-Jewish Committee.

Hofstein, S. 1978. Perspectives on the Jewish Single Parent Family. *Journal of Jewish Communal Service* 54:229–40.

———. 1985. *The One-Parent Family in the 1980's*. Toronto: University of Toronto Press.

Schlesinger, B. 1987. *Jewish Family Issues*. New York: Garland Press.

Waxman, C.I. 1976. The Centrality of the Family in Delivering Jewish Identity and Identification. *Journal of Jewish Communal Service* 53:170–87.

CYRIL LEVITT

Is Canada a Racist Country?

Is Canada a racist country? There is an old Yiddish expression that goes: *Az men fregt a shayle, iz treyf.* Freely translated this means: If you have to ask a question, then you'll get the answer you don't want to hear. This question, however, has been asked in recent years, and more forcefully than ever in recent months. The supposed race riot that occurred in Toronto on 4 May 1992, following the shooting of a black man in the course of an undercover drug operation, called world attention to the race question in Canada. Concern was magnified, of course, on account of the timing of this event, coming as it did on the heels of the eruption of violence in Los Angeles only a few days earlier. I want to present a number of observations and several arguments concerning the charge of racism in the Canadian context.

Antipathy between and among human groups is surely a very ancient phenomenon. The concept of a common humanity as an abstraction is not very old. Indigenous peoples often use one term to describe the members of their group, other terms to describe members of other groups with no common term that includes both. Some refer to themselves as "true people," as if humanity meant only those with membership in their group. Western conceptions of a general humanity and, by extension, of human equality, are derived from the reality of ancient empire, especially that of Rome, where diverse peoples were brought together within a political-economic system. Christianity gave religious expression to these "humanist" impulses that had already been developed by Stoic philosophy and Roman law.

If antipathy between groups is as old as the existence of human group differentiation, then sympathy within groups, or what my late colleague Howard Brotz called "the prejudice on behalf of one's own"(personal communication) is probably of equal antiquity. In theory these two matters may be treated separately; in practice they are often indistinguishable. Sigmund Freud brought them together in his theory of the "narcissism of small differences" between groups. His argument in *Civilization and its Discontents* asserts that groups distinguished from one another by small degrees and in minor ways bear the most antipathy towards one another. More recently, sociobiologists have explained in-group solidarity/out-group antipathy in terms of strategies of gene pool survival.

Racism has had an enormous impact upon twentieth-century history. It does not appear to be a very ancient phenomenon, however. True, the classical Greeks divided peoples into Greeks and Barbarians. But this was in the first instance a linguistic division; the term barbarian signified someone who spoke confusedly, i.e., someone who didn't speak Greek. [Modern English takes revenge upon the ancients, for something that is unintelligible is "Greek" to the modern English speaker.] Race hatred as we understand it was unknown in the ancient world. In Book II of the *Politics*, Aristotle praised Carthage, a city that was not only non-Greek but was non-white as well. Greek thinkers who concerned themselves with the physical differences among human groups attributed these differences to the effects of different environmental factors.

The word "race," and by extension "racism," has an obscure etymology. The word exists in many European languages suggesting a classical origin. It first appears in English writing in the sixteenth century. Thackeray used it in *Vanity Fair* to distinguish one lineage from another. In this original meaning race referred to something wholly concrete—a specific line of descent. In this original sense race was hardly to be distinguished in meaning from what the Greeks called the *ethnos* and the Romans *natio*.

The seventeenth-century French physician and ethnographer François Bernier was the first to use the term to classify peoples by physical characteristics (Banton and Harwood 1975, 13). The growth of the slave trade gave rise to a theory of the inferiority of the black race. Systematical racial classifications were made by Blumenbach in the late eighteenth and by Prichard in the early nineteenth century. In developing human types, the early nineteenth-century French anatomist François Cuvier divided the races of the human species into white, yellow and black.

When Kant looked at the different races of man in 1775 he attributed them to environmental factors, as had Rousseau before him. In Hegel we find Spirit developing through different peoples at different times in human history. Accordingly, morality developed in the Orient, ethics (*Sittlichkeit*) in Greece. Fichte, like others, developed a passionate concern for national character and for the advancement of the Germanic, which he considered superior. But what was missing in all of this was the rooting of culture in biology. Only when this link was systematically established by writers like Gobineau in the middle of the nineteenth century do we have the development of a more insidious theory of race. With Gobineau and Chamberlain and others, we find a racialist determinism where culture and character are seen as inevitable excrescences of blood and individuals are powerless to act in any other way than by following the dictates of race. It was precisely this crass materialism and determinism which turned De Tocqueville against the *Essai* of his friend Gobineau. For example, in his letter to Gobineau of 17 November 1853 de Tocqueville wrote:

> Votre doctrine est plutôt en effet une sorte de fatalisme, de prédestination si vous voulez; différente toutefois de celle de saint Augustin, des jansénistes et des calvinistes (ce sont ceux-ci qui vous ressemblent le plus par l'absolu de la doctrine) en ce que chez vous il y a un lien très étroit entre le fait de la prédestination et la matière. Ainsi, vous parlez sans cesse de races qui se régénèrent ou [se] détériorent, qui prennent ou quittent des capacités sociales qu'elles n'avaient pas une *infusion de sang différent*, je crois que ce sont vos propres expressions. Cette prédestination-là me parâit, je vous l'avourerai, cousine du pur matérialisme et soyez convaincu que si la foule, qui suit toujours les grands chemin battus en fait de raisonnement, admettait votre doctrine, cela la conduirait tout droit de la race à l'individu et des facultés sociales à toutes sortes de facultés. (Mayer 1958, 202)

At the same time, it must be recalled, Gobineau did not provide the foundation for racial antisemitism, and his few statements about the Jews, which were by and large positive, were suppressed by his latter-day followers. Chamberlain's writings in German provide a much clearer foundation for later biological antisemitism.

This kind of racialism was later honed and fine-tuned by Nazi racial doctrine. The strong reaction of the world to manifestations of racism following the Second World War can only be understood as a reaction to the horrors which had been carried out in the name of this theory. The experience of the world with the practical side of racialism constitutes the basis for all developments in race relations in the post-War period.

Canada, like most Western societies, has had a history in which racial undercurrents have often played a not insignificant role. Historians have recalled the anti-oriental riot in Vancouver in 1907, which was in part instigated by organized labour. The history of the Chinese in Canada presents a picture of prejudice and discrimination (*see* Li 1988a). Historians have also documented the treatment of Japanese Canadians as enemy aliens who lost their land and possessions as well as their civil liberties during the Second World War (*see* Sunahara 1981). Abella and Troper's classic work on Canadian immigration policy in the thirties and forties, *None is Too Many* (1982), shows antisemitic prejudices operating at the highest levels of the Canadian government, while my own work with Bill Shaffir, *The Riot at Christie Pits* (1987), paints a picture of Orange Toronto in the thirties in which Jews, Italians, other immigrant groups and Catholics met with discrimination and, on occasion, violence. Others have drawn equally lamentable portraits in relation to the treatment of Native peoples (Frideres 1988; Miller 1989), Blacks (Winks 1971), French Canadians (Jones 1972) and others.

Until 1968, Canadian immigration policy was plagued with racial assumptions about the "character" of certain peoples. This is the "official" face of racism and antisemitism. But it was not codified in law. Canada has not had a system of legal Apartheid as did South Africa or parts of the United States. There can be little doubt that Canadian society evinced elements of racism, antisemitism and xenophobia—which even extended to people of English background during the dirty thirties. But to describe Canada as a racist country, even in the 1930s, is problematic since this would prevent us from finding a means to distinguish between Canada and Nazi Germany. That widespread racist, xenophobic and antisemitic prejudice *and* discrimination was present is clear; that life was difficult at times for Jews, Italians, Blacks and Catholics in Toronto is recognized; yet Canada was not, I maintain, a racist country.

The watershed event in Canadian history was the Second World War. The democratic fight against the racist Axis powers and the revelations of the extermination camps led to dramatic changes in the socio-political landscape. By the early 1950s fair employment and fair accommodation practices legislation were on the books and the Supreme Court had struck down restrictive covenants in the sale of residential properties. True, social practices did not change overnight as restricted clubs continued to exist and only certain clientele was desired at many summer resorts. But the new atmosphere was signalled by the popular Prime Minister John Diefenbaker who was a champion of human rights, and more concretely by the changes in Canadian immigration policy in 1968. The adoption of the official policy of multiculturalism in 1971 went far beyond tolerance of racial, religious and ethnic minorities. It marked an official departure from the Anglo-conformity model of majority-minority relations.

When people talk about "racism" they refer both to prejudicial attitudes and to discriminatory behaviour. The two may not always go together. One can engage in discriminatory behaviour without prejudice and one can be prejudiced without discriminating against the objects of prejudice. There is also a body of literature that deals with social and economic inequality among ethnic and racial groups and that treats this inequality as a result of hidden or systemic discrimination. Thus, according to this view, it is possible to have a racist society without racists.

Before the Second World War "racism" was understood to be a doctrine that had a biological foundation. Culture and character were seen to be the necessary products of genetically grounded racial features. Races were classified as higher or lower according to the physical features apparent or imputed, which supposedly gave rise to cultural traits. Furthermore, racist societies were identified as those in which this ideology had been translated into state policy. In other words, a racist society, *sensu strictu*, was defined by the nature of the public sector, not the private sphere. According to this view, Nazi Germany was a racist country; Canada in the thirties, was not.

After the War, the meaning of racism was broadened considerably as it moved beyond the confines of the biological. With the growing concern for human rights, racism came to refer to all kinds of prejudice and discrimination—religious, ethnic, cultural, ideological. Any kind of group preference could be seen as evidence of racism. It was in the light of this all-encompassing notion of racism that the infamous "Zionism is racism" resolution was proposed and passed by the United Nations. In fact, any inequality in condition between non-economically defined groups in society was viewed by some, especially by intellectuals and minority community activists, as evidence of racism.

What do the statistics tell us? The first direct measure of racist behaviour might be based upon reports of racist slurs and racist assault. Indeed, the League for Human Rights of the B'nai Brith has been keeping statistics on racist-motivated acts in Canada. It has noted that in recent years the number of such reported acts has increased. However, there are two problems associated with this measure. 1. How do we know when an act is motivated by racist attitudes? 2. We have no way of knowing the ratio of reported to unreported acts. In fact, it is possible that the number of acts in general has decreased while the number of reported acts has increased.

This might be due to a change in climate, heightened concern on the part of the community or even an oversensitivity to the issue on the part of many.

Other studies have concentrated on measuring the attitudes of Canadians towards specific minority groups. For example, the research committee at Concordia University in Montréal led by H. Taylor Buckner has been conducting national surveys for the League for Human Rights of the B'nai Brith Canada annually since 1983. Prejudicial attitudes were operationalized by means of responses to questions posed in relation to opinions concerning a number of minority groups. From 1983 to 1985 the minority groups included were Jews, Italians and Poles. Blacks were added in 1986, Chinese in 1988 and Pakistanis in 1989. Respondents were asked whether these groups had too much power, whether they would vote for a person from one of these minority groups if he or she were running as a candidate for the party they normally supported at elections, whether the respondents believed that anti-Jewish sentiment was increasing or decreasing among the people they knew. When the researchers controlled for age by birth cohort they discovered that prejudicial attitudes were inversely correlated with birth cohort. Younger generations tend to harbour less prejudicial attitudes towards minorities than do older generations. This is explained partly in terms of higher educational levels among most recent cohorts and the different generational experiences affecting attitudes towards minorities. Furthermore, level of prejudice towards minorities was also shown to be inversely correlated with contact with members of the particular minority. Earlier cohorts lived in more ethnically homogeneous environments, many in rural areas where contact with minority group members would have been limited. It was also demonstrated that education and contact decrease prejudice regardless of birth cohort and independently of one another. The researchers find the increase in levels of prejudice in 1989 alarming but in spite of this they make the following optimistic observations:

> Expressions of prejudice have been declining in Canada and the U.S. over the last fifty years as the population became more educated and had more contact with minorities. As the average level of education in Canada rises we should expect to see a further reduction in the expression of prejudice, unless this trend is confounded by public figures making disparaging remarks about minorities, thus legitimizing the expression of prejudice. (Buckner Taylor, forthcoming)

In another recently published study by Brym and Lenton on antisemitic attitudes in Canada, based on a secondary analysis of the data from the National Election Study of 1984, it was shown that some 86% of Canadians had positive attitudes towards Jews, more than showed positive feelings towards French Canadians. The province of Alberta showed the least antipathy towards Jews (7%) while the highest levels of dislike were found to exist in Newfoundland (29%), New Brunswick (23%) and Québec (21%). High levels of antisemitism were positively correlated with poverty, low levels of education, and being Francophone Catholic. But like H. Buckner Taylor, Brym and Lenton optimistically conclude:

> ...that the overall level of antisemitism is quite modest in Canada as a whole. The only populous province with a relatively high level of antisemitism (and a large Jewish population) is Québec. Moreover, one is to be optimistic about the long-term outlook, at least outside Québec. (Brym and Lenton 1991, 411–18)

The issue of antisemitism in Québec was brought to international attention through the publication of an article in the *New Yorker* magazine on 17 September 1991 by Mordecai Richler, one of Canada's best-known novelists. In the article, and later in a book (1992), Richler accused the Québecois of unrepentant antisemitism, citing a number of scholarly and journalistic works as evidence of his claim.

However, he called special attention to one large-scale public opinion survey, the Charter of Rights Study completed in 1988, that was specifically concerned with beliefs about civil liberties. As a result of the storm of protest unleashed by the accusations of Richler, critics attacked the study for providing a faulty French translation of a key indicator of antisemitism, rendering it in such a way as to give it a positive instead of a negative meaning. ["Most Jews are pushy"/"La plupart des Juifs se frayent un chemin."] In the light of the controversy the authors of the study released a follow-up paper in which they reiterated the main points of the original work. In fact this one item was only one of a number of other items measuring antisemitic attitudes. In the case of each item French Québeckers were shown to be twice as likely as other Canadians to agree with negative stereotypes of Jews. Furthermore, French Québeckers are less likely than other Canadians to agree with positive portrayals of Jews. The study also showed that French-speaking Québeckers were also more likely to hold negative stereotypes of minorities in general.

Nevertheless, the authors are careful to point out that

> [t]o say that Quebeckers are more likely than English-speaking Canadians to dislike Jews is not to say that all, or even most, Quebeckers are anti-Semitic. On every test except one, a minority of Quebeckers expressed dislike of Jews, and although the proportions observed agreeing with a negative stereotyping cannot be given an absolute construction, the weight of evidence runs against the suggestion that most Quebeckers are anti-Semitic. (Sniderman 1992)

Perhaps further analysis of the data will show what happens when education, income, and other variables are controlled. This was not done here. With the possible exception of Québec then, recent studies paint quite an optimistic picture for the future of Canada.

Other studies are concerned with the issue of race or ethnicity and inequality. In Canada this line of investigation has its roots in the famous work of John Porter, *The Vertical Mosaic*. In that seminal book, Porter argues that ethnicity was a major determinant of socio-economic class in Canada. In his words, "[i]mmigration and ethnic affiliation (or membership in a cultural group) have been important factors in the formation of social classes in Canada. Unlike the United States, Canada was an ethnic mosaic which hinders the process of social mobility for immigrant groups." Bernard Blishen argued that the "blocked mobility" thesis could be accounted for either in terms of the low achievement orientation of the immigrant groups themselves or by prejudice against immigrants on the part of the British majority (Darroch 1992, 60–61). Porter modified his position in 1974 by suggesting that ethnic identities could weaken and the block to mobility be eliminated in this fashion. There are two issues that emerged from this original work that have continued to be a focus of research down to the present. The first question concerns the nature of the relationship between ethnicity and class, i.e., is it a stable feature of Canadian society or is it a dynamic process whereby ethnic and racial groups shift positions within the economic structure? The second question asks whether income and occupational differences among ethnic and racial groups are to be attributed to discriminatory practices in society or whether the lack of mobility of some groups is due to cultural factors having to do with the history and traditions of the groups themselves.

In a study of ethnic mobility in Hamilton, Ontario in 1987 that I conducted with my colleagues Howard Brotz, Peter Pineo and William Shaffir, we showed that, for most of the 16 ethnic groups that we considered, economic success varied directly with the length of time since immigration to Canada. We also studied the different strategies different ethnic groups used to achieve upward mobility.

Conrad Winn, in an important article, presents an analysis of ethnic mobility based on 1981 census data. He demonstrates that income and occupational differences among ethno-racial groups are less than income differences within these groups. For example, after adjusting for one anomalous group in the sample, the ratio of mean incomes of the highest and lowest ethnic groups is 1.8. But blacks in New Brunswick earn two-and-a-half times what they do in Nova Scotia and Japanese in Newfoundland make five times what they do in Nova Scotia. He also shows that the over-arching categories "white" and "non-white" or visible minority are far too general and portrayed as far too homogeneous categories to do justice to the reality. He shows, for example, that

> Asians are the second-highest income earning category in 1971 while Japanese are the third highest earners in 1981. In 1971 Asian Canadians earned 8 percent more than the British, 13 percent more than the average Canadian, 24 percent more than the French, and twice as much as the Natives. (Winn 1988, 196)

Furthermore, by using a relative measure of mobility Winn is able to show the direction of changes in rank for mobility of select ethnic groups. He demonstrates that for the 1971 census "[a]ll the upwardly mobile groups are low-prestige White groups or Asians. All the high-prestige White groups...experienced downward social mobility." For the 1981 mobility scores he was able to show that "the seven non-White groups in the sample of 16 were greatly overrepresented among the upwardly mobile group."

But the question may be asked, are income and occupational differences among ethno-racial groups in Canada attributable to racist practices, conscious or systemic? Peter Li, for example, in a recent work (1988b), criticizes the view that these differences are cultural in origin. Instead he argues that there exist in Canada different labour markets that provide differential rewards. Different ethnic groups enter different labour markets according to their qualifications. Ethnicity is a means whereby people are assigned to different labour markets. But by looking at a variety of control variables, Brym, in a review of the book, shows that the correlation between ethnicity and income and ethnicity and education is weak. Brym concludes:

I interpret Li's data to show that there is no vertical mosaic, that ethnicity per se is not a significant determinant of education and income for Canadians. That, of course, is what nearly all of the research on the subject has shown for the past two decades. (Brym 1989, 127–8)

And yet there is a widespread view, one has to say prejudice, that differences among ethno-racial groups are attributable to systematic or structural discrimination. This is often asserted without the slightest evidence. To suggest that different cultures have different patterns of socialization, value systems, historical experiences and the like has been dismissed by many sociologists as an attempt to "blame the victim." But, as Thomas Sowell points out:

By making the issue *who* is to blame, such arguments evade or pre-empt the more fundamental question—whether this is a matter of blame in the first place.

Clearly today's living generation—in any group—cannot be blamed for the centuries of cultural evolution that went on before they were born, often in lands that they have never seen. Nor can they be blamed for the fact that the accident of birth caused them to inherit one culture rather than another. In causal terms, it would be a staggering coincidence if cultures evolving in radically different historical circumstances were equally effective for all purposes when transplanted to a new society. Blame has nothing to do with it. (Sowell 1989, 31)

So predominant is this view within many quarters of Canadian sociology that honest researchers, whose data clearly support the cultural hypothesis, feel that they must apologize for doing so. For example, in a recent article, Carl Grindstaff discovers that marital status and age at marriage are clearly more important than ethnicity in determining economic outcome for women. But early marriages and thus lower income are culturally specific. And so Grindstaff concludes:

In general, it is probable that economic differences observed along the ethnic dimension are related to normative and value systems within the group rather than to any structural inequities in the social system. The analysis presented here would seem to lend support to the subcultural hypothesis. This type of subcultural interpretation is in contradiction to the vertical mosaic concept....

In such an argument there is a danger of being caught in the 'blaming the victim' trap. However, given the range of economic outcomes across the various ethnic measures, the specific cultural interpretation seems most appropriate. (Grindstaff 1990, 341)

Finally, a study released in March of 1992 shocked its author because it violated one of the cherished views of many sociologists. According to a report in the *Hamilton Spectator*, 18 March 1992:

The results of the comprehensive study, which concluded that there is no evidence of systematic discrimination, came as a shock not just to rights groups, but also to its author—Arnold deSilva, a Sri Lankan-born economist. "Surprised is not the word—I was shocked," Mr. deSilva told the media. "[But] I double-checked and triple-checked before releasing these results."

What did deSilva's study show? It shows that once immigrants get hired they do not suffer systematic wage discrimination. It shows that the reason why immigrants are slow to find work has to do with the undervaluation of their foreign credentials and not their colour. It also shows that the overall unemployment rate for the immigrant is lower than that for the native-born. Finally, although it takes immigrants a long time to catch up to the incomes of native-born Canadians, they do eventually catch up. In deSilva's own words:

The main conclusion to emerge is that there is no significant discrimination against immigrants in general. There is one possible exception discussed in the next paragraph. More important, there is no detectable general tendency to discriminate against immigrants originating from Third World regions. That can be interpreted as there being no generalized tendency to discriminate against visible minorities. While two particular nontraditional immigrant groups—people from East Asia and from the Caribbean—have not done well relative to the native-born and to other immigrants, immigrant groups from other Third World regions—West Asians, Southeast Asians, South Asians, Africans, South and Central Americans—have done as well as native-born Canadians.... (deSilva 1992, 37)

Conclusion

Canadian society has a history in which racist undercurrents were a major factor in group relations and policy decisions. But Canada has made enormous strides forward over the last 50 or 60 years. This is not to deny that a significant minority of the population harbours prejudicial attitudes towards groups not their own. Nor is it to suggest that minority group members do not suffer forms of discrimination. Nor is it a call to let down our guard against racial bigotry. But I am suggesting that Canada is a country that has come to deal with the problems of race and ethnic relations in a generally enlightened way.

There is a problem here, but the problem is not with Canada but with some of those who study it. Many sociologists bemoan what they take to be the racism and systematic discrimination rampant in Canadian society. Why is this the case? Much of sociology has turned into what one of my colleagues calls "victimology." There is some moral superiority attached to the status of being a victim or identifying with a victim. Why this should appeal to intellectuals today is a question that cannot be answered here. Suffice it to say that there is a large body of literature on the sociology of intellectuals.

Immigrants themselves, being eminently practical people, know just how much Canadian society has to offer them relative to what they experienced in their own countries. Throw open the doors to Canada and the wretched of the earth would vote with their feet.

Critics of John Stuart Mill pointed out that he published his book *On Liberty*, which was concerned with the freedom of individual expression, at a time in which the individual had never been as free to differ from the norm. With all the talk about racism in Canadian society, Howard McCready's words ring true. The black NDP Member of Parliament said in the aftermath of the Toronto unrest that Canadian society is probably the least racist on earth. For those of us still awaiting the Messiah, that's not too bad.

References

Abella, Irving, and Harold Troper. 1982. *None Is Too Many*. Toronto: Lester and Orpen Dennys.

Banton, Michael and Jonathan Harwood. 1975. *The Race Concept*. London: Newton Abbott; Vancouver: David and Charles.

Brym, Robert J. 1989. Review of *Ethnic Inequality in a Class Society* by Peter Li. *Canadian Ethnic Studies* 21:3.

Brym, Robert J. and Rhonda L. Lenton. 1991. The Distribution of Antisemitism in Canada in 1984. *Canadian Journal of Sociology* 16:4(November):411–18.

Buckner Taylor, H. Forthcoming. Attitudes Towards Minorities: Seven Year Results and Analysis.

Darroch, A. Gordon. 1992. Another Look at Ethnicity, Stratification and Social Mobility in Canada. In *Debates in Canadian Society*, edited by Ronald Hinch. Scarborough, Ont.: Nelson Canada.

deSilva, Arnold. 1992. *Earnings of Immigrants: A Comparative Analysis*. Economic Council of Canada.

Frideres, James S. 1988. *Native People in Canada: Contemporary Conflicts*. Scarborough: Prentice-Hall.

Grindstaff, Carl F. 1990. Ethnic, Marital and Economic Status of Women. In *Ethnic Demography: Canadian Immigrant, Racial and Cultural Variations*, editied by Shiva S. Halli, Frank Trovato and Leo Driedger. Ottawa: Carelton University Press.

Jones, Richard. 1972. *Community in Crisis: French Canadian Nationalism in Perspective*. Toronto: McClelland & Stewart.

Levitt, Cyril, and William Shaffir. 1987. *The Riot at Christie Pits*. Toronto: Lester and Orpen Dennys.

Li, Peter. 1988a. *The Chinese in Canada*. Toronto: Oxford University Press.

———. 1988b. *Ethnic Inequality in a Class Society*. Toronto: Wall and Thompson.

Mayer, J.P. ed. 1958. Correspondence d'Alexis de Tocqueville et d'Arthur de Gobineau. *Alexis de Tocqueville Oeuvres Complètes*, Tome IX. Paris: Gallimard.

Miller, J.R. 1989. *Skyscrapers Hide the Heavens: A History of Indian-White Relations in Canada*. Toronto: University of Toronto Press.

Richler, Mordecai. 1992. *Oh, Canada! Oh Quebec!* Toronto: Penguin Books.

Sniderman, Paul M. et al. 1992. Antisemitism in Québec. Mimeographed paper.

Sowell, Thomas. 1989. Affirmative Action: A Worldwide Disaster. *Commentary*. December, 31.

Sunahara, Ann. 1981. *The Politics of Racism: The Uprooting of Japanese Canadians During the Second World War*. Toronto: James Lorimer and Company.

Winks, Robin. 1971. *The Blacks in Canada*. Montréal: McGill-Queen's University Press.

Winn, Conrad. 1988. The Socio-Economic Attainment of Visible Minorities: Facts and Policy Implications. In *Social Inequality in Canada*, edited by James Curtis et al. Scarborough, Ont.: Prentice-Hall Canada.